The Social and Political Thought of George Orwell

From the playing fields of Eton College to the slums of Wigan and the battlefields of the Spanish Civil War, George Orwell led a unique life that found expression in a prose style of uncompromising brilliance.

Stephen Ingle captures this range of social experience and political vision in this fascinating new study, showing that although Orwell is often read as a socialist, he is best understood as a moralist and imaginative writer. This new reading, supported by detailed and thorough analysis, enables the reader to explore key topics such as:

- the myths of working-class socialism
- socialism, family values and poverty
- the threat of totalitarianism
- patriotism and imperialism
- the nature of revolution
- power and the Intellectuals.

This is a stimulating new view of one of the most influential figures of the twentieth century.

This book will be of interest to students of political history, political theory and literature, as well as keen readers of George Orwell's writing.

Stephen Ingle is Professor at the Politics Department, University of Stirling. His main academic interests are in the relationship between politics and literature and in adversarial (two party) politics, especially in the UK.

Routledge Studies in Social and Political Thought

The Social and Political Thought of George Orwell

A reassessment

Stephen Ingle

Routledge
Taylor & Francis Group

LONDON AND NEW YORK

First published 2006
by Routledge
2 Park Square, Milton Park, Abingdon, Oxon, OX14 4RN

Simultaneously published in the USA and Canada
by Routledge
270 Madison Ave, New York, NY 10016

*Routledge is an imprint of the Taylor & Francis Group,
an informa business*

Typeset in Sabon by RefineCatch Limited, Bungay, Suffolk
Printed and bound in Great Britain by
Biddles, King's Lynn, Norfolk

British Library Cataloguing in Publication Data
A catalogue record for this book is available from the British Library

Library of Congress Cataloging in Publication Data
Ingle, Stephen.
    The social and political thought of George Orwell : a reassessment /
Stephen Ingle.
      p. cm.—(Routledge studies in social and political thought ; 45)
    Includes bibliographical references and index.
    ISBN 0–415–35735–7 (hardback : alk. paper)   1. Orwell, George,
1903–1950—Political and social views.   2. Politics and literature—
Great Britain—History—20th century.   3. Literature and society—
Great Britain—History—20th century.   4. Political fiction, English—
History and criticism.   5. Social problems in literature.   I. Title.
II. Series.
    PR6029.R8Z71165 2005
    828′.912309—dc22

                                       2005018904

ISBN10: 0–415–35735–7
ISBN13: 978–0–415–35735–7

To the memory of one James Ingle and to the future health and happiness of another James Ingle.

Contents

Acknowledgements

I have been teaching in the areas of politics and literature for a number of years and have been fascinated especially by the work of George Orwell. In the early 1990s I began work on a book on Orwell and thought at the time that my interest in him would be satisfied. However, *George Orwell: A Political Life*, published by Manchester University Press in 1993, left me feeling that I wanted to say more than the essentially hybrid format of that book had allowed me to say about his political ideas. In 2003, Orwell's centenary year, I was invited to give a number of papers on aspects of Orwell's thought and was disingenuous enough to imagine that these could easily be brought together to make a book. Routledge were good enough to express an interest in the project, and so I immediately began to work on my individual papers. But of course I discovered that a great deal more work had to be done on each, and gaps between them, too, had to be filled. I am very grateful to those at Routledge who expressed an interest in the original project and to those, especially Harriet Brinton, who bore with me when it became clear that the task would be more difficult than originally envisaged.

I would also like to express my gratitude to two friends, Claire Lightowler and Stanley Kleinberg, who read most of the original draft – in fact, in Stanley's case, all the original draft. Their comments were very helpful and caused me frequently to rethink my approach. I am not a good proofreader; in fact, if I were any younger I would have been classified as dyslexic. In those days, however, that option was not available – only indolence. It has been my great good fortune to have a friend who is a meticulous proofreader and I am most grateful for the help that John Stewart offered and gave. Finally, my wife has been enormously and unstintingly supportive of my work. This project would not have been possible to complete without her help. All of these people are partly responsible for the successful completion of what follows, but only I am responsible for its deficiencies.

Stephen Ingle, Stirling, May 2005

1 In search of Orwell

That Trotskyite with the big feet.

(H. G. Wells)

'It's the pigs I remember most. Napoleon, Squealer – especially Squealer – and when I look round the Chamber, there they are.' So said a back-bencher in response to a survey on Labour MPs' reading habits.[1] He claimed that his politics had been decisively shaped by reading Orwell. For his own part, Orwell acknowledged the influence of other writers. The world would have been perceptively different, he said, if H. G. Wells, the hero of his youth, had not existed.[2] This is a substantial claim to make in respect of any individual, especially a writer, and yet it is a claim that might be advanced equally seriously on behalf of Orwell himself. There is no comparison between the amount that the two writers published, or indeed between the length of time over which both were writing. Wells established an international reputation comparatively early in his career, went on to write some seventy novels and short stories as well as two extremely widely read world histories and a celebrated textbook on biology, met and claimed to have influenced a number of world statesmen and worked productively into his eighties. Orwell, on the other hand, achieved fame only near the end of his life, died at the age of forty-six after several years of debilitating ill-health, had the ear of no politicians or statesmen and wrote only nine major works (two of which he subsequently sought to suppress) and a number of seminal long essays (one of which he sought to suppress). On the face of it, then, any claim that Orwell might have changed the world would appear to be fanciful. But only a little digging would allow a fuller, and different, picture to emerge.

Orwell's books have earned twice as much as all the writers on Secker and Warburg's entire list (including Gide, Kafka, Mann and

Colette), says Jeffrey Meyers.[3] Three of his works – *Keep the Aspidistra Flying*, *Animal Farm* and *Nineteen Eighty Four* – have been made into popular films. Much of Orwell's enduring reputation was the consequence of his anti-totalitarian, and specifically anti-Stalinist, polemics. When he originally took this stance it was by no means popular or expedient. From the Spanish Civil War onwards, Orwell had difficulty getting some of his more partisan writing published. *Animal Farm* was a case in point: because the book was so clearly aimed at Stalin and his regime, and because until 1945 the USSR was such an important ally in the war against Hitler, it was difficult to rouse publishers' interest on either side of the Atlantic. When the Western allies broke with their former brothers-in-arms, this graphic fable of Soviet brutality suddenly became very apposite and T. S. Eliot's earlier judgement regarding its political inappropriateness was turned on its head.[4] The publication a few years later of *Nineteen Eighty Four* could scarcely have been better timed. *Nineteen Eighty Four* was recently described as 'the canonical text' of anti-communism, 'the key imaginative manifesto of the Cold War'.[5] The book, together with *Animal Farm*, was translated into more than sixty languages, the two selling more than forty million copies between them. *Nineteen Eighty Four* received the supreme populist accolade, abridgement for the *Readers' Digest*. In a survey of university-bound students in Britain and the United States, *Nineteen Eighty Four* was amongst the most 'personally significant books'.[6] In 1983 a Harris Poll discovered that no fewer than 27 per cent of Americans claimed to have read *Nineteen Eighty Four* – wishful thinking perhaps, but at least indicative of the book's reputation with the American public. In the first six months of 1984 itself, 301,000 copies of *Nineteen Eighty Four* were sold in Britain alone, together with 132,000 copies of *Animal Farm*. In the USA in the same year the novel was selling 50,000 copies a day. But some twenty years after the passing of that totemic year and twelve years after the end of the Cold War, the centenary of Orwell's birth brought a number of biographies, a small and generally distinguished cluster of hagiographies,[7] new editions of all his major works, television profiles and international conferences. The following year the US National Council of Teachers sponsored a nationwide reading and discussion project on *Nineteen Eighty Four*.

No doubting, then, the extent of Orwell's influence on the English-speaking world and the significance of his contribution to Western morale in the Cold War. No doubting either the extent to which his critical stance *vis-à-vis* the Soviet Union was taken out of context: Orwell was trying to save the world for socialism as he understood it, and not for Western capitalism or for right-wing individualism. The enthusiastic adoption of *Nineteen Eighty Four* by the right-wing John Birch society[8] would have infuriated Orwell beyond measure, though his many opponents on the Left might have felt vindicated. Even worse for Orwell's *amour propre* perhaps would have been Rupert Murdoch's claim, in a lecture to the Centre for Independent Studies, that, in the struggle between free markets and totalitarianism, it was News International that had kept alive Orwell's 'crystal spirit'.[9]

Orwell's popularity did not disappear with time, even after the collapse of the Berlin Wall. More than half a century after they were written, Orwell's books are still much in demand. In fact in 2005 London's Royal Opera House put on a production of Lorin Mazel's opera *Nineteen Eighty Four*, whose themes, according to the composer, were 'seemingly ever more relevant'. Why is his social and political thought still so influential? What is the nature of Orwell's influence? This book constitutes an attempt to address these questions by means of a detailed analysis of Orwell's social and political thought. Where to begin? The obvious starting point must surely be a consideration of some of the main products of the 'Orwell industry', the key commentaries on and biographies of Orwell that have emerged since his death. Our focus is on Orwell's social and political thought, and so we will not be much concerned with the details of his life, except where they bear directly upon his thought. In reviewing some of the key commentaries and biographies, not only will we extract important insights into our subject, but we will introduce the main themes to be explored in the body of this study. The continuing popularity of a writer dismissed by some as simply one of the most martial of the Cold Warriors implies that there must be something more to Orwell than the good fortune of being the right person in the right place at the right time with the right message for the Right.

1

Sir Bernard Crick, Orwell's first and, according to Julian Symons, definitive biographer, agreed to undertake that task because he wished to acknowledge, to celebrate, Orwell's success in achieving his goal of making political writing into an art. Sir Bernard would have warmed to the kind of political writing that Orwell wished to make into an art: what Orwell called democratic socialism. Indeed, Crick called Orwell a supreme political writer 'both for what he said and how he said it'.[10] However, the biography shows clearly that Crick was primarily interested in what Orwell had to say rather than in how he said it. Had he chosen, Crick could have concentrated more on Orwell's works as literature, but his interest was principally biographical and his exploration of Orwell's life was undertaken to enrich our understanding of his politics. Crick set himself the task of coming as close as he could to understanding Orwell through observing his life closely. Acknowledging the shortcomings, as he saw them, of psychological analysis – 'none of us can enter into another person's mind'[11] – he set out systematically to gather and corroborate the available evidence. Unlike a number of biographers who followed him, for example Michael Shelden, who left no stone wittingly unturned,[12] Crick was not much concerned with what Samuel Johnson called 'domestic privacies', primarily because he had concluded that Orwell had no great secrets to hide and that, anyway, they would not have impacted greatly on what Orwell had to say.[13] This strategy seems to amount to fighting with one's arm tied behind one's back. We cannot know that Orwell had no secrets that might have affected his work without first carefully looking. Abstemiousness can be a virtue when we choose not to include some secrets merely because they are titillating, but it can also turn out to be a vice if we decide not to include some secrets that might have provided a clue to some action or event because they might impugn the integrity of the subject. An a priori decision not even to consider such things, however, can surely only be regarded as a vice in a biographer. Crick was quite clear in his own mind that the most important thing about Orwell was his supreme ability to render the spirit of democratic socialism as art, but he gave more attention to the socialism than the art. Crick has argued that Orwell scholars who see their subject as, for example, a Christian socialist, or as a Trotskyite, are actually finding in Orwell chiefly a reflection of their own political preferences, whereas Crick assures us that as a matter of fact, when all is said and done, Orwell was a plain Tribunite socialist. *Quod erat demonstrandum?* Even so, we should not give up the attempt to categorise Orwell's social and political thought as objectively as we can, and in any case I do not believe that Orwell was a Tribunite socialist, and I shall try later to show why. Crick's main contribution to Orwell scholarship was to provide a carefully crafted portrait of the man, skilfully set within the background of the main events and ideas of his times.

Sir Bernard was by no means the first of Orwell's biographers. Orwell himself sought to prevent the writing of a biography (an odd thing for a man with no 'secrets', a man whose own writing was so patently autobiographical), but he was not successful, for a number appeared. Lionel Trilling included a perceptive chapter on Orwell in his 1955 book *The Opposing Self*, and he entitled it significantly 'George Orwell and the Politics of Truth'.[14] Orwell, like Cobbett, to whom he is often compared, did not dream of new kinds of men but contented himself with 'the old kind' of man, and passionately wanted for these men 'freedom, bacon and proper work'. Trilling declared that Orwell *was* what he wrote: he acted out his beliefs in the world and so could be considered, in short, a virtuous man. This theme of virtue became a leitmotiv for many who wrote about Orwell, including Crick himself; we shall return to it. For Trilling, Orwell's virtue as a writer lay in his not being a genius, in his 'fronting the world with nothing else than [his] simple, direct, undeceived intelligence'. Although this analysis is consistent with Trilling's picture of the man and the writer being one and the same, it is not of itself convincing. In 1989 a personal, annotated copy of *Down and Out in Paris and London*, which Orwell had sent to an old flame, Brenda Salkeld, came to light. Michael Shelden read the annotations with care and his conclusions throw a different light on the relationship between the man and his work. 'It is the moment in Orwell's career when we can see the split. As Eric Blair he is saying "George Orwell said this, but I as Eric Blair felt this." He had seized upon a way of *creating* himself as Orwell, of hiding Blair almost perfectly for the rest of his life.'[15] Eventually 'Orwell' came to represent what Rodden called a 'persona of such style and simplicity ... the Common Man arguing plain Common Sense'.[16] From 1930 onwards, then, Blair (Orwell-the-man) had begun to create a fictional character, Orwell-the-writer, a device which, as Raymond Williams put it, enabled him to get inside the experiences he was writing about. 'Orwell' was to remain Orwell's finest literary achievement, one that as it blossomed would transform his prose style and allow his politics to develop. (I had the pleasure of spending a weekend in the house of Orwell's nephew Henry Dakin some years ago. It was as clear as could be that the George Orwell I knew from his writings and the Eric Blair he knew as an uncle were quite different men. My man was Trilling's 'Orwell of the undeceived intelligence', a literary contrivance that enabled its creator to champion the values of ordinary people.) In response to Trilling, then, to say that Orwell *was* what he wrote, whilst not entirely wrong, is to miss a trick. Nevertheless, Trilling's picture of Orwell as common-sensible, forthright, virtuous and truthful has been influential.

In 1961 Richard Rees, formerly editor of *The Adelphi* for whom Orwell frequently wrote, and a long-time friend, wrote a biography poignantly entitled *George Orwell: Fugitive from the Camp of Victory*.[17] Rees also wrote a biography of Simone Weil, for whom much the same title would have been appropriate, and he argued about Orwell, as he would about Weil, that a concern for justice and an understanding of the balance of society made him ready to add his weight to the lighter scale, to change sides. Rees offered as an example Orwell's championing of the industrial working-class, especially the unemployed, but he could have chosen Orwell's joining the Partido Obrero de Unificación Marxista (POUM) militia when fighting in the Spanish Civil War. Although he scarcely knew enough about the situation for this to have been an entirely conscious decision, there seems to have been something quite natural about his siding with the party that would be treacherously attacked by its former allies and then generally demonised. As we shall see, when Orwell returned to Britain he declared that his championing of POUM's cause, which earned him the distrust and enmity of a number of former friends, was prompted not so much by the belief that POUM was right as that it was unfairly treated. This fire for justice was fanned by a general disregard for his personal safety. Orwell's attitude towards his own health seems to represent a disdain for the sensible and comfortable in favour of the dangerous and uncomfortable in pursuit of his mission. His decision to live on Jura towards the end of his life is a specific example. Here was a man who was tubercular and who had been told that he needed easy access to a good hospital and the benefit of a dry climate, so he made for one of the most inaccessible parts of the Inner Hebrides, to live in what Rees described as 'the most uninhabitable house in the British Isles'.[18] Orwell wrote to his friends in London that the journey was quite easy really, though they would have to walk the last eight soggy miles. But he completed *Nineteen Eighty Four* there.

Rees found it difficult to account for Orwell's fame. As we have seen, he was hardly prolific. His lack of an informed knowledge of philosophical and psychological issues limited the scope of his writing; and his style, Rees suggested, was nothing like as brilliant as Joyce's. For Rees, then, Orwell's cult status could be explained only by his personal appeal, 'the man he was'. Plausible though this might have sounded in 1961, it can hardly account for his continuing popularity half a century later. Neither, as we stressed, can the timeliness of his anti-totalitarian political stance. Nevertheless, Rees did try to elaborate on the kind of man he took Orwell to be: he reminded us of Orwell's description of Dickens in his celebrated essay as a man who was 'generously angry . . . a nineteenth century liberal, a free intelligence, a type hated with equal hatred by all those smelly little orthodoxies which are now contending for our souls'.[19] Orwell could have been describing himself, said Rees. There is something in what

Rees says, though the concern with equality that marks out the socialist was more central than the concern with individual liberty that marked out the liberal. However, there was nothing generous about Orwell's anger, even though he might have placed on record his inability to hate Hitler.[20] His criticism of his opponents, especially on the Left, was often vicious. A request from the *New Left Review* seeking authors' responses to the Spanish Civil War drew this unpublished reply from Orwell: 'By the way, tell your pansy friend Spender that I am preserving specimens of his war-heroics and that when the time comes when he squirms for shame at having written it . . . I shall rub it in good and hard.'[21] Later Orwell met and formed a friendship with Spender, who asked how Orwell could have attacked him without knowing him. Orwell responded that he had not 'exactly' attacked him but might perhaps have used the phrase 'parlour Bolsheviks' (in fact fashionable pansies), and that knowing someone made it difficult to criticise them. He seems nevertheless to have managed in Cyril Connolly's case without too much difficulty: his criticism of his friend's novel *The Rock Pool* was devastating.[22] Orwell said he wanted to retain the right to be intellectually brutal,[23] though his frequent criticisms of the 'nancy poets' would score more highly for brutality than intellect. No critique of Orwell himself, from a representative of any of the smelly orthodoxies he detested, was more splenetic or vindictive than his own critique of W. H. Auden – that 'sort of gutless Kipling' – and especially of his poem 'Spain'.[24]

So, Orwell was not a generously angry man. On the other hand, the opprobrium that settled on his reputation after it was disclosed that Orwell had provided a list of 'fellow travelling' public figures to the security services seems largely unearned. A headline in *The Guardian* during his centenary wondered whether he hadn't been a government stooge.[25] More damning was the charge that Orwell had supplied the list to his old friend Celia Kirwan to secure what might be called romantic favours. As a matter of fact, at the time he compiled the list Orwell was too ill even to receive visitors, let alone plan unlikely amorous adventures.[26] The purpose of the list had been to identify those whom it would not have been appropriate to consider for pro-British propaganda purposes, and it contained, along with Chaplin, Michael Redrave, E. H. Carr and the Labour backbencher Tom Driberg, the name of Hugh McDiarmid, the stridently anti-English Scottish Nationalist. None of these made any secret of their sympathies and they were well known to the security services. Nevertheless, Orwell gave the matter a lot of thought and made no bones about providing the information. All things considered, it is not surprising that Richard Rees called Orwell a good hater. In more general terms, however, Rees confirmed the view of Orwell as truthful and virtuous, and added that his chief concern both as a writer and a man was with moral values.

An acquaintance who knew Orwell for a long period of time was fellow Etonian Christopher Hollis. A Catholic convert, Hollis was the Conservative MP for Devizes from 1945 to 1955, and he wrote *A Study of George Orwell* on his retirement from Parliament. Hollis' approach to his subject provides an excellent example of Crick's point, that those who write about Orwell actually write about themselves; it was Kingsley Amis who noted that Hollis could not resist drawing Orwell very much in his own image. Hollis' Orwell, then, is at heart a Conservative and a Catholic fellow-traveller, of whom he concluded: 'Orwell never doubted that man was fundamentally a moral being and that this world was a testing place.'[27] His Orwell was a subconscious Christian with a deep sympathy for the conservative ideals of tradition and organicism.

Another important biography appeared in the following decade, with an evocative title, George Woodcock's *The Crystal Spirit*.[28] Woodcock and Orwell had remained on good terms despite the former's pacifism, which made them ideological opponents during the war. Woodcock regarded Orwell as a far more complex character than he liked to present himself: Woodcock describes him as 'in his own way a man of the left',[29] an 'ambivalent anarchist',[30] a radical individualist (*à la* Hazlitt)[31] and a Swiftian Tory dissenter.[32] Indeed, in his essay on Swift, as Woodcock shows, Orwell displayed a Tocquevillian fear of public opinion. 'When human beings are governed by "thou shalt not", the individual can practice a certain amount of eccentricity: when they are supposedly governed by "love" or "reason" he is under continuous pressure to make him behave and think in exactly the same way as everyone else.'[33] No wonder, then, that conservatives, anarchists, Trotskyites, socialists and liberals found encouragement in his work; but as Woodcock shrewdly observed, they must all be missing something. Woodcock's Orwell, then, was essentially a complex figure whose politics reflected a series of 'highly idiosyncratic' reactions to the experiences of life[34] but who lacked any ideological frame by which he might readily be identified. This is only part of the story, because we know that Orwell, more than most of us, actively *chose* the experiences to which he responded 'idiosyncratically'. Perhaps his years in Burma were a terrible mistake (though in retrospect even this is open to doubt), but he chose to enlist. He chose to go down to the 'bedrock of Western civilisation' on his return from Burma, chose to go to the north of England, to fight in Spain, and finally to wrestle with his last book in greater discomfort and solitude than was strictly necessary. And to a considerable degree he chose his responses to these experiences. Although Woodcock argued that these responses did not offer ideological coherence, they did sustain a consistent moral force. Woodcock's contribution to the depiction of Orwell is not radically different from Trilling's or Rees', though in specifically political terms it is significantly different to Crick's: Orwell was always an outsider and 'at the most an unwelcome guerrilla on the flank of the regular army'.[35]

An early US analysis of Orwell's work, though not a biography, was Robert A. Lee's *Orwell's Fiction*.[36] This was no hagiography. 'In many ways', says Lee:[37]

> Orwell was the antithesis of what his admirers hold him to be: strains of orthodoxy and conservatism often outweigh his vaunted radicalism; meanness of spirit is often apparent in the man admired for largeness of vision. His often remarked rancour towards socialists and his not-so-thinly veiled distaste for the real people whose abstract causes he championed are part of the antidemocratic strain in his writing that . . . is indisputable.

Even Orwell's being wounded in Spain was seen by Lee to be 'perversely satisfying' because it gave him a badge showing him to be on the side of the oppressed. It enabled him to say without fear of contradiction that not merely had he sought to comprehend tyranny and dramatise it in his literature, but he had actually fought it in Spain.[38] Perhaps, if Orwell had been killed – which he so nearly was – Lee would have seen this as especially perverse. Although Lee clearly admired Orwell's writing, especially *Animal Farm*, his picture of Orwell was far more ambiguous: it portrayed a political thinker whose principal ideas were 'thematically limited and parochial'.

More generally critical of Orwell was Raymond Williams, who, in 1971, managed to damn his subject with faint praise in a short book in Fontana's Modern Masters Series.[39] He saw Orwell's going off to Burma as very conventional (for the son of an Imperial civil servant), and so too was his stay in Paris (for an aspiring writer). Orwell's position in the social hierarchy, lower-upper-middle-class, gave him a 'double vision, rooted in the simultaneous positions of dominator and dominated'.[40] This double vision was compounded by Orwell's analytical shortcomings. True, through his response to his experiences, he could conjure up a 'climate' of injustices, but this missed out the important analytical component, and as Williams concluded, 'a social structure is not a climate'. Williams claimed that Orwell imagined class differences to be principally about accent, food and clothes and that he managed to sell this lie to a whole generation, an argument so perverse as to be simply not worth pursuing. Even where Williams acknowledged Orwell's integrity as a witness, he still saw him in his early career as an outsider with 'no social function'. Williams' point was that to opt for literature instead of politics, and this is indeed what Orwell claimed to have done, was to put oneself into a compartment which by definition 'has no direct concern with social reality'.[41] On this reading, to seek detachment in the sense of abjuring smelly little orthodoxies is to choose to cut oneself off from social reality and thus opt for political impotence. Nevertheless, Williams acknowledged Orwell's political commitment in Spain and called *Homage to Catalonia* Orwell's most important and moving book. From Williams' perspective, Orwell was now too committed – to revolutionary socialism. But during the Second World War Orwell abjured revolution and, in Williams' cutting phrase, 'reverts to type'. The apotheosis of this reversion to type was *Nineteen Eighty Four*, in which, whatever Orwell said himself, 'all modern forms of repression and authoritarian control' were attributed to a single political tendency, socialism, which Orwell misrepresented.[42] We shall be considering these points at greater length later, but to conclude for the present: Williams applauded Orwell's ultimately successful attempts to write about his experiences from the inside but castigated his lack of understanding of the economics of class exploitation. Orwell's fixation on the potential evils of totalitarianism prevented him from addressing the new contradictions of developing capitalism. Hence Orwell helped to prepare the mainstream Left for post-war accommodation to capitalism by virtue of his pessimism. So it seems that in opting for literature over commitment Orwell had not, after all, chosen political impotence. Williams cannot have it both ways. Williams' picture, on the whole, is not a flattering one. He depicted Orwell as a species of bourgeois ingénue who flirted unsuccessfully with and finally forsook socialism.

In 1972 Stansky and Abrahams produced an Orwell biography whose title, *The Unknown Orwell*, excited expectations which, to some degree at least, were realised.[43] We discover more about Orwell's childhood and school days, but the apparent discrepancies between Orwell's own later accounts and those of people who knew him, or indeed his own letters home, were by no means resolved. Many of the former were taken by the authors at their face value, his prep school bedwetting for example, whereas his letters showed 'the ordinariness of schoolboy life in so ordinary a fashion – with a full quota of jolly chaps and ripping games of footer'.[44] By and large the authors accepted Orwell's own conclusion about his days at St Cyprian's, that they gave him 'an economic explanation of affection and society'.[45] Orwell at Eton was pictured as being rather aloof, without close friends, and also without any great academic aptitude; after three years he was placed 117th out of 140 in his year. The authors were persuaded that Orwell's choice not to try to go on to university was a sensible one. For Crick and others the decision was more problematical. For our purposes, the matter is of consequence only to the extent that a decision between a university education and a career in the Imperial Police would have a profound consequence on the kind of writer he would become. Given his very average academic performance and his tutors' lack of enthusiasm concerning the further pursuit of his education, a career in the Imperial Police made sense if only as a *pis aller*, but perhaps Orwell was truly fired by the prospect of following in his father's footsteps and 'going East'. For several reasons, then, his decision to join the Imperial Police made sense. In the development of Orwell's social and political thought, the decision would have profound consequences. Stansky and Abrahams' book has little to say about the development of Orwell's career or his politics, and at the end we might feel that the unknown Orwell has remained, if better known, still enigmatic.

There have been, over the years, a number of assessments of Orwell's work that have been only tangentially biographical, one of the best being an early one, Jeffrey Meyers' *George Orwell: The Critical Heritage*.[46] What was particularly useful about this book was that most of the contributors knew Orwell and knew his age, and both were still reasonably fresh in their minds. This volume, if generally rather laudatory in tone, nevertheless brought together a wide range of critical comment and was generally more illuminating than the same editor's *Reader's Guide*, published in the same year.

One of the most comprehensive and scholarly treatments of Orwell's political influence, published in 1989, was John Rodden's *The Politics of Literary Reputation: The Making and Claiming of 'St. George' Orwell*, to which I have already referred. This still provides the fullest account of Orwell's relevance to the modern age, and Rodden deals in considerable depth with the differing responses to Orwell's social and political ideas in both the United Kingdom and the United States. It is an impressive achievement, but perhaps more for the breadth of the scholarship on which it is based than for any particular insight into

Orwell's thought. It is strange nevertheless that the later biographies do not refer more to Rodden.

Orwell's reputation, as we have seen, did not survive unscathed. One of the most comprehensively critical analyses of aspects of the man and his politics was *Inside the Myth, Orwell: Views from the Left*.[47] Of the contributions to this collection, the most trenchantly critical were two on Orwell's treatment of women and women's issues, by Beatrix Campbell and Deirdre Beddoe. Their themes were taken up in the last of the older works on Orwell that I shall turn to, if only briefly: Daphne Patai's *The Orwell Mystique: A Study of Male Ideology*,[48] which was published in the same year, 1984. Patai was trenchantly critical of Orwell's 'traditional notion of masculinity, complemented by a generalised misogyny'.[49] My reference is brief not because I regard Patai's book as short-sighted in its reductionist interpretation of Orwell's thought, though I do, nor because I think the feminists' case against Orwell[50] is weak, but rather the opposite: because I think the case is irresistible, even if Christopher Hitchens tried half-heartedly to resist it.[51] Newsinger, whose work we shall shortly be discussing, was obdurately, and to my mind mistakenly, defensive of Orwell: if Orwell were really so convinced of male superiority, he argued, this would have made him a conservative, or even a fascist. If that were true for Orwell, then it would have been true for half of the contemporary Labour Party and most Tories would have been fascists. Stephen Spender later said that Orwell despised women and thought of them generally as inferior.[52] Kay Ekeval, with whom Orwell had an affair, also noted Orwell's 'ultra masculine tendencies'. Though he enjoyed their company, Orwell did not think women to be 'a force in life'.[53] I profoundly disagree, however, with Patai's assertion that Orwell used his 'generalised misogyny' consciously for broader political purposes, to signal to liberal and conservative intellectuals that he was 'safe', one of them, a man who would not 'rock the boat'. There is no evidence to suggest that Orwell wished to soften his political stance to make it more appealing, and it is hardly conceivable that he of all people would have selected misogyny as his means had he made any such attempt. However, from a feminist perspective, Orwell's position was even more condemnable; he simply was not intellectually interested in women. This is an important consideration, and we shall have cause to return to it on several occasions.

I now want to turn to some of those books that came out in anticipation of, or were timed to coincide with, the centenary of the writer's birth in 2003. I shall be selective for, as Stefan Collini observed, in some cases the 'new facts' do not add much to our understanding and simply 'do not justify the bold conclusions which [are] derived from them'.[54]

2

The first is John Newsinger's *Orwell's Politics*, published in 1999.[55] This book, to coin a phrase, does just what it says on the tin. It is a systematic account of the development of Orwell's political thought, in fact, according to Bernard Crick, as good an account as we are likely to get in this generation. It is particularly valuable in providing the political background to Orwell's work; indeed, it does so more successfully than any of the biographies, and so it deserves our detailed attention. On the other hand, it can be said to have one major drawback: Newsinger does not consider Orwell as an imaginative writer. That is to say, he does not concern himself with the crucial fact that Orwell's primary motivation was to write, and where literary integrity came into conflict with political commitment, Orwell's primary allegiance was to the former. A study that fails to recognise this fact is bound to be correspondingly deficient, as the following small example shows. *Animal Farm* is commonly regarded as the greatest political satire since *Gulliver's Travels*. Newsinger devoted three pages to it. I have already conceded that the author was very clear about his appointed task, and this did not include analysing Orwell's status as an imaginative writer or its implications. But Orwell *was* an imaginative writer, and, as we shall discover, imaginative writers have an unusual relationship to politics.

Newsinger's analysis begins with Orwell in Burma, and he attempts to make sense of Orwell's changing attitude towards imperialism. We shall be considering what he has to say in more detail later, but he recognised that Flory's view of the Empire in *Burmese Days*, as being a despotism motivated by theft, did not represent Orwell's final judgement. Orwell became convinced finally that, whatever its faults, the British Empire was a lesser evil, and Orwell's views were not static.[56] We shall have the opportunity to pursue this debate in detail in Chapter 2. On his return to Britain, Orwell went 'down and out', says Newsinger, quoting Orwell, to absolve himself from the stain of the exploitation associated with imperialism. But Orwell went down and out with his pen, as a writer, and not as a volunteer social worker. He went, in part at least, to garner new experiences. And to very good effect: it was because Orwell had earned himself a reputation as one who could write tellingly about the poor that Gollancz approached him to undertake a survey of working-class life in the north of England.[57] But Gollancz was to get more than he bargained for. In the second half of *Road to Wigan Pier*, the book that grew out of Orwell's diaries of his six weeks in Yorkshire and Lancashire, he 'unleashed a sustained idiosyncratic diatribe against the British left'. (Newsinger's words.)[58] A more favourably disposed commentator likened that second half to 'a brick through the window of the upper class party faithful'.[59] Unlike many on the Left, Newsinger seems willing to forgive Orwell, but only because his 'theoretical understanding of the crisis of British capitalism and of the socialist alternative was weak'.[60] Particularly difficult to forgive was Orwell's rumbustious, take-no-prisoners style. The image of middle-class socialists 'flocking towards progress like bluebottles to a dead cat'[61] was trenchant, vituperative, unfair and unforgettable.

When Newsinger discussed Orwell's experiences in Spain, he was especially assiduous at filling in the crucial political background, pointing out to the reader, for example, via Trotsky, that in its early days the Spanish Revolution achieved even more than the Russian. Newsinger rightly concluded that Spain convinced Orwell that to be anti-fascist one had to be anti-capitalist,[62] which is to say revolutionary. Just as he had earlier imported his 'imperialist' model into his analysis of British society, so when he returned from Spain he imported his Catalonian model: 'only revolution can save England', he was to write.[63] Moreover, Orwell concluded with some justification that leading British left-wing intellectuals were almost exclusively pro-communist, so that he found it very difficult to put across the revolutionary point of view publicly. As late as 1942, in his essay 'Looking Back on the Spanish War', Orwell wrote that the question confronting the Left in Spain was essentially the same as that confronting the Left in Britain in its struggle with the fascists: were ordinary people to be allowed to live fully human lives or were they not?[64] But as Newsinger showed, the question proved to be no simple one, and when Britain was under grave threat Orwell was quick to jump to its defence and to discard the pacifism that had led him to take out his brief membership of the Independent Labour Party. When he first joined the Home Guard, Orwell urged all socialists to do the same, and to turn that body into a 'democratic guerrilla force'. Although Crick suggests that the Home Guard did indeed acquire a political dimension,[65] the idea of its becoming a guerrilla force out to establish a socialist republic surely belongs to another world. Orwell had miscalculated fundamentally the revolutionary potential of the wartime situation, as he later admitted. Nevertheless, he contributed a short work, *The Lion and the Unicorn*, to a series known as *Searchlight*, which was aimed at bringing international socialism to terms with (British) nationalism. Newsinger argues that in this extended essay Orwell established a feasible 'third way' between reform and revolution. I hope to show later that this is wishful thinking. Even Newsinger agrees that the essay Orwell wrote two years later, *The English People*, constituted a 'pretty decisive repudiation of the revolutionary politic [of] less than three years earlier'.[66]

Before the end of the war in Europe, Orwell owned up to his miscalculations about the importance of revolution to the war effort. He had been consistently wrong. Yet he continued to think himself consistently right in his anti-Stalinism; indeed, he was already working on *Animal Farm*, a book characterised by Newsinger as an assault on Russian communism 'from a Trotskyite "in the wide sense" point of view'.[67] I shall try later to argue that it is hard to envisage a sense wide enough to make such a description appropriate. Newsinger quotes a letter from Orwell to the editor of *Partisan Review* in which he wrote: 'You can't have a revolution unless you make it for yourself: there is no such thing as a benevolent dictatorship.'[68] Newsinger went on to quote Orwell's 'enigmatic but vitally important' comment on Koestler's novels *Darkness at Noon* and *The Gladiators*: 'all revolutions may be failures but they are not all the same failure'.[69] This sententious, even cryptic, aphorism offers an example of the manner in which an imaginative writer operates. Newsinger understood it to be an important observation, but he was not certain what it meant and Orwell did not go on to elaborate. We would not allow a political thinker such latitude. But its meaning can be shown by example, and the most appropriate example also shows that Orwell was wrong: in fact, Koestler was well aware that not all failures are the same. His Spartacus attempted to make his own failed revolution a nobler failure by refusing the Roman General Crassus' offer of flight to Alexandria. He symbolically drained his wine: 'One must not leave any dregs . . . So that one may hand it [the chalice of revolution] in a clean state to the Next One who will come.'[70] But the last word was with Spartacus' counsellor, the Essene, who came close, surely, to capturing the essence of Orwell's own final verdict on the nature of revolution: 'Man comes and man is gone, and knows nothing of the fate of his fathers and has no knowledge of the future of his seed. The rain falls into the river and the river drowns in the sea, but the sea becomes no greater. All is vanity.'[71] This seems to offer a suitable valediction for the history of the revolution on Animal Farm, whose animals, after all, *had* made their own revolution, only for it to fail, in every sense.

Newsinger turned next to Orwell's last book with a disarming: 'What of *Nineteen Eighty Four?*' What indeed. Newsinger turned on Orwell's critics, especially Raymond Williams, who had failed to acknowledge that Orwell was not attacking British socialism, by pointing out that Williams had decided that by the time he wrote *Animal Farm*, Orwell had ceased to be a socialist. Ironically, several pages further on in the same work, Williams justified as necessary what he called the 'harsh discipline' of Cambodia's Khmer Rouge regime. A revealing comparison, Newsinger pointed out: Pol Pot's Killing Fields did not invalidate his claim to be a socialist but Orwell's *Nineteen Eighty Four* was more than enough to disqualify him.[72] For Newsinger, *Nineteen Eighty Four* had been written primarily to alert the British managerial class to the excesses of totalitarianism; these were the people Orwell had sought to engage with *The Lion and the Unicorn*. His last book, however, was hijacked by its own international success, achieving, as we have noted, iconic status in the rhetoric of the Cold War, and so Orwell's own intentions simply ceased to signify. Newsinger's chapter title constituted an attempt to restore the balance: 'A Doctor Treating an All but hopeless Case'. This indicates what Newsinger took to be Orwell's view about the future of the West; ironically, it was also how the medical world felt about Orwell. Newsinger's Orwell died an enemy of tyranny and a fighter for a better world. Was he at his death a 'Tribunite socialist' *à la* Crick? Certainly not, says Newsinger, he was a literary Trotskyite: someone who debated the ideas of the revolutionary Left within a fictional framework.[73] Unfortunately, Newsinger did not elaborate on this definition. As I said at the outset, he was primarily interested in Orwell's political thought and not in his status as an imaginative writer, but was Orwell, as Newsinger suggests, a Trotskyite? John O'Callaghan was right to refute Crick's assertion that 'the nature and spread of fascism' were Orwell's major concerns after 1936.[74] It is undeniably the case that Orwell devoted far more time to criticising Stalin's Russia than he did to criticising Hitler's Germany, or indeed fascism generally, as would befit a Trotskyite. It is also true that some of Orwell's more general beliefs were held by Trotskyites and that he remained as great a foe of Stalin's Russia as any Trotskyite. We shall consider this question in more detail later, but in directing the reader predominantly to Orwell's revolutionary-left side, Newsinger redressed the balance of our picture of the writer.

3

In the year 2000, Jeffrey Meyers brought out *Orwell: Wintry Conscience of a Generation*,[75] described by one reviewer as the new authoritative biography. I shall not discuss this book, however, because comprehensive and well written as it is, it adds very little that is distinctive or new to our knowledge or understanding of Orwell's social and political thought, and anyway it was destined soon to be overtaken by two biographies that appeared in Orwell's centenary year of 2003. The first of these was Gordon Bowker's *George Orwell*.[76] Unlike Newsinger, Bowker confronted Orwell's literary status head on. In his first sentence he tells us that Orwell was a writer of great power and imagination, was indeed 'one of the greatest writers of the twentieth century'. The decisive ingredient of Orwell's reputation, he went on, was his writing ability; he created a 'window pane of transpicuous prose'.[77] However, Bowker's interest, we soon discover, was not focused on Orwell's transpicuous prose; rather he was predominantly concerned to explore the ramifications of some of the ambiguities concerning Orwell's life and his reputation. The latter was characterised by his 'crystalline honesty' but the former by a 'deceptive streak'. Orwell had a partly repressed dislike of women; he possessed a deeply ingrained religiosity that hardly fitted with his vaunted atheism; his marriage was a rather loose one, each partner tolerating the other's infidelities (though Eileen did much more tolerating than George did). In short, Orwell was not what he seemed. Bowker provided details of Orwell's family background, which are not relevant to our purposes, except to say that it is worth remembering that this supposedly quintessential Englishman was actually qualified to have represented France on the rugby or soccer field. His mother was half French.

Bowker claims to have thrown light upon something of a mystery in Orwell studies: his rampant anti-Catholicism, strong enough to be remarked on by a number of his acquaintances. Now, it is known that as a young boy Orwell attended his sister's convent school. According to Bowker, though others have assumed that this was an Anglican establishment, it can only have been a Catholic convent run by French Ursulines. If he is right, then Orwell was taught as a lone boy in a Catholic girls' school run by nuns. This might account for the fact that he acknowledged a well-developed consciousness of sin by the age of eight and subsequently acquired his dislike of women.[78] Orwell's subsequent days at his prep school, St Cyprian's, unlike these earlier experiences, have been very well turned over and drawn upon by biographers, but Bowker emphasised more than most the great effect that the writings of H. G. Wells had upon the growing boy. It was a wonderful experience, Orwell said later, to be included as a boy in a conspiracy that foretold the shape of things to come.[79] Bowker also noted how admired an English teacher the despised Flip (the headmaster's wife) was: she had a passion for simple and clear prose. However exaggerated Orwell's later picture of St Cyprian's might have been, it is clear that he disliked it increasingly and did not trouble to hide his dislike. As his contemporary Cyril Connolly wrote: 'I was a stage rebel, Orwell a true one.'[80]

At Eton Orwell did not stand out academically or indeed in any other way. One contemporary described him as having a face like a hamster, another as 'a bit of a bastard'.[81] He had no close friends but pursued his love of reading, consuming the works of Bernard Shaw and discovering the writing of Jack London. Bowker repeats the story in which Orwell and Runciman (the future historian) got their revenge on a senior boy who had been unpleasant to them by making his image in candle wax. Orwell had wanted to pierce it with a pin but Runciman insisted on only breaking off a leg. Soon after, the older boy broke his leg: indeed, within a year he had died of leukaemia. Perhaps this is one of those secrets that *is* worth knowing. It throws some light on Orwell's paranoia later in life: one of the reasons Orwell gave to Richard Rees for adopting a *nom de plume* was that his enemies could do him a mischief by using magic if they knew his real name.

Bowker suggests that Orwell proposed to his childhood sweetheart Jacintha Buddicom before setting off for Burma, but that she rejected him and he left disconsolate. It is true that much later, when they had re-established contact, Orwell had chided Jacintha with blighting his life, hinting that he had gone out to Burma to forget her, thus 'outraging' his true nature, but he could not have been serious. He was only eighteen at the time and we know that he was set on joining the Imperial Police. It is possible, however, that over a period of time Orwell had concocted a future for himself and Jacintha but had omitted to inform her of his plans, and so had been stung by her rejection. Bowker uncovered more Orwellian secrets in Burma, claiming that Orwell indulged himself with Burmese women to a greater extent than earlier biographers allowed, and he hinted at affairs with the wives of absent colleagues. At one of his less salubrious postings, Katha, Bowker tells us, one of Orwell's superiors, on a tour of inspection, denounced him in the club as a disgrace to Eton.[82] If true, this is another secret that helps us better to understand the enigma of Orwell the Empire builder, as described by his visiting Etonian friend Christopher Hollis and others, and Orwell the scourge of the 'Pox Britannica'. Orwell took sick leave in 1927, following a bout of dengue fever and, as we know, quitted the Service on his return to Britain. Burma had been a mistake, but then, as Bowker discerningly observed, Orwell might already have conceived of making failure his *métier*.[83]

Orwell told his distraught family that he intended to write for a living, and we know that he was well read so far as British, French and American leftist writers were concerned. There is no indication, says Bowker, of his having read Marx, except for the *Communist Manifesto*, but in any case there is no indication either that at this stage in his career he saw himself as becoming a political writer. His stay in Paris turned out to be very fruitful, thanks chiefly to his well-connected Aunt Nellie Limouzin. Back in London, Orwell continued his tramping missions and was also introduced to an older woman, Mabel Fierz, with whom he had an affair: another important secret. It was Mabel who bullied the literary agent Leonard Moore, of Christie and Moore in the Strand, to take Orwell on. It was she who, when Orwell's manuscript of *Days in London and Paris* was rejected by T. S. Eliot, took it personally round to Moore and insisted he read it and get it published.[84]

Although Bowker does not significantly add to our knowledge of Orwell in Spain, his judgement on *Homage to Catalonia* bears repeating. It was, he said, 'not just a work of shining integrity, but the clearest expression of Orwell's version of socialism ... the quintessential expression of Christian socialism'.[85] Bowker's account of Orwell's career through the Second World War is conventional, though he does remind us that as a war correspondent in Europe Orwell was to meet many celebrated intellectuals, including Malcolm Muggeridge, Harold Acton, A. J. Ayer, André Malraux and Ernest Hemingway. Ayer is said to have remarked that Orwell appeared not to care much for philosophy, a deceptive impression thought Bowker, since 'a key philosophical argument' lies at the heart of *Nineteen Eighty Four*.[86] In fact, there are several such arguments, though as we shall see it is not certain that any is pursued rigorously or knowledgeably. I referred earlier to Orwell's paranoia. Bowker informs us that Orwell borrowed a revolver from Hemingway for self-protection and later swapped Hemingway's rather inferior revolver for a Luger that he bought in London from the owner of a newly established periodical, *Polemic*, for which he wrote. Orwell explained to the owner that he feared he could be a target for communist assassination.[87] He later mentioned to a friend, Geoffrey Gorer, that he thought that Gollancz might arrange to have him killed and he tried to find out more, from Warburg, about how Trotsky had been assassinated.[88] Bowker tells us that Orwell carried a large hunting knife around London at this time. Ever since Barcelona, Orwell had believed that he had cause to watch his back, and indeed a number of political murders were carried out in Paris and in America around this time. Given this frame of mind, Barnhill seems not so strange a choice of home after all.

Bowker's Orwell, unlike Crick's, is not shorn of 'domestic privacies', but for the most part they are used judiciously and add to our understanding of his work. Bowker is right to conclude that Orwell was consumed by his own concerns, if only because he thought of them as supremely politically important, and this tended to make him unsympathetic regarding others' concerns. This in turn led to a lack of insight that left his novels one-dimensional. But the sheer force of his imagination and the unequalled quality of his prose, says Bowker, made him the great writer he had boasted, as a boy, that he would become.[89]

The last biography I want to refer to is D. J. Taylor's *Orwell: The Life*, winner of the Whitbread Biography Award for 2003.[90] Elegantly written, it covers much the same ground as Bowker, and if I refer only to those details and points of discussion omitted by Bowker, this is not because I consider it a lesser work. Taylor gave more emphasis to Orwell's early concern with what he calls 'displaced religious sensibility', that is the channelling of religious sentiment into merely social relationships with the decline of organised Christianity. How did traditional concern with the afterlife translate into concern with the fate of the world after our death? Orwell's major foray into these matters was the novel *A Clergyman's Daughter*,[91] the acknowledged aesthetic failure of which should not obscure his deep concern with the subject matter, spiritual belief and Christianity as a value system. Taylor's perspectives on Orwell's northern pilgrimage and the Spanish Civil War do not constitute departures from accepted wisdom, but they contain additional insights. For example, we learn that after several weeks spent in Yorkshire and Lancashire Orwell pined for the south but had to make do with a long weekend in Bramley with his sister; that the working-class author Jack Hilton, whose advice on the trip Orwell had sought, concluded that Orwell had 'wasted money, energy and wrote piffle';[92] that in Spain Orwell spent 115 days on the Aragon front trying half-heartedly to take impregnable positions and regarded this time as 'one of the most futile periods of my life'.[93] Taylor points out that those who knew him in Spain thought that Orwell had little political consciousness, hence his readiness, if they would have him, to join the International Brigade.[94] More poignantly, he tells us that even in the socialist paradigm of the POUM militia Orwell could not bring himself to use the communal wine bottle, the *porrón*, but had to ask for his own cup.[95] Shades of Miss Mayfill. We are also reminded of Orwell's story of his sheer horror at being asked to drink from a communal beer bottle that was making its way around a railway carriage, from working-class mouth to mouth: 'I felt certain I should vomit.'[96]

Later Taylor referred to Orwell's skills as a carpenter, of interest to us because of Orwell's claim that working with our hands formed an important part of our consciousness.[97] Orwell knew the son of a timber merchant, through whom he had acquired some cherry wood to make bookshelves. The son was invited to inspect the finished article. His judgement: 'awful beyond belief!' The wood had been painted white and the shelves 'curved like a hammock'.[98] If Taylor's judgement on Orwell gave preference to his political achievements, he was nevertheless well aware of Orwell's literary achievements. He referred to something that Orwell had said to Sonia Brownell at one of Cyril Connolly's dinner parties: one should never write anything that a working man could not understand. Orwell achieved this, and it is the mark of his genius, to which everything else in his life, more or less, was sacrificed.

Finally, the most significant development in recent Orwell studies was unquestionably the publication in 1998 of Peter Davison's twenty-volume collection of Orwell's published and unpublished work.[99] The great advantage that Davison's labours afford the scholar is not merely that he has brought together the corpus of Orwell's work, including some pieces not previously readily available, but that he included responses invoked by some of the essays and journalism, adding a new dimension to our understanding of Orwell's work in these genres.

We take from these more recent additions to Orwell studies a more complex picture than the earlier work suggests, but none, not even Newsinger's, considers the extent to which and the manner in which Orwell's polemics were shaped by his literary talents and ambitions.

This completes our survey of a selective sample of some of the major biographies and commentaries on Orwell. I want now to draw together some of this material to form a picture of Orwell that might enable us to answer the question with which we began; why has Orwell been so influential, and indeed why is he still so influential? Judging by what we have discovered, there appear to be three *prima facie* reasons for Orwell's continuing international status. The first is that his political message was not only strong but enduring and applicable far more generally than to the Cold War world – indeed it is applicable to the modern world where individual rights and basic privacy are increasingly at risk from state vigilance. This is a theme, explored in detail in Shelden but also in the later biographies, that has assumed considerable importance in the modern age when governments suborn our liberties the better, they say, to protect them. It is no coincidence that Michael Moore's documentary film *Fahrenheit 9/11* concluded with a lengthy quotation from *Nineteen Eighty Four*.

The second is that Orwell's writing and, if Rees, Hollis, Spender and others are to be believed, his life, promoted a moral view of the world, based upon Trilling's 'freedom, bacon and proper work' for all – a morality based on common decency. This picture of Orwell has been reinforced by the frequency with which his personal moral status, his integrity, was referred to. Jennie Lee, the Labour politician, wrote: 'The only thing I can be quite certain of is, that up to his last day George was a man of utter integrity; deeply kind, and ready to sacrifice his last worldly possessions – he never had much – in the cause of democratic socialism.'[100] Orwell's personal integrity was weighed in the balance by many critics when assessing his work – he *was* what he wrote. In the modern age when many of the certainties of formal religion, especially in the West, have been eroded by scepticism, relativism and technological development, there is a perceived need for some moral system that can make sense of our changing world.

The third is that Orwell was a major writer whose work would naturally outlive him and his times. His exquisite prose style, though not brilliantly innovative like Joyce's, was the product of a lifetime's struggle. Together with the sheer force of his imagination, this 'transpicuous prose' provided us with several works that will last as long as books are read. This dimension of Orwell's legacy is the most widely acknowledged but the least developed. In the very act of drawing these distinctions concerning Orwell's legacy, we become immediately aware that they are likely to be closely interwoven, each contributing to Orwell's status. Interwoven then, but not indistinguishable. Rodden argued in 1989 that Orwell was 'alive today' because the themes about which he wrote were alive today, and this is equally true in the twenty-first century.[101] The 'spectre of totalitarianism, the agonies of the Left, the advent of the "media age", the rise of the "organisation man" ' all these themes demand our attention and make Orwell relevant. But what Rodden did not trouble to make clear is that what makes Orwell, rather than some of his contemporaries, alive today is the quality of his writing. Perhaps that was why his prediction, that Orwell's centenary in 2003 would be an exclusively academic celebration, turned out to be so wide of the mark.[102]

4

In this account of Orwell's social and political thought, we shall buck the trend of earlier studies and explore the third dimension of Orwell's continuing reputation, his greatness as a writer. It was primarily his last two works that established his reputation, and they provided a bridge to his earlier work. Here we find superlative essays, journalism of the highest quality, documentary writing of sheer brilliance, and novels that, for all their faults, contain memorably incisive passages. He possessed the ability to bring the issues about which he wrote so forcefully to our attention that we are obliged to take notice. Although the biographers and commentators whose work we have discussed all acknowledge, to varying degrees, Orwell's status as an imaginative writer, none, even Rodden whose focus was probably closer than that of any of the others, seems prepared to take account of what this might imply in terms of analysing Orwell's social and political thought. In shifting the traditional focus of Orwell studies more squarely onto Orwell the writer, I am not abandoning the study of his politics. Quite the opposite: this book is *about* Orwell's politics. I wish to elucidate, clarify and classify what it was that inspired Orwell to write. One consequence of giving prominence to Orwell as primarily an imaginative writer is that in analysing his social and political thought, it makes sense to concentrate primarily upon his major works. In the next chapter, then, we shall be looking at inequality and imperialism primarily through *Burmese Days* and a number of the better-known essays. In Chapter 3 we shall explore Orwell's attitudes to poverty, family and the working-class through *Down and Out in Paris and London, Keep the Aspidistra Flying* and *The Road to Wigan Pier*. In Chapter 4 we shall be considering Orwell's views on the nature of revolution, principally through *Homage to Catalonia* and *Animal Farm*. In Chapter 5 we shall be examining Orwell the patriot, primarily through *The Lion and the Unicorn* and *Coming Up for Air*. Chapter 6 will be concerned with Orwell's reaction to the threat of totalitarianism, principally through *Nineteen Eighty Four*, and essays such as *No Orchids for Miss Blandish*. Chapter 7 will consider Orwell's general theories on the nature of socialism as a political and moral system. The chief work studied here will be *A Clergyman's Daughter*. Finally, Chapter 8 will summarise Orwell's socialism, categorise it and assess its significance for modern social and political thought generally.

One last point before we begin. I believe it is essential, when discussing Orwell's work, to try to make a distinction between the imaginative and the non-fictional work. I have opted for imaginative and not fictional as a descriptor because so much of his work is based on personal experience and reportage and is therefore not strictly fictional, and yet this material is filtered through perspectives that are both aesthetic and political. We know that the diaries he compiled when in Yorkshire and Lancashire, for example, were manipulated and reordered for greater literary effect in the (therefore) essentially imaginative *Wigan Pier*. The key to the distinction I wish to make is intentionality. Where the intention is at least partly aesthetic, where Orwell is consciously using his narrative and imaginative powers to take us beyond the particular and to make a general, usually political point, I class this as imaginative. Where the intention is rather to discuss the particular in an unadorned, factual manner, to describe discrete events, I shall call this non-fictional. Again, let us take an example from *Wigan Pier*. The picture Orwell painted of a young woman unblocking a drain is described by the US scholar Ronald Thiemann as 'realistic narrative at its best'.[103] In fact, as we shall see in some detail, that picture has been substantially edited from the original diary entry, for aesthetic (and political) effect. Why attach importance to this difficult distinction? Because in non-imaginative writing, canons of accuracy, objectivity, soundly based knowledge and judgement are of primary importance, and Orwell was often wrong, biased and lacking in knowledge. Michael Foot, who was, after Aneurin Bevan, general editor of *Tribune* when Orwell was literary editor, suggested that 'George Orwell', the public persona, was a 'consciously cultivated *alter ego*.'[104] As he gained in experience as a reviewer and essayist, this *alter ego* came more to the fore and Orwell made a fetish of the hard-hitting, straight-talking style that had helped to make his reputation.

This style had much to commend it. Eagleton, for example, spoke of Orwell's 'Enlightenment conflation of truth, language, clarity and moral integrity [which] may have involved some questionable epistemology, but politically speaking it is worth a lot more than the work of those whose subversion of Western Reason is to write unintelligibly.'[105] Others saw in Orwell's clean style a riposte to 'opaque, jargon-laden writing' and 'the treatment of the past as a collection of fictional texts in history'.[106] On the other hand, the clear, robust style to be found in Orwell's non-fictional work offers no guarantee of impartiality, accuracy or special knowledge. He would frequently begin an argument with:

> 'Everyone who thinks at all . . .'
> 'All people who are morally sound . . .'
> 'Almost anyone who has travelled will confirm this . . .'
> 'All the more thoughtful members of the British working-class are . . .'
> 'Question any thinking person. . . and you will usually find . . .'
> 'Anyone who actually talked to working men at the time would . . .'
> 'A child of six would be able to see that . . .'

'Any soldier reading a book would . . .'
'It is universally agreed that . . .'.

These sweeping claims would be followed by arguments that would seldom bear them out. For example:

'It is universally agreed that the working-classes are far more moral than the upper classes;'[107]
'No decent person cares tuppence for the opinion of posterity.'[108]

This last preposterous assertion was marshalled against Vera Brittain's pamphlet *Seeds of Change*, in which she had opposed the carpet bombing of German cities because, as she explained, the 'unrestrained infliction of cruelty' might lead to general moral deterioration.[109] Orwell claimed that talk of limiting war was 'sheer humbug'. It seemed no bad thing that others should be killed beside young men. Was Brittain anxious to win the war or not? Later Orwell was to write: 'it seems to me you do less harm by dropping bombs on people than by calling them Huns'. Under which canon, common sense, decency or truthfulness, does this fall?

Orwell's claims were sometimes simply banal. In arguing that the British have no taste, he declared: 'You could see more ugly things in Oxford Street in half an hour than you could see among all the savage tribes in the world.'[110] This from a man who had hardly made a career of globe-trotting. Again, writing about the *New Statesman*, he claimed: 'I have . . . never . . . once found any coherent policy or constructive suggestion.' Not one – *ever*? There are many examples of Orwell being taken to task for factual inaccuracy. In one 'As I Please' article, Orwell took an edition of *Common Wealth* (the organ of Sir Richard Acland's new political party) to task for treating the important argument on birth rates in 'a slapdash way'.[111] He made two specific points: the German birth rate had been raised to 'unheard-of' levels under Hitler and the same had happened earlier in Kemalist Turkey. A statistician replied two weeks later saying that as a matter of fact Orwell was entirely wrong about Germany and that there were no reliable sources at all to support his claim for Kemalist Turkey. He concluded that Orwell was right to call for the scientific treatment of such important issues: 'Many *Tribune* readers will hope, as I do, that Mr Orwell will himself set an example.' Indeed, many *Tribune* readers were upset by what they took to be the frivolousness of some articles and the bias of others. Frivolity, bias and inaccuracy are not negligible charges, but one American Anglophile reader accused Orwell of bias, inaccuracy *and* falsification in a piece on US soldiers in Britain.[112] Orwell had asserted, typically, 'the general consensus seems to be that the only American soldiers with decent manners are Negroes'. This generalisation was based upon an experience involving two drunken US soldiers. His American critic accused Orwell of 'taking advantage of an unpleasant situation [from which he had generalised] to air one's specious knowledge of a subject'. How had Orwell arrived at his consensus? In a scientific way no doubt, jibed the reader. But worse: Orwell specifically referred to these soldiers attacking 'perfidious Albion'. His American critic wondered, as well he might have, how many GIs would have had the use of such words!

Orwell's dalliance with bias and lack of judgement, almost invariably advanced with complete assurance and spleen, surfaces elsewhere. An early champion of Henry Miller's work, he nevertheless came to the conclusion that 'no more that is of any value will come out of Henry Miller'.[113] One Miller expert took strong exception to this, referring to Orwell's 'insolent air of know-all and tell-all, which, coupled with his excellent style and show of intelligence, is capable of persuading innumerable readers that what he says is true'. Instead of reviewing Miller's latest book properly, Orwell, said the critic, chose to 'parade his knowledge in support of extremely silly generalisations'. The critic praised Orwell's prose but was offended by the no-nonsense, know-all style. Another example I wish to consider is chosen because it is generally regarded as a model essay, indeed praised by some as one of the best early examples of the new discipline of Cultural Studies, 'Boys' Weeklies'.[114] Frank Richards, the begetter of many of the better-known characters and the main target for Orwell's criticism in the essay, wrote a lengthy rebuttal of Orwell's principal arguments, to which Orwell did not respond.[115] Richards had two main criticisms. The first was that Orwell failed to do his homework and made some basic factual errors. For example, Orwell had written that 'Frank Richards' had been writing too long to be one author. As a consequence, the stories attributed to him 'must be written in a style that is easily imitated'. In fact, all the stories were written by Richards himself. Orwell, said Richards, had proceeded from an 'erroneous premise to an even more erroneous conclusion'. Whatever the merits or demerits of the style, Richards continues, it was his own and 'if I may say so with due modesty – inimitable'. Orwell had also accused Richards of 'lifting' words, and indeed characters, from other stories. Richards offered evidence to disprove the charge. Finally and more substantively, Orwell had stated that working-class characters enter into Richards' stories only as 'comics and semi-villains'. 'This is sheer perversity on

Orwell's part', Richards replied, 'I would like Mr Orwell to indicate a single sentence in which Frank Richards refers disrespectfully to the people who keep him in comfort'. Orwell did not accept the challenge.

Critics and men of letters will disagree profoundly and it is in the very nature of reviews and essays to be provoking and controversial. Orwell did not habitually lie or seek to mislead in his essays and reviews: far from it. But his prose, like a window pane, did not always look out onto the truth. Lucidity, Asquith said once, is the enemy of the man who has nothing to say. It is not a good friend to those who readily forsake impartiality, good judgement and sound research in their writing either.

One last brief example. In an unpublished essay entitled 'New Words', Orwell assured us that 'everyone who thinks at all' knows that the English language is deficient when describing mental acts. In pursuing his argument, he declared: 'I notice that many people never laugh when they are alone.'[116] Now Big Brother might say this, but it is logically absurd for Orwell to venture such an opinion.

I trust I have made clear why I think it is important to distinguish between Orwell's imaginative and non-fictional work, and why, in trying to elucidate the principal themes of Orwell's social and political thought, I shall be concentrating mainly on the former. However, as well as major works that are readily identifiable as imaginative, I shall also have recourse to discussing hybrid works of reportage in which those canons of accuracy, objectivity, soundly based knowledge and judgement may prove contentious. This issue cannot be ducked and is best confronted *in situ*. So let us begin.

2 The shadow of imperialism

Better hang wrong fellow than no fellow.
District Superintendent Westfield, George Orwell, *Burmese Days*
(Harmondsworth: Penguin, 1969, p. 228).

When Orwell sailed for Rangoon on the SS *Herefordshire* in October of 1922 he was little more than nineteen years old. He had left Eton, an environment about as different as one can imagine from the one he was going to, just over a year before. The ambiguity concerning Orwell's motivation to go East has been touched on already and I have suggested that a mixture of motives was almost certainly involved. A friend at Eton, the future historian Sir Steven Runciman (Orwell's collaborator in the experiment in the Black Arts), was convinced that Orwell had set his mind on going East fairly early. 'He used to talk about the East a great deal, and I always had the impression he was longing to go back there. I mean it was a sort of romantic idea . . .'[1] Romantic certainly, and in the full sense of that word: Orwell was not two when he left India and his father was hardly the man to have filled George's head with colourful tales of imperial derring do. R. W. Blair had devoted his life to an undistinguished and rather obscure branch of the service, the opium department. It was the task of this department to oversee the production, collection and distribution of Indian opium to China. In his thirty-seven years with the Department, Richard Blair rose from the position of assistant sub-deputy opium agent to sub-opium agent (class one). Michael Shelden referred to the opium trade as 'one of the worst evils of the British Colonial system' and as he grew up in the privileged and sheltered atmosphere of Eton, Orwell must have had some doubts concerning the nature of the specific paternal contribution to the great imperial enterprise. Yet, however he came by it, his ambition when leaving Eton was to join the Service. No doubt the expectations of both his parents, who regarded a career in the Imperial Civil Service as highly prestigious, would have helped to reinforce the romantic notions of the young Orwell. Moreover, Orwell's undoubted patriotism sought an outlet. Like many of his generation, he regretted having 'missed' the First World War and he did want to prove himself.

None of the biographers or commentators we have looked at entertained the possibility that Orwell might have regarded his chosen course of action, perhaps only subconsciously, as an excellent opportunity to gain experience from which to write. Yet everything we know about Orwell speaks of the centrality of writing in his life and ambitions. Why should it not have been included among his concerns and ambitions in 1922? After all, we should not forget that Orwell had read, and indeed written, more before the age of eighteen than befits either a putative man of action or indeed an academic failure (his other career possibility). Military experience in an exotic country was no bad platform from which to write. And it seems that he did write, though not a great deal, even when training in Burma, and later on almost certainly made sketches for his first novel.[2]

Whatever attitude Orwell might have entertained on boarding the *Herefordshire*, he could have had no notion of the reality awaiting him. At the time, he was one of some ninety British police officers responsible for maintaining civil order in a country that generally despised its British masters. Newsinger reports that a revolutionary nationalism had begun to make its presence felt in the 1920s,[3] though on nothing like the same scale as in India. According to Jacintha Buddicom, Orwell very soon came to loathe his life in Burma.[4] Others tell a different story of these early years.[5] Old Etonian Christopher Hollis visited him in 1925 and found him to be a man divided between the conventional imperial policeman and the radical critic of imperialism. He told Hollis that freedom and liberty 'don't agree with niggers'.[6] As usual it becomes impossible to pigeonhole Orwell, and his conversation with Hollis might have represented only the articulation of a debate going on in Orwell's own head, and he was confused. We know that he took Middleton Murry's journal *The Adelphi*, for example, showing his radical credentials; but we also know that he used some of its trendier articles for target practice.[7] Orwell later became convinced that his experience in the police had given him a clear edge over other left-wing critics in understanding the problems of empire. In *Burmese Days* Flory found it increasingly difficult to speak his mind at the expat's club because of his radical views; no doubt as a young Imperial Policeman Orwell began to find himself in just the same trap. Flory was lonely and homesick; so was Orwell. But for all Orwell's distaste of his life in Burma, Flory's comment to Elizabeth, that Burma could be paradise if one weren't alone, only points up the ambivalence to which I have referred. Orwell's description of the train journey northwards from Mandalay gives a further inkling of this ambivalence. 'White egrets stood poised, motionless, like herons, and piles of drying chillis gleamed crimson in the sun. Sometimes a white pagoda rose from the plain like the breast of a supine giantess.'[8] He was moved by the beauty of the country and the grace of its people, and perhaps if he could have shared these rich experiences and his misgivings with a close companion, such as Jacintha, life, as Flory hinted, might have become quite different.

If we cannot be entirely certain about Orwell's complex attitude towards Burma or his job, at least we have his fiction to turn to, and here we are on somewhat firmer ground. In his writings on Burma Orwell sought to use his own experiences, worked on by a powerful imagination, as a kind of metaphor for the whole imperial experience. Later, I shall suggest, he began to construct a model of social and political relations in capitalist society from the same metaphor, reflecting the same 'imperial' nexus quite unambiguously. I wish to pursue two objectives in this chapter. First, to tease out the constituent themes of Orwell's imperialist model and to examine it for consistency, and to go on to consider briefly whether the model sheds any light on the relationship between leaders and led, a relationship which exercises political thinkers as much today as ever it did.[9] Secondly and much more briefly, I wish to make some comments upon what it was that Orwell contributed to this debate as an imaginative writer which a political philosopher or historian, for example, might not have done. But first, and more substantively, we turn to the development of the imperialist model.

1

Burmese Days, Orwell's first published novel,[10] tells the story of a middle-aged timber merchant John Flory and his relations with the expatriate community in a small outpost in upper Burma, Kyauktada. Flory is an archetypal Orwellian hero, an outsider whose status as such is indicated by a disfiguring birthmark on one side of his face, a physical manifestation, it might be thought, of his alienation from society. His friendship with an Indian doctor in the community earns him not only the contempt of the expatriates at the local club but also enmeshes him, unknowingly, in the machinations of a ruthlessly ambitious

Burmese magistrate, U Po Kyin. The latter has a habit of taking bribes from both sides in a dispute and then adjudicating cases strictly on legal grounds. He had thus gained a reputation with the British and the local Burmese for impartiality. This suited him, for even when a child he had decided that his interests would best be served by fighting on the side of the British, by making himself useful, perhaps indispensable, to the imperial rulers. His intention was to amass wealth and influence in this role and then, at the end of his life, to endow pagodas and do good works so as to ensure a comfortable reincarnation.

The expatriates' club at Kyauktada had been advised to give membership to an Asian, as a manifestation of a new government initiative, and U Po Kyin had set his sights on being that member. His only competitor was the Indian doctor befriended by Flory, Veraswami, and the magistrate set about discrediting the doctor, and in the end Flory, in order to achieve his objective. As a sub-plot, Flory, too, had an objective: to marry Elizabeth, the niece of the Lackersteens, an attractive but small-minded young woman, who took Flory seriously only after the departure from Kyauktada of an arrogant patrician military policeman whom she vastly preferred. Flory's marital prospects were suddenly enhanced by his proving instrumental in putting down a minor revolt which actually threatened the club and its members. His equally sudden humiliation and disgrace was engineered by U Po Kyin. Elizabeth spurned him and Flory took his own life. Without the support of his white friend, Veraswami was undermined by the magistrate and U Po Kyin achieved his objective of membership of the club and indeed all his other worldly ambitions (except that of becoming a great benefactor before his death: we are left wondering, with his widow, whether he had not come back on the earth as a rat or a frog). This is a story without heroes, a story of mendacity, treachery and hypocrisy, of racial and social repression and hatred. It is a story of the empire.

The story provides the author with the opportunity to expose the imperial elite to ruthless analysis. Amongst the ex-pats was Ellis, an intelligent and able timber executive who felt sincerely for all Asians 'a bitter, restless loathing as of something evil and unclean . . . any hint of friendly feeling towards an Oriental seemed to him a horrible perversity'.[11] Ellis' feelings were roused to a fury by the government's new policy of encouraging the admittance of non-Europeans to clubs. He found it unpalatable that Flory should befriend an Asian, go to his house and drink with him, but the prospect of Flory proposing Veraswami for the club completely infuriated him: 'By God, he'd go out with my boot behind him if ever I saw his black snout inside that door.'[12] Orwell makes it clear that Ellis' attitude, though paranoid, was not without some imperialist rationale: 'Here we are', he said, 'supposed to be governing a set of damned black swine who've been slaves since the beginning of history, and instead of ruling them in the only way they understand, we go and treat them as equals.'[13] Indeed, his attitude was not so very far from the axiom Orwell propounded to Hollis, that freedom and liberty 'don't agree with niggers'.

Only the Lackersteens amongst the expats are as fully drawn as Ellis. Mrs Lackersteen's views on race relations in Burma signalled the connection that Orwell began to make after his return to Britain between overseas and domestic 'imperialism', though probably he had already seen it whilst in Burma: 'Really I think the laziness of these servants is getting too shocking', she complained. 'We seem to have no authority over the natives nowadays, with all those dreadful reforms and the insolence they learn from the newspapers', said Mrs Lackersteen. 'In some ways they are getting almost as bad as the lower classes at home.'[14] As for Lackersteen himself, he was shown to be a drunkard and a lecher, part of an empire described by Flory as cemented together by booze (perhaps not Orwell's most apt metaphor).

Flory's own political position was manifested primarily through his discussions with Veraswami. The doctor argued that in building up the infrastructure of the subject nations in terms of transport and communications, irrigation, health, education and the legal system, the imperialists had contributed to the well-being of those they governed. They 'set up hospitals, they combat plague, cholera, leprosy, smallpox, venereal disease'.[15] He went on to argue that if the British were not consuming the resources of Burma, somebody else would, and far more selfishly. British businessmen actually develop the resources of the countries they control and British civil servants endeavour to run them with justice. 'At least you have brought us law and order. The unswerving British Justice and the Pax Britannica.'[16] 'Bosh', retorted Flory, declaring his own position to be not so much anti-empire as anti-humbug (a very Shavian position[17]). He, too, wanted to make money but not to the extent of participating in the 'slimy white man's burden humbug'.[18] Let's not pretend, he argued, that the white man was in Burma to uplift the Burmese; he was there to rob them. Living the imperial pretence 'corrupts us . . . There's an everlasting sense of being a sneak and a liar that torments us and drives us to justify ourselves night and day'.[19] The whole business of empire, Flory concluded, may be summed up as follows: 'The official holds the Burman down while the businessman goes through his pockets.'[20] That, said Flory, was the reality of the 'Pox Britannica'.

On one level Flory surely deluded himself, for at base the humbug he attacked was the lubricant of the imperial machine, allowing both enthusiastic and reluctant imperialists to convince themselves that they were involved in a mighty enterprise for the good of all. As Arthur Koestler pointed out and Orwell himself later acknowledged, that 'humbug' constituted a cushion of decency and constitutionality, the difference between the British Empire in the East and that of the Japanese. At another level this 'humbug' did nothing to alleviate the burden on both participants of the underlying relationship of exploiter and exploited, and indeed could be seen, though Flory did not actually suggest this, as largely a long-term investment; minimalist philanthropy would facilitate exploitation over a far longer period.

At root Orwell was bitterly critical of a system in which louts fresh from school (as Orwell was himself) whose song would be something like Flory's own, *The Scrum of Life*, could kick grey-haired servants; a system in which not only the natives but also the masters had no liberty. Free speech was impossible when every white man was a cog in the wheels of despotism. The only freedoms that existed for the masters were the freedom to drink and to fornicate. Like most of the single British men (apparently including Orwell himself), Flory had taken a young Burmese woman, Ma Hla May, as a mistress. He had no feelings towards her but simply used her for sex and otherwise treated her with distaste. All other public actions and pronouncements were dictated by the code of the white ruling class, the *sahiblog*. Flory, as a sole rebel, found that 'in the end the secrecy of your revolt poisons you like a secret disease',[21] especially when he discovered that he lacked the courage to stand up for Veraswami. When the club members signed a notice urging against native membership, he too signed. Only later, when it became clear that the club, if it voted unanimously, could block the membership of an Asian, did Flory stand up for his friend, earning Ellis' bilious rant: 'You oily swine! You nigger's Nancy Boy! You crawling, sneaking, – bloody bastard!'[22]

The arrival at Kyauktada of Elizabeth, the niece of the Lackersteens, gave rise in Flory's mind to the possibility of some release from his solitude. Free of any 'excess of intellect', she was hardly the kind of woman he would have chosen for himself. But she was young, attractive and British, and the Lackersteens were anxious to find a husband for her. After all, the only alternative for Elizabeth would have been working for a living, a notion that Mrs Lackersteen found repulsive. So Flory undertook to escort Elizabeth and to try to interest her in those aspects of Burmese life that interested him – 'how you could love this country if you were not alone'[23] – but she withdrew within the fastidious and platitudinous certainties of the tribal behaviour pattern of the European woman in the East, the *burra memsahib*. He could interest her only in tiger hunting. Flory's courtship, however, was massively derailed by the arrival of a young Military Policeman, Lieutenant Verrall, who was everything that Flory was not, as 'elegant as a picture with his white buckskin topi and his polo-boots that gleamed like an old meerschaum pipe'.[24] He was, in fact, the very epitome of aristocratic self-assurance like Auden's iconic 'splendid person' who stood 'In spotless flannels or with hand/Expert on trigger'.[25] Naturally the Lackersteens saw Verrall as the better catch, especially on discovering that his name was prefaced in the Civil List by those magical words 'the Honourable'. And to clinch the matter Elizabeth was told that Flory was keeping a Burmese woman. 'What on earth for?' had been her initial response. For his part, Verrall was a man who took whatever he wanted, whenever he wanted it, and in Kyauktada Elizabeth provided some small and fleeting distraction. But one day, to the Lackersteens' and their niece's lasting consternation, he was gone without a word.

The world of Kyauktada was thrown into turmoil by the murder of one of the club members. Club members suggested to the police that they should beat information out of the villagers, but this was firmly rejected as being against 'our own silly laws'. Nevertheless, the club was reassured: there will be an arrest. 'Much better hang wrong fellow than no fellow.'[26] U Po Kyin organised a minor revolt against this blatant injustice, though entirely for his own purposes, in the course of which Flory acted with considerable valour and perspicacity. His new reputation led him to hope, after all, to win Elizabeth. But U Po Kyin was intent on securing club membership; that meant discrediting Veraswami and that, in turn, meant discrediting his friend and supporter Flory. He contrived to persuade the aggrieved Ma Hla May, Flory's former mistress, to embarrass him in front of Elizabeth. This plan was brilliantly successful. Flory was disgraced, and indeed consequently took his own life, leaving Veraswami without a friend. U Po Kyin became the first non-European member of the club.

Burmese Days represented a savage indictment of empire. It did this not so much through the discussions that Flory and Veraswami had on the nature of empire but simply by depicting those who run the real thing. Whether it is the unchallengeable nature of their power that corrupts these men and women or whether corrupt men and women are attracted to these positions of power is immaterial. What matters is that simply by telling their story, Orwell confronts us with a state of affairs that is very difficult to defend on any moral grounds. How much of Orwell himself is in the story is an interesting but in the end insignificant matter. We do know, though, that Gollancz was originally very concerned about the possibility of libel actions, and so we may draw our own conclusions.

2

'A Hanging', which first appeared in print in 1931,[27] was a less overtly didactic essay, and dealt with the execution of a prisoner in Burma. We are not told of what crime the man was guilty; neither is any inference drawn by the writer from the events that are described. What Orwell does, however, is to oblige the reader to confront the harsh realities of empire. The policeman in the story was none other than Trilling's 'Orwell of the undeceived intelligence', the ordinary moral man. He noticed that the condemned man, walking to the gallows in the early morning, actually stepped aside to avoid a puddle.[28]

> It is curious, but till that moment I had never realised what it means to destroy a healthy conscious man. When I saw the prisoner step aside to avoid the puddle I saw the mystery, the unsupportable wrongness, of cutting a life short when it is in full tide . . . He and we were a party of men walking together, seeing, hearing, feeling, understanding the same world; and in two minutes, with a sudden snap, one of us would be gone – one mind less, one world less.

What is more, the man was endowed with reason: even in his parlous situation he reasoned 'even about puddles'. For the reader the important, untold part of the story is that 'justice' is always the prerogative of the imperial power, the exploiter, and that the recipient of justice is always the exploited nation. There are social implications too. Justice is the prerogative of the owning class, embodied in a system that is structured above all to protect the property and status of that class: to protect the strong from the weak, the rich from the poor. On the other hand, the condemned man represented the powerless and although we know nothing of his crime we are invited to believe that it was likely to be somehow consequent upon his social disadvantage. Justice is carried out by a disillusioned young British officer and a group of Indians, unenthusiastic for their task but anxious to gain the favours of the British officer. The prisoner wins our sympathy. We learn from a young Eurasian that when he had discovered, a few days earlier, that his appeal had been rejected, the prisoner had wet himself. We hear his supplication to his God; even when the mask was fitted over his head the bell-like, 'Ram! Ram!

Ram!' intoned sombrely. We note that when the hanging party was besieged and finally invaded by a friendly dog, it was the prisoner's face it tried to lick. Orwell cleverly used the dog to help stitch the story together. It later ran to the back of the gallows after the hanging and was immediately cowed by what it found. It knew that something unnatural had happened. At the end Orwell tells us ironically that it was the dog that was 'conscious of having misbehaved itself'. We note finally the attempts of the Eurasian to ingratiate himself with his colonial master, offering Orwell a cigarette from his 'classy' European-style case. The whole exercise, in short, provided a sordid example of the exploiter/exploited relationship that characterised imperialism and it is told with force and an economy of style that arouses our sympathy but, more importantly, helps us experience at first hand, as it were, the real nature of the imperial relationship.

In *The Road to Wigan Pier* Orwell wrote: 'I watched a man hanged once; it seemed to me worse than a thousand murders.'[29] It was part of the system of 'so-called justice', characterised by the cowed faces of the long-term prisoners, the scarred buttocks of men who had been flogged with bamboos, the horror of arrests. The thieves whom the imperial police imprisoned never thought of themselves as criminals but as victims of a foreign power. He wrote: 'I thought then – and I think now, for that matter – that the worst criminal who ever walked is morally superior to a hanging judge.'[30] Some might consider such a statement merely sentimental and sententious, a charge that Orwell himself seemed half-inclined to accept later on, when admitting that the real alternative to the state applying strict laws might prove to be Al Capone applying his own brand of law.[31] If Orwell was an enemy of capital punishment as such, he never said so. Neither did he assemble a single line of argument in support of his indictment of imperial law, beyond the claim that imperialism was itself an injustice. Nevertheless, the American scholar the late Jorge Fernandes did flesh out such an argument. He wrote apropos racial inequality that the act of discrimination was never simply a matter of inconvenience; it always constituted a 'spiritual murder'.[32] Even if we accept this position, spiritual murder is not the same thing as murder and we do not have to be convinced Hobbesians to reject the idea that an agent of the state, even a state not freely chosen by its citizens, should be relegated *ipso facto* to a worse moral category than any criminal. Perhaps Orwell's intention was more than anything to make his readers think; to that extent he succeeded.

'Shooting an Elephant', which appeared in 1936,[33] was a much more didactic piece. Although just as forcefully written, it does not leave us to make our own minds up, as in 'A Hanging', but presents us very clearly with the conclusions we are supposed to draw from the story. The story concerned an elephant on the rampage, an event reported to Orwell, the young imperial policeman, by the local Burmese, so that this representative of law and order might go and kill the offending animal and minimise the damage it was causing. But before these events unfolded we are already privy to Orwell's feelings about his role as an imperial guardian. He was 'all for the Burmese and all against their oppressors, the British'.[34] And yet he had no love for the oppressed. He hated their 'sneering yellow faces', their constant baiting of him. He was, he felt, stuck between his hatred of empire and his 'rage against the evil-spirited little beasts' who made his job so difficult. All this gave him 'an intolerable sense of guilt'. It was with such a state of mind that this guardian of the empire set out to deal with the problem of the elephant.

We discover that the elephant was a young male, which had not gone wild but had been subject to an attack of must, an intermittent sexual frenzy. Consequently it had been chained up but had somehow broken free. Orwell followed the trail of destruction and we are soon brought up sharply by the description of the body of a Dravidian coolie horribly mangled by the elephant. On went Orwell, followed now by a growing band of Burmese anxious to see the action. Finally, Orwell discovered the animal in a paddy field looking no more dangerous than a cow. He knew then that to shoot the elephant in such circumstances would be reprehensible. What weighed in his decision was not so much the morality of taking life unnecessarily but the fact that in killing the beast he would be destroying a 'huge and costly piece of machinery'. However, he was not a free agent in this affair; he was part of the imperial system. And here he was, confronting a docile animal, but willed forward by the crowd, willed to kill: he, the man with the rifle, with the authority, they an unarmed and apparently powerless group of natives watching 'a conjuror about to perform a trick'. But in reality, he went on, he was no more than 'an absurd puppet pushed to and fro by the will of those yellow faces behind'. It was then that Orwell realised the irony of imperialism, that the imperialist needed to create a mask of ruthless, God-like omniscience and 'his face grows to fit it'. The truth is, that when 'the white man turns tyrant it is his own freedom that he destroys'.[35] The account of the actual shooting of the elephant is a gripping piece of writing that fully brings home the enormity, and indeed immorality, of this act of wanton destruction. What Orwell tells us emphatically is that *this* is the real nature of the imperial relationship. *This* is the white man's burden. Orwell wrote this piece a number of years after the event (in which he may or may not actually have participated) and he mentions then that at the time of the event he was unaware that the British Empire was on its last legs or that it was, in his later judgement, a great deal better than the empires that might supplant it. It is hard to believe that such awareness would have affected his attitude at the time but it is nevertheless worth noting. We shall be returning to this point.

Were Orwell's stories 'true' (that is, reasonably accurate accounts of real events in which he had himself participated)? It is not easy to be sure. There is no evidence that Orwell participated in a hanging and Orwell's version is similar to an event depicted in Somerset Maugham's 'The Vice-Consul', with which he would have been familiar and which he might have used as a model. Taylor suggested Thackeray's 'Going to See a Man Hanged' as another possible model.[36] As for 'Shooting an Elephant', Bowker concluded that this indeed happened,[37] and since it involved the unnecessary loss of a major financial asset, a working male elephant, it may have been the reason for Orwell's being dispatched from his comfortable posting at Moulmein to the far less congenial Katha in the far north. Taylor, however, was less confident, referring to a report in the *Rangoon Gazette* of just such an event and at the right time, but the policeman involved was not Orwell.[38] Later we shall discuss the nature of truth in literature, but for the moment it is enough to say that Orwell was intent on conveying the truth, as he saw it, of imperialism. In that wider sense, the stories were certainly true; or at least Orwell believed them to be so.

Supporters of imperialism had always acknowledged that the white man's burden was a heavy one, entailing in Kipling's famous words merely 'the blame of those ye better, the hate of those ye guard'. Yet the assumption had always been that, in the long run, the relationship was of mutual benefit, bringing to the subject races all the advantages of modernisation and Christianity, and to the imperial race not merely clear economic gains but also the opportunity of serving the great cause of civilisation. Orwell's view may be summarised as accepting the Marxist analysis of the economics of imperialism and as rejecting totally any notion of moral or cultural gains for either side: imperialism debased both sides utterly. Both sides were obliged to adopt policies and attitudes which they privately found distasteful. It was the very condition of the imperialist's role, said Orwell, that 'he shall spend his life in trying to impress the "natives", and so in every case he has got to do what the "natives" expect of him'.[39] So the nature of the imperialist relationship was an intensely alienating one; both sides were alienated from each other and from their roles (i.e. from themselves).

Flory, like Orwell, came to the realisation that empire was despotism motivated by theft, but Orwell himself also reached another crucial conclusion: that 'the overwhelming bulk of the British proletariat does not live in Britain but in Asia'.[40] The universality of the imperial relationship was thus underlined.

When Orwell returned to Britain he may originally have believed that he personally was exchanging the tyranny of imperialism for the sweet smell of liberty, but he apparently did not believe this for long; soon enough he was beginning to use imperialism as a metaphor not merely for the relationship between the classes in Britain but also for any relationship between those with and without power. Every such relationship was based implicitly or explicitly upon exploitation, and he devoted the rest of his life to exploring the nature of that relationship, bringing to bear that sharpness of focus and intimidating directness for which he became justly renowned.

An excellent example of the use much later of this imperial metaphor is his account of his school days at St Cyprian's, with the ironic Blakean title 'Such, Such Were the Joys',[41] which he wrote in 1947.[42] Orwell portrayed himself as the victim of an imperialist system. Although St Cyprian's was a fee-paying boarding school, Orwell was on reduced fees (as a potential scholarship boy), a fact of enormous economic and political importance; he was a native. If the Head behaved with forbearance to the sons of the wealthy, he was almost brutal with the poorer scholarship boys. The relationship was purely an economic one, the boys' abilities representing a long-term investment (though in the short term they could be underfed and ill-treated), just like the people of Burma; and the governing principle of the relationship, as it was with the empire, was not love or even respect but, as Orwell portrayed it, fear. Young boys were dropped from the comfort and security of their families into a world of power relations, dishonesty and hypocrisy, 'out of a gold-fish bowl and into a tank full of pike'.[43] The determining element of the imperialist model was that it was quite impossible for the exploited ever fully to join the exploiters, whatever their achievements. 'If you climbed to the highest niche that was open to you, you could only be an underling, a hanger-on of the people who really counted.'[44] That indeed had been the summit of U Po Kyin's ambition, and what Orwell, as a young scholar, pitifully aimed for. The decisive factor, said Orwell, was class and the cornerstone of class was wealth. Money, he continued, was synonymous with goodness, with moral virtue. The rich and the strong – the same thing really – always won, and since morality was their agent, they always deserved to win. The depiction of his school days after nearly forty years represented one obvious illustration of the attempt to apply the imperialist model to a different setting. It was one illustration, but not the chief one: that was to be his exploration of the nature of class relations in Britain, and it was the one to which, following his return from Burma, Orwell devoted his life and sacrificed his health. We shall be looking at the fruits of his experiences in Chapter 3.

3

To summarise the argument so far: I have suggested that Orwell's political perspective was shaped by his formative Burmese experiences, which provided him with a framework of analysis of the relationship between the rulers and the ruled, a framework that he adapted to analyse contemporary capitalist society in his homeland. It must be borne in mind that he had gone to Burma with two conflicting sets of values concerning imperialism. The first was the product of his upbringing. It esteemed the traditional imperialist qualities almost as a modern adaptation of the classical concept of *virtu*. The second was the product of his intellectual nourishment at Eton and was iconoclastic, dismissive, Shavian. As we have seen, those who met him in Burma, such as Christopher Hollis, described him as torn between these two visions of the imperial project. He had misgivings about the ends of imperialism (or at least some of them) and anyway his personal experiences rendered him increasingly incapable of willing the means. Some aspects of imperialism might be justified politically, and British imperialism might legitimately claim to be less unacceptable than most other forms – Orwell accepted both of these possibilities – but it necessarily involved so much inhumanity, so much 'dirty work', as to be ultimately morally unjustifiable. Orwell's analysis of empire shows him to have been primarily concerned not so much with a political, and certainly not an ideological, critique, as with a moral critique, and to have focused on and made judgements about human conduct rather than political conflict. It was his achievement to reduce political problems to their fundamentals, and in his imaginative work imperialism was forensically reduced to the exploiter/exploited nexus. He was not so much concerned here to unravel the ambiguities and complexities of imperialist political relationships as to lay bare what he took to be its essential moral constituents. The resulting imperialist model needed to be simple; it had to expose actions as either morally right or wrong. His was a bipolar monochrome world: black and white but no greys. Grey was the casuist's colour. Orwell claimed elsewhere that if ever he saw working men struggling with their 'natural enemies', the police, he knew instinctively which side he was on.[45] This is nothing other than the imperialist model in operation. One was either exploiter or exploited and, as he said unequivocally, in that model the exploited were always right and the exploiters always wrong.

Orwell's basic concern here, then, appears to have been not so much with political values as such, as with the moral values that could be seen to buttress them. If humanity was the part-angel and part-beast of traditional dualism, it could nevertheless be transformed by the nature of the social relationship. Imperialist, and indeed all capitalist, social relations were founded on power, and for Orwell it was immaterial whether those who held power believed themselves (erroneously no doubt) to be motivated by a desire to improve the lot of their fellows or by a naked, cynical desire for theft or other gratification; the effect was the same. To base one's expectations of justice on the powerful adopting self-denying ordinances as, for example, Confucius and Plato or Hegel and Marx had done, was simply illusory. Power itself had to be defused and imperialism as the base of all capitalist social relationships had to be replaced by equality.

Does the imperialism model contribute anything at all to the development of political theories of the ruler–ruled relationship? There would be general agreement that at first sight the model seems demonstrably simplistic, as consequently does Orwell's analysis of power relations. The motives that impelled so many to participate in the imperial enterprise could not realistically be written off as invariably exploitative. The intentions of schoolteachers in even scholarship factories like St. Cyprian's were seldom uncoloured by genuinely good intentions for their pupils. Most socialist intellectuals and ideologues who strove to improve the lot of the poor (their 'imperial' enterprise) could not plausibly be represented as simply attempting to exercise power for its own sake. Contrary to the assumptions of the model, the oppressors are not always wrong. Nor does the evidence (even Orwell's evidence) lend much substance to the claim that the oppressed are always right. Does the opposition in Burma today believe that their government is less imperialist than were their British former masters? Have not some of the oppressed become oppressors themselves, like modern U Po Kyins? Are criminals not to be punished because they are sentient human beings with the power of reason, even though they may have used that reason, as Hobbes would have anticipated, to secure the most antisocial of objectives?

These are important questions, but there are others: did Orwell remain true to his anti-imperialist moral position; did his later non-fictional writing have the same unequivocal moral message? In 1942 he wrote a revealing essay on Kipling.[46] In it Orwell employed a style that he commonly used when dealing at length with an issue, event or personality on which he might be thought to hold a controversial view. That is to say, he starts by identifying himself with what he takes to be the common view, in this case a condemnation of Kipling's imperialism, and then works towards a more contentious position. So: 'It is no use pretending that Kipling's view of life, as a whole, can be accepted or even forgiven by any civilised person.' And again: 'Kipling is a jingo imperialist, he is morally insensitive and aesthetically disgusting.'[47] On the other hand, Kipling was seriously misquoted by the sniggering 'pansy-left circles'. The imperialism that Kipling represented was not in any way comparable to the gangsterism of the twentieth-century fascists and totalitarians. Imperialists like Kipling may have been patronising, but they had a 'sense of responsibility that "enlightened" people" seldom or ever possess'.[48] The Anglo-Indians, for example, 'did things'. In fact, they 'changed the face of the earth'. Moreover, Kipling extolled the virtues, if in a patronising way, of the ordinary soldier at the expense of his leaders, those 'flannelled fools at the wicket, those muddied oafs in the goal'. In his writing Kipling might have dealt in platitudes, said Orwell, but at least he confronted issues of action and responsibility, unlike the socialist Wilde's 'enlightened' epigrams or the socialist Shaw's 'collection of cracker-mottoes' in *The Revolutionist's Handbook*. In short, this essay, which begins with an attack on Kipling, turns into a clever defence not simply by giving some support to those whom Kipling supported but by denigrating the fashionable Left. Orwell's defence of Kipling might (inelegantly) be called an exercise in subtle Veraswami-ism and unsubtle intellectual-bashing. In Kipling's day, Orwell had written earlier, you could still be an imperialist and a gentleman, and Kipling was personally decent.[49]

Orwell spent part of the Second World War working for the BBC Indian Service.[50] He edited a radio magazine which comprised a journal of literature and ideas that included contributions from a range of literary and philosophical figures. The programme, indeed the Service, was aimed at the educated Indian, and Orwell knew very well that its propaganda purpose was to help to keep India within the imperial fold at least until after the war. He also happened to believe that this was in India's best interests. In 1943 he was asked by *Tribune* to write a background note to Duval's 'Whitehall Road to Mandalay', what modern diplomatic jargon might identify as a road map, which was designed to give a measure of independence to Burma partly in an attempt to scotch Japanese anti-British propaganda. Orwell wrote: 'Burma is a small, backward, agricultural country, and to talk about making it independent is nonsense in the sense that it can never be independent. There is no more reason for turning Asia into a patchwork of comic-opera states than there is with Europe.' Moreover, Burma was politically backward, with no trade unions and no grasp of modern political ideas. It was, he concluded, dangerous to transpose European habits of thought to Asia.[51] This evoked the following pointed response from one reader: 'When I read George Orwell's "footnote" to Duval's "Whitehall Road to Mandalay", I began to wonder whether I had stumbled on the *Daily Telegraph* rather than the *Tribune*.' He went on to wonder whether Orwell imagined that the British Raj would introduce the trade unions and socialist ideas 'whose absence in Burma he makes the excuse for the retention of empire'.[52] The writer pointed out that Europe itself was a patchwork of states. Orwell, stung by this, replied that whilst this was true to an extent, one could hardly imagine states like Luxembourg or Lithuania becoming independent. Or Wales. I mention this reply because it illustrates the limitations of Orwell's grasp of political realities. His general point about small European states is untenable and to introduce Wales as an example in an argument against Burmese independence is entirely inappropriate, and likely, moreover, to have brought a small Celtic hornet's nest about his head. Which it did. What Orwell argued for was spheres of influence. 'I would place the whole mainland of southeast Asia, together with Formosa, under the guidance of China, whilst leaving the islands under an Anglo-American-Dutch condominium.'[53] This 'guidance' would entail the loans of experts, technical guidance and so on. In a word, as Alok Rai concludes, it would constitute 'imperialism as welfare'.[54] In *The Lion and the Unicorn*, Orwell put the point with his customary forcefulness: 'In the age of the tank and the bombing plane, backward agricultural countries like India and the African colonies can be no more independent than can a cat or dog.'[55]

In a *Horizon* review written in 1943, Orwell pursued this theme, declaring that India was 'very unlikely to be independent in the sense that Britain or Germany is now independent'.[56] She could not aspire to becoming a sovereign state because she could not defend herself. The author of the book being reviewed, Lionel Fielden, replied with a disheartening conclusion: 'But, when all is said and done, there remains in Mr Orwell's writing a rancour that is hard to explain.'[57] In fact, Orwell saw himself as the Left's expert on Asia and found it hard not to criticise even those views that were close to views he had himself advanced. But there was another reason for Orwell's rancour: he was totally opposed to Gandhi's pacifism and did not want to see India move out of the orbit of British influence. He attacked Gandhi on several occasions, earning a rebuke from one reader that his criticisms were 'full of mistakes and inaccuracies'.[58] Orwell was advised to go into the matters more thoroughly before circulating 'dirt' about the ashram. 'And what is it about Gandhi's career that makes you think him a bit of charlatan?' the reader asked. The honest reply would have been that Gandhi was a pacifist and Orwell could admit no justification for pacifism at such a time.[59] Orwell's argument against Indian independence might be construed as some kind of reluctant acceptance of neo-imperialism; but there is more than this *realpolitik* in his thinking. As he wrote in 1941: 'It is a fact that many of the events which the jingo history books make the most noise about are things to be proud of.'[60] In his non-fiction, then, Orwell the patriot proved unable entirely to reject the imperial project and all its works. We therefore cannot collude with Christopher Hitchens' ambition to establish Orwell as one of the founders of the discipline of post-colonialism.[61] As we have seen, Newsinger conceded that Orwell's views on empire were not static. What we might wish to conclude from this discussion, however, is that his views on empire were probably more static than Newsinger allowed, but equally probably less consistent.[62] Orwell's imaginative literature was fiercely anti-empire, but his non-fictional writing showed an ambivalence that damages Hitchen's case fatally.

4

I have argued that the quality of Orwell's contribution to social and political thought was shaped very largely by its quality as literature, and it is to this theme that I shall now turn. Eagleton and others might wish to argue against such a proposition. 'Literature', he says, 'in the sense of a set of works. . . . distinguished by certain shared inherent properties, does not exist'.[63] If this were true then perhaps we would need to invent literature, rather like Voltaire's God. Fortunately, this will not be necessary, since I share the view of the prolific Peruvian writer Mario Vargas Llosa, who was certain of literature's existence and called all arguments to the contrary 'complete buggles'.[64] In earlier times literature included every serious discipline, its concerns encompassing the whole of knowledge. By the nineteenth century, however, knowledge had fractured into specialisms and intellectual activity quickly became differentiated. There emerged kinds of writing that were consciously instrumental and consciously non-literary. But there was also writing that intended to 'influence by characteristically non-objective techniques, our perception of the world and our moral understanding'.[65] It is in this sense that Orwell's analysis of imperialism should be viewed. The author attempts to share his experiences of imperialism with us in the form of imaginative literature. He has, quite literally, reorganised these experiences so as to represent to us a view of life that many will perceive to be essentially 'true'. This idea of sharing an experience was of fundamental importance to Orwell's project; it was probably the only method open to him to expose us to 'the truth' of imperialism. Where he employed the more orthodox philosophical, economic or ideological form of analysis, he was soon sucked into the murky world of *realpolitik* in which the dominant colours were those despised shades of grey, and he becomes less convincing. Moreover, from Orwell's own perspective he was obliged to take on the mantle of an intellectual, a pejorative label Orwell used in the political sphere to include ideologists. His intellectual was a spokesman for a system of thought whose exclusive nature could be penetrated only by other intellectuals, and only they had the right key. As an imaginative writer sharing his experiences rather than an intellectual advancing an ideology, Orwell was committed not so much to giving a duplicate key to anyone who might be interested as to leaving the door wide open for everyone and doing his best to oblige them to be interested. That is the nature of imaginative literature, and it represents a medium of communication ideally suited to the writer who wishes us to realise that political issues are at their core moral issues, and that to deny the appropriateness of morality to the issues of governance, as Machiavelli preached and many have practised, would represent the first decisive step in establishing imperialism.

Orwell attempted to provide us with a metaphor depicting how human relationships should *not* be structured. We shall need to examine the nature of imaginative literature more deeply before we complete this study of Orwell's social and political thought, but it is enough for the present to establish clearly what medium Orwell was working in. Sartre once famously argued that Picasso's great anti-fascist, anti-war painting *Guernica*, won not a single convert to the Republican cause; W. H. Auden was of the view that his own poetry of the 1930s had had no political influence whatever.[66] Both would presumably have agreed that Orwell's project was doomed to failure, yet the quality of Orwell's imaginative writing, especially his powerful use of metaphor, leaves the door open to the possibility of our being influenced politically, which was undoubtedly Orwell's objective.

3   The poor, the workers and the 'decency myth'

We have got to fight for justice and liberty, and Socialism does mean justice and liberty when the nonsense is stripped off it. It is only the essentials that are worth remembering.

George Orwell, *The Road to Wigan Pier* (Harmondsworth: Penguin, 1963, pp. 193–4).

Orwell returned from Burma on sick leave in the late summer of 1927. The news that he was to resign his commission and that he had no intention of returning came later, and as a complete shock to his family. It must have been doubly galling for his parents to realise that their considerable sacrifice over a number of years appeared to have been in vain and that they would have to live with the opprobrium of having a son who seemed to be determined to shirk his social responsibilities and adopt a bohemian lifestyle. Orwell's declaration that he intended to earn his living as a writer would hardly have softened the blow. What sort of living? What sort of writer? He was later to tell the story of the young man down from Oxford who informed his family that he intended to write. 'About what?' asks an aunt. His reply was that one didn't write *about* anything, one just wrote.[1] It goes without saying that throughout his career Orwell held such an attitude in contempt. It was always certain that Orwell would write about *something*; the question was what? Much had happened to the Europe that Orwell had left in 1922. The rise of the Nazis in Germany had begun, following the Munich rally in 1923; in the USSR Stalin had strengthened his grip on power and Trotsky had been expelled; in Britain a Labour government had taken office, if only briefly, in 1924. In 1926 the country had experienced what radicals such as Georges Sorel and Henri Barbusse (whom Orwell was soon to meet) had confidently identified as the first step on the road to revolution – a General Strike.

Orwell was probably right to argue that he and his contemporaries lived in a political age and that any writer who took no cognisance of that fact was 'either a footler or a plain idiot'.[2] In short, Orwell, who was neither, would write principally about politics.

1

Orwell left Burma with more than the aftermath of dengue fever; he brought back a sense of injustice that could also be described as fever-ish. He felt, he said, an immense weight of guilt as an exploiter, not just in the racket of empire but in the racket of the British class system. He had the need to sink to the lowest, to the bedrock of Western civilisa-tion, in order to expiate this sense of guilt.[3] There is no reason to doubt that these guilt feelings were genuine, but I want to suggest that they were judiciously mixed with a canny realisation that the bedrock of Western civilisation could provide good subject matter to write about. His eyes were wide open when he set out for his tramp expeditions from the Portobello Road. He kept his tramp's uniform at 'head-quarters', in that first-floor flat in Notting Hill. Unlike his comrades on the roads, he could always retreat back to this world whenever he wished. A family friend, Ruth Pitter, who had organised his flat for him, was shown the first fruits of his writing in the early days. They were full of obscenities which Orwell could not spell: the result, she thought, of an Eton education.[4] Many have criticised Orwell's attempts to sample a life of poverty in and around London and then later in Paris (where he was to spend three months in 1928) as an exercise in fantasy or make-believe. But these experiences gave him an empathetic understanding of how the poor lived, which he gained at no small personal cost in terms of ordinary creature comforts and indeed health. This much is undeniable. On the other hand, it is also undeniable that contact with well-to-do friends in London and with his aunt Nellie Limouzin in Paris was directly beneficial to his career. In Paris Orwell was able to act as the impoverished young artist, visit-ing the haunts of the Parisian bohemians, and yet also to meet, through Nellie, members of the intelligentsia who were able to help him. He explored the famous cafés, bars and restaurants, including the obliga-tory *Deux Magots*, and was introduced by his aunt to Henri Barbusse, who edited the left-wing periodical *Monde*, which was subsequently to publish his first piece. He also published in *Le Progrès Civic* and in *GK's Weekly* in Britain. Nellie also introduced him to Eugene Adam, an ex-communist who had gone to Russia but fallen foul of the régime and had consequently torn up his party card. This Parisian interlude was important to the construction of Orwell's literary career, both in terms of the material he acquired for his subsequent book and also in terms of the contacts he made.

Back in London, Orwell continued his tramping expeditions and began writing for *The Adelphi*, the erstwhile target of his shooting practice in Burma. In 1931, as we have seen, T. S. Eliot, who acted as a reader for Faber and Faber, had returned Orwell's manuscript entitled *Days in London and Paris*, largely on structural grounds.[5] Through the intervention of Mabel Fierz and Leonard Moore, *Down and Out in Paris and London* was duly published in 1933. The book constituted an autobiographical account of Orwell's experiences in those cities. These experiences were consciously manipulated not so much to win our sympathy for the characters, who appear only as insubstantial thumb-nail sketches for the most part, but to provide us with an understanding of their social predicament. The writer operated as a sociologist *à la* Jack London: observing, enumerating, measuring, comparing, and finally pushing the reader forcefully towards conclusions about the nature of the society in which so many were obliged to live the kind of miserable, cramped lives that he depicted. In the introduction to the French edition, Orwell claimed that he had invented nothing; though he went on to admit that in selecting what to include and to omit he would certainly have exercised bias. Of the writer himself, we remain uncertain as to whether he wished us to see him primarily as an observer or a participant. For example, he observed that a man who exists for even a week only on bread and margarine is not really a man any longer, only a 'belly with a few accessory organs'.[6] On the previous page, however, he told us that he himself, having spent his last eighty centimes on a bottle of milk, threw it away because a bug had dropped into it whilst he was boiling it. It is doubtful that one of those few accessory organs left to most starving men would be the one responsible for producing fastidiousness. Here Orwell was participating in the story and himself becoming the object of our attention. Perhaps it was the tension between observation and participation that gave the book its interest, with Orwell both 'telling it like it really is' on the one hand but also at times telling it like the middle-class might imagine that it would be for them.

Some of the characters sketched in the book, especially in the first, the Parisian half, are of intrinsic interest. Boris, the émigré White Russian officer, emerges both as an individual in his own right but also as a kind of exemplar of discarded social failures from whose ranks were recruited the plongeurs of Paris. Charlie, on the other hand, was a 'curious specimen ... I describe him just to show what diverse characters could be found flourishing in the Coq d'Or quarter'.[7] In truth, he turned out to be the literary device that allowed the author to tell a tale of Huysmanesque debauchery in a passage of prose that is almost a pastiche of that brand of nineteenth-century voyeurism. Where Orwell's intentions were principally literary, as they were with Charlie, he was less secure in his writing than when dealing with social realities and attitudes. For example, when Orwell turned down the offer of a month's work at a hotel because of a promise made to a previous putative employer, Boris rounded on him for his obtuse honesty: 'Honest? Honest? Who ever heard of a plongeur being honest? . . . Do you think a plongeur can afford a sense of honour?'[8] Here Orwell was writing with intent and conviction. Boris hated looking for work because he knew that people recognised that he was out of work. 'It is fatal to look hungry. It makes people want to kick you.'[9] Again, Orwell's acute observation of the philosophy of waiters is just as convincing: they do not despise those on whom they wait but rather envy them. Their ambition is to be one of those waited upon. Orwell was later to enlarge upon this important point, when reviewing Robert Tressell's *The Ragged Trousered Philanthropists*.[10] He endorsed Owen's conclusion that the working-classes sometimes see themselves as unsuccessful capitalists rather than as hapless victims of an unjust social system.[11]

Orwell was at his most didactically successful when drawing or allowing us to draw political and social conclusions from close observation, as with the morality of the plongeurs or the philosophical proclivities of waiters, and at his least successful when generalising on weak evidence. One hotelier of long experience claimed that Orwell had libelled all of Paris' luxury hotels and restaurants. The conditions he (Orwell) described were inconceivable, said the hotelier.[12] Orwell replied that he did not refer to Paris hotels in general but to one in particular, and so his critic had no basis to doubt the veracity of his reports. This letter was the first to which Orwell added, by way of a signature, his newly adopted pseudonym, but this is not the only reason to focus on it. If Orwell was actually doing what he claimed, writing only about one particular hotel, then the work would have had some literary value but not the general social or political value that Orwell clearly wished to vest in it. In any case, it would be hard to accept his abject defence, which he himself blew to pieces with one short and very explosive sentence: 'Roughly speaking the more one pays for food, the more sweat and spittle one is obliged to eat with it.'[13] It is in fact abundantly clear that what Orwell was doing was to use his apparently authentic fly-on-the-wall observations as a basis for a much wider and more trenchant criticism of the nature of society. We do not need 'posh' hotels or restaurants, Orwell was saying. We have them only because they perpetuate 'useless work', which the wealthy need to 'keep the mob off the streets'.[14] But when challenged on the facts which underpinned this particular argument by an expert, admittedly an entirely partisan one, Orwell scurried for cover: he was really only writing about one hotel.

Briefly to return to Orwell's pseudonym. I have referred already to the significance of that process: it represented the successful creation of a literary persona. Most critics recognised the importance of this transformation in Orwell's style and the change in his approach to his writing,[15] and were fully aware that it did not happen suddenly; the literary persona 'Orwell' was a long and hard time in the creation, but it was worth it. He said elsewhere: 'it took me nearly thirty years to work off the effects of being called Eric.'[16] And the actual choice of pseudonym was crucial. Could the anodyne Kenneth Miles or the faintly risible H. Lewis Allways ever have written *Nineteen Eighty Four*?

By comparison, the second half of *Down and Out* was rather dull. We might conclude that Orwell's principal purpose here was to educate us. He took it that the tramps about whom he wrote were generally regarded as being the authors of their own misfortunes, but he tried to show the tramp as victim, with no reasonable hope of escaping his destiny. Orwell's case was that a man with no money had no ambition, no pride, no self-respect; he was fit for nothing. Only Bozo the pavement artist excited Orwell's admiration rather than pity. Bozo believed that a man always had choices so long as he could say to himself: ' "I'm a free man in here" – he tapped his forehead.'[17] An incident, unimportant in itself, that would eventually lead Orwell to a new understanding of the poor took place when, dressed in his tramp's uniform, he helped a hawker with an upset barrow. ' "Thanks mate", he said with a grin. No one had called me mate before in my life.'[18] As we shall see later, mateship was to be a defining feature of the Promised Land that Orwell was later to call upon us to build. Orwell concluded his account of being down and out in Paris and London by declaring that he would never again think of tramps as scoundrels, never expect gratitude from a beggar, nor be surprised at the lethargy of the unemployed, and he would never again enjoy a meal at a smart restaurant. 'That is a beginning', he concluded. And so it proved: the beginning of a mission to explore, understand and champion the interests, as he saw them, of the powerless, those who spoke of each other as 'mate'.

At the conclusion to Chapter 1, I spoke of the importance to our study of hybrid works in which reportage is mixed with imaginative literature. In *Down and Out* it is likely that the 'behind the scenes' picture that Orwell painted of large hotels, though not invented, was in some respects consciously manipulated, shaped by the writer's political agenda. Moreover, when he reached his political conclusions, Orwell requires us to leap further than is wise from the particular to the general if we want to follow him. Yet his descriptions could surely be said to stand on their own: on the whole they, like his Burmese pictures, often possess a general truth or validity, and we could, if only he would just leave us to it, draw our own social and political conclusions from this work, some of which might well be similar to his.

Orwell's next book, *A Clergyman's Daughter*,[19] will be discussed in another chapter. Its pictures of the destitute and the working-class, who provide the background to the story as it unfolds, though vivid, add nothing new to our understanding. *Keep the Aspidistra Flying*,[20] on the other hand, explores new aspects of poverty. Again in part autobiographical, the novel covers that period in Orwell's life when he worked in a bookshop in London. Comstock, the central character, like Orwell, was an aspiring poet. He had thrown in his job with an advertising agency in order to escape the rat race and to concentrate on his poetry. Like the hero of Gissing's *New Grub Street*,[21] Comstock has chosen poverty; he was not born poor, he had expectations of life which the ordinary poor do not have. His life was constrained in so many ways by this self-imposed poverty: nobody without money in their pockets, he mused, could be considered, or could consider themselves, to be a complete person. It is lack of money that alienates man, possession of money that allows a person to be whole. 'And now abideth faith, hope, money, these three; but the greatest of these is money.'[22] Comstock was consumed in equal measure by his hatred of poverty and of wealth. He commented to his well-to-do friend Ravelston (a less than flattering portrait of Richard Rees): 'Don't you see that a man's whole personality is bound up with his income? His personality is his income.'[23] The centrality of money in people's lives was ordained primarily by women, for whom good and evil meant simply money and no money. Women needed financial security and man's liberty was the price that had to be paid. Comstock's fiancée Rosemary sought to save him from the 'abyss where poetry is written',[24] to reinstall him in his former job, set up home with him, marry him and have children. Ironically, she managed to achieve all these but in the reverse order. Rosemary lost her surname, Waterlow, but it was Comstock who played the part of Bonaparte. His personal defeat was represented by a respectable villa with an aspidistra set in the window, and the loss of his soul.[25]

Keep the Aspidistra Flying was an unsubstantial novel. Raymond Williams argued that Orwell had not a good enough grasp of socialist ideology to conceive of a form of society in which his characters could integrate without having to admit failure and neither had he the literary ability to depict such a society even in microcosm.[26] Williams was probably right but then, few writers could have met these challenges successfully.[27] George Woodcock's criticism was more apposite: some of Orwell's early books were spoilt by self-conscious theorising and by social and political commentary that come to no great harm in works of reportage but 'merely disfigure his fiction'.[28] There was a dimension to *Keep the Aspidistra Flying*, however, that had nothing to do with money and only indirectly to do with socialism. Comstock will settle down in his villa with Rosemary and they will be comfortably off but not wealthy, but how long before Comstock transmogrifies into George Bowling and takes on his bitterness? What both characters lack is a sense of belonging, of being part of a community. We catch a glimpse of Comstock looking into the window of the *Crichton Arms* and musing: 'To be in there, just to be in there! In the warmth and light with people to talk to, with beer and cigarettes and a girl to flirt with!'[29] He did not go in, but like Bowling and indeed Orwell himself, preferred to stay on the outside looking in. Had he gone in, somebody without much money might have called him 'mate'. What Ruth Pitter said of Orwell at this time might equally well have been said of Comstock or Bowling: 'It wasn't just poverty, it was suicidal perversity.'[30]

If Orwell's writing so far was considered by some critics to be deficient, Compton McKenzie thought it incomparable in 'directness, vigour, courage and vitality'[31] and more significantly it convinced Victor Gollancz to commission Orwell to travel to the north of England to write about the lives of the poor. This was to prove a breakthrough for the struggling young writer.

2

'The road to socialism for George Orwell went via Wigan Pier', wrote Bowker.[32] Orwell's commission was to explore the north, that 'other country', to write about the lives of the poor and unemployed in the north of England for the readers of Gollancz's Left Book Club. Orwell was in many ways an obvious choice: after all, he had a track record of writing about the lives of the poor: this was what he did best. Moreover, he had been pursuing an active interest in socialism. In his 1938 essay

'Why I joined the ILP' (Independent Labour Party), Orwell wrote that 'for perhaps ten years past I have had some grasp of the real nature of capitalist society'. This would take him back to the later 1920s. Moreover, before venturing north, he had been writing for *The Adelphi*, the unofficial mouthpiece of the ILP, and naturally met socially those involved in its production. It would have been natural for Orwell to have picked up almost by osmosis some basis of a socialist critique of contemporary society. What is more, the Westropes, who owned the bookshop in which Orwell worked, introduced him directly to the politics of the ILP which encompassed revolutionary and pacific socialism. Southerner, socialist sympathiser, and analyst of great vigour and clarity who had written about the lives of the poor; who better to send on this mission? But who would have predicted that his northern pilgrimage would affect him so profoundly; that, to all intents and purposes, Orwell would go native?

'The filthy bloody bastards!' a Cockney travelling salesman confided to Orwell, recognising him intuitively as a fellow southerner, a man who would share his instinctive animosity towards the north and its people.[33] It was true that the household in which they found themselves was 'a beastly place' and not typical; in fact, that was precisely why Orwell had chosen it. It enabled him to provide a lengthy and unflattering description of the house and of the lifestyle of its owners, the Brookers. He concentrated on the squalor, attributing it not so much to poverty as to sloth. He captured the habits of the Brookers with all the sharp focus of a 'reality television' show; the meanness of spirit, the self-pitying, the 'endless muddle of slovened jobs', and perhaps above all their habit of repeating themselves over and over again as if each phrase were trapped in a Pinter play with no possibility of exiting the stage. And the landscape of industrial Lancashire was as unremittingly squalid as the Brookers' house. The north of England, Orwell tells us, was a region defined by an industrial squalor and an ugliness so arresting that you were obliged to come to terms with it, as it were.

According to Orwell, who was not a man to allow his almost complete ignorance on the subject to be a constraint, Sheffield was 'the ugliest town in the Old World'. He made this claim for a specific purpose: to confront his chiefly southern middle-class audience with the realisation that this industrial dereliction was qualitatively different from the down-at-heel inner cities with which they might have been familiar. He posed two questions for the reader: was this stultifying ugliness inevitable, and did it matter? Well, actually, it was not inevitable: it was possible to build factories and houses that were aesthetically pleasing; but it did matter because of the exploitative nature of the reality that it symbolised. Even pleasant factories would not have disguised the domination of an entire race of people that the industrial system had called into being, reminiscent of the Morlocks of Wells' *Time Machine*.[34] It was to this race of people that Orwell now turned his attention.

Housing was his first subject. He deployed squadrons of statistics and measurements, but it was the arresting generalisations to which these gave rise that seize our attention. Great numbers of the houses he describes were simply not fit to live in, but those who lived in them thought themselves lucky because there weren't enough of even these 'dreadful holes' to go round. Local council redevelopment programmes produced regimented rows of dwellings that were barely adequate in terms of facilities and numbing in their soullessness. In Chestertonian terms he concluded: 'I sometimes think that the price of liberty is not so much eternal vigilance as eternal dirt.' Yet his main point was that in the north of England it was more common to be dirty but not free.[35]

Orwell's next theme was unemployment, and he began by dispelling what he believed to be a common misconception amongst the comfortable: that if the unemployment rate stood at two million then there were two million people without enough to eat. These figures ignored not only those who had never registered but also the dependants of those who had. Quoting government sources, Orwell estimated that the total number of underfed people would be well over ten million.[36] Having established the extent of poverty arising from unemployment, he analysed what the poor spent their money on. Again it was his general conclusion that captures our attention: it was not so much poverty that ruined the unemployed but the resultant loss of self-esteem. They could no longer provide for their families or contribute to their communities: they were in fact no longer men.[37] He confronted the prejudice of 'the old ladies in Brighton' directly; when the unemployed marry and have children despite their condition this is no selfish, antisocial act. It is an attempt to cling on to their very humanity, indicating to the world that they have blood in their veins and not money, as Gordon Comstock had put it.[38]

Although his approach was workmanlike, reminiscent of that of Jack London in the East End when he prepared his *The People of the Abyss*[39] in the early years of the century, Orwell was no trained sociologist and not even an especially gifted amateur. His surveys, his accumulations of factual evidence, his assemblage of motley statistics would hardly pass muster as scientific. But they did represent an honest attempt to give a factual account of the lives of the poor upon which he felt it appropriate to make the social and political statements for which the book is generally remembered. What distinguished *Wigan Pier* from the other early works that cover the subjects of poverty and the poor and powerless, was that Orwell made a profound discovery in the north of England: the people of this abyss possessed a value system that he came greatly to admire. No mere Morlocks these, after all! And Orwell sought to explore these values and show their social and political importance. Typically he did so by first aligning himself with the imagined prejudices of his readers. There is a cult of northernness, he said, in which 'you and I and everyone else in the South of England is written off as "fat and sluggish". Yorkshiremen in the South will always take the trouble to let you know that they think you are inferior.' 'The Northerner has "grit" ', he went on, 'he is grim, "dour", plucky, warm-hearted, and democratic; the Southerner is snobbish, effeminate and lazy'.[40] Yorkshiremen are members of a 'small, rustic, rather uncouth tribe whose members secretly believe all the other peoples of the earth to be just a little inferior to themselves'.[41] When Yorkshiremen came to London, he warned, they were like barbarians after loot. So the writer establishes his *bona fides*: he is 'one of us' and we can trust him in this matter of nationalism in miniature, and no doubt much else besides. Philip Toynbee was to write that *The Road to Wigan Pier* 'reads like a report brought back by some humane anthropologist who has just returned from studying the conditions of an oppressed tribe in Borneo'.[42]

Thus established, Orwell felt free to lead us out of our provincial laager to explore the 'real' differences between the north and the south. For climatic reasons the 'parasitic' dividend-drawing classes had tended to settle in the south, so that there was indeed some truth in the picture of the south as 'one enormous Brighton inhabited by lounge lizards'.[43] The embourgeoisement of the northern working-class was happening at a much slower pace than in the south, and so the northern accents persisted whereas the differentiated southern ones were collapsing. An educated accent stamped a person as an incomer rather than as a representative of the local petty gentry. This turned out to be a great advantage for Orwell because it made it easier for him to get to know working-class people. And anyway, as he said, it was easier to meet working-class people in the north on 'approximately equal terms' than it would have been in the south, where class differences were felt more sharply. Those he met in Yorkshire (and Lancashire), he felt, took a different attitude towards family life. These working-class families hung together more, had a fundamentally different conception of family loyalty. No insignificant point this, because 'the fact that the working-classes know how to combine and the middle-class don't is probably due to their different conceptions of family loyalty. You cannot have an effective trade union of middle-class workers, because in times of strikes almost every middle-class wife would be egging her husband on to blackleg and get the other fellow's job.'[44]

In one of the best-known passages from *The Road to Wigan Pier*, Orwell wrote:[45]

> In a working-class home . . . you breathe a warm, decent, deeply human atmosphere, which is not so easy to find elsewhere. I should say that a manual worker . . . has a better chance of being happy than an 'educated' man. His home life seems to fall more naturally into a sane and comely shape. I have often been struck by the peculiarly easy completeness, the perfect symmetry as it were, of a working-class interior at its best.

The most immediately apparent, and indeed most durable, characteristic of working-class decency was its equality, and how memorably Orwell captures it: 'In a Lancashire cotton town,' he wrote, 'you could probably go for months without once hearing an "educated" accent, whereas there can hardly be a town in the South of England where you could throw a brick without hitting the niece of a bishop.'[46] This sense of equality, he said, was deeply rooted in working-class family life, for family relationships were far less tyrannical. Moreover, working men did not have that millstone of family prestige hanging round their necks. Orwell linked the strength of working-class family life to the sense of solidarity and equality of the class as a whole in a causal relationship, and there can be little doubt that he responded to the warmth of working-class family life throughout his career, continually drawing sustenance from it in his prose style, continually stressing its broader social and political significance. He came to believe that working-class family life was the basis of the integrated community in which the same values of togetherness and equality were fostered.[47] Of all working men Orwell chose the miner as a model for the kind of virtues he sought to encapsulate. He described the miner as a kind of 'grimy caryatid upon whose shoulders nearly everything that is not grimy is supported', and forces this point home with typical directness:[48]

> You and I and the editor of the Times Lit. Supp. and the Nancy poets and the Archbishop of Canterbury and Comrade X, author

of Marxism for Infants – all of us really owe the comparative decency of our lives to poor drudges underground, blackened to the eyes, with their throats full of coal dust, driving their shovels forward with arms and belly muscles of steel.

Unlike the parasitic occupations of many intellectuals, Orwell's worker was engaged in an activity that was vitally important to the community and also physically demanding. It was the habit of being of use to the community which made unemployment such a hard cross to bear for Orwell's working man.

Orwell appeared to be captivated by what he took to be a living value system rooted in equality and emphasising the traditional Christian values of decency and justice. This value system was captured, he was later to write, in the cinematic art of Charlie Chaplin[49] and in the cartoonist's art of Donald McGill.[50] In his essay 'The English People', Orwell wrote that Chaplin's comedic success stemmed from his ability to represent the little man. He was a modern version of those Jack the Giant-Killer figures that were amongst the most enduring heroes of the English-speaking peoples' folk-tales. It was no surprise, said Orwell, that Chaplin's films were banned in Germany when the Nazis came to power. Chaplin, he said, represented the 'concentrated essence of the common man'. Whereas an intellectual could make out a conceptually coherent case for, say, smashing German trade unions or torturing Jews, the common man, operating from instinct not intellect, would know that 'it isn't right'.[51] In his essay on the cartoonist McGill, Orwell explored these ideas in some depth. The world that McGill depicted was the world of the oppressed, a world in which all those with incomes of much above or below £5 per week were figures of fun. It was a world of equality and of vigour. Superficially it was a world of obscenity, well exemplified by McGill's much-loved seaside postcards. These postcards and their mottoes, however, possessed a meaning only within the context of a fairly strict moral code, the backbone of which was an incorrigible belief in the institution of marriage and in the value of family life. This was a world in which family was put first, a world, Orwell noted, 'more traditional, more in accord with the Christian past than [that of] the well-to-do women who still try to look young at forty'.[52] All the *double entendres* of McGill's world actually implied a common culture strong enough not to see them as threats. They reflected a world, said Orwell, in which ordinary people want to behave decently and be good, though perhaps not too good, and not necessarily all the time.[53]

Though this common culture was deeply patriotic, it had no time for extreme nationalism, or indeed for any extremism. Orwell wrote that he found himself unable to listen to proclamations by 'great men', pious moral platitudes from self-righteous left-wing party leaders, Papal pronouncements and the like without also 'imagining the sound, in the background, of a chorus of raspberries from all the millions of common men'.[54] Elsewhere he wrote: 'one must conclude that in this matter the English common people have lagged behind their century. The have failed to catch up with power politics, "realism", *sacro egoismo* and the doctrine that the end justifies the means.'[55] Theirs was that ancient wisdom that Orwell sought to portray as a fundamental commitment to decency, equality and justice.

These values were essentially pragmatic rather than ideological and they rose naturally from the culture of working people. The northern working-class was moved not by systems of ideas but by egalitarian fellow feeling, by a sense of common decency. The social and political significance of this value system could hardly be more profound: 'All over England, in every industrial town, there are men by scores of thousands whose attitude to life, if only they could express it ... would change the consciousness of our race.'[56]

3

If Orwell had left matters there, at a broadly cultural level, he would still have been open to criticism. Orwell himself wrote in a letter to Henry Miller only a month or so after his return from the north, that 'it is dreadful to see how the people have collapsed and lost all their guts in the last ten years'.[57] This was by no means the picture he had chosen to paint in *Wigan Pier*. Wyndham Lewis wrote: 'I consider Orwell's romanticising about [the working-class] an insult to them, for he really thought they were marked off in some mysterious way ... which they are not. The whole of the *Wigan Pier* business was a very stupid affectation.'[58] He went on to call Orwell's picture, with its virile workers and nineteenth-century values, 'medieval and guildish'. He believed it had long since lost any relevance even in the 1930s. Walter Greenwood, whose *Love on the Dole* was made into a film, wrote that although *Wigan Pier* held his interest from cover to cover, 'I cannot remember being so infuriated for a long time by some of the things he says here ...'[59] Samuel Hynes wrote that Orwell's working-class values amounted to nothing more than 'emotional liberalism' which said people can behave decently and that if more people would be decent the world would be decent. But really this is a superficial judgement, because Orwell said much more than this. First, the moral system that Orwell sought to articulate belonged predominantly to one class, the industrial working-class. What is more, Orwell made it abundantly clear that his moral system required equality as a *sine qua non*. 'Working-class decency', then, though by no means a precise concept, was more closely defined than the phrase 'emotional liberalism' implies. Several other critics suggested more simply that Orwell was deluding himself by attributing any special moral virtues to the working-class.

Newsinger argued to the contrary: Orwell's panegyric for the miners was much more than a 'personal idiosyncrasy'; it constituted a serious political position.[60] On the other hand, he continued, it suited Orwell's purpose to show the working-class as honourable victims. The network of activists who populated the diaries upon which the book was based somehow failed to appear in the final version. Orwell was concerned to show that the working-class had only a limited capacity for leadership, that it was, and here Newsinger borrows Marx's words, a class in itself but not for itself. Orwell wanted to depict a working-class culture that was confidently strong enough to enable the workers to come to terms with unemployment and its consequences, whereas Marxists might want to stress the influence of a more hegemonic cultural pattern with its bread and circuses, imposed to keep the working-class falsely conscious and in its proper place. Nowhere, Newsinger criticised, did Orwell acknowledge the revolutionary potential of the 800,000 miners, failing even to mention that at the time of his sojourn these miners were contemplating strike action. On a more personal level, judging from his novel *Sons and Lovers*,[61] D. H. Lawrence would have found grounds to dispute Orwell's cosy image of the miners' family life. And Lawrence was the son of a miner.

The reader might suspect that Orwell's picture of working-class decency owed at least something to his attempt to come to terms with his own deep-seated class prejudices. In an extraordinarily revealing autobiographical section to the book, Orwell explained that as a child he was brought up to believe that the working-classes smelled, that 'there was something subtly repulsive about the working-class body'.[62] He set himself the task of exploring the 'vitally important' matter: do the 'lower classes' smell?[63] He seemed to believe that they probably did but that we (the middle-class potential socialists) should embrace their values just the same. After all: 'why should a man who thinks all virtue resides in the proletariat still take such pains to drink his soup silently?'[64] As we have heard, Orwell was (sometimes) what he wrote: he is reported to have made a habit of ostentatiously drinking his tea in the BBC canteen out of the saucer, with what he thought were the appropriate working-class slurps.[65] This was to prove a point: he had written earlier how ridiculous it was that a bourgeois socialist, an old Etonian even, though he might be ready to die on the barricades for the working-class, would nevertheless find it physically impossible to drink his tea out of a saucer.[66] Following his return from the north, when they got married, he told Eileen that he wanted to live like the workers, but then became upset when she put a marmalade jar on the breakfast table. He insisted that she buy a proper pot.[67] Newsinger's defence notwithstanding, there is indeed something of a 'personal idiosyncrasy' about Orwell's description of and extrapolation from working-class values here.

But in fact Orwell did not leave us with only this problematical picture of the northern working-class living by a system of values that he professed profoundly to admire. He bequeathed us something far more ambitious and immeasurably more controversial: a myth of socialism based upon these values. I use the concept of myth here in the sense of a formalised statement of values whose function is intended to promote a sense of solidarity through self-awareness. Orwell's working-class, or what I shall call 'decency', myth of socialism sought to embed and to anchor these northern working-class values and to proselytise them, so that the middle-class might recognise that its own interests and values could best be realised in alliance with Orwell's working-class.[68] Thus socialism, which alone offered a viable alternative to fascism, might triumph.

Orwell's 'decency' myth of socialism, then, foresaw the incorporation into the public sphere of working-class decency, and conversely it recognised that working-class decency represented the clearest expression of basic socialist values. He wrote:[69]

> His [the working man's] vision of the Socialist future is a vision of present society with the worst abuses left out, and with interest centring around the same things as at present – family life, the pub, football and local politics. As for the philosophic side of Marxism, the pea and thimble trick[70] with those three mysterious entities, thesis, antithesis, and synthesis, I have never met a working man who had the faintest interest in it.

Orwell took for granted, not unreasonably, that retention of the basic framework of its culture would be a prime objective of working-class socialism – how else could his myth be sustained? – and that consequently the utopianism of some socialists would be anathema to the working-class socialist. Orwell claimed never to have met a miner, steel worker, textile worker, docker, or navvy who could be described as 'ideologically sound'.[71] He continued: 'The working-class Socialist, like the working-class Catholic, is weak on doctrine and can hardly open his mouth without uttering a heresy, but he has the heart of the matter in him.'[72] The working-class decency myth, then, depicted a kind of essentialist socialism that was shorn of ideology, shorn of utopianism, shorn of intellectualism. It could not be elaborated into a programme of action any more than it could be formulated into a systematic ideology because it represented the way of life of a community. This myth contrasted with the intellectuals' version of socialism where poverty and the cramped style of life associated with poverty were things to be abolished from above, by violence if necessary; or perhaps even preferably by violence. He concluded that for the intelligentsia (and he had in mind not so much Soviet aparatchiks as home-grown socialists such as Bernard Shaw and the Fabians), socialism was something for 'the clever ones' to impose upon 'the Lower Orders'.[73] As for the Lower Orders themselves, they understood this kind of socialism to be bound up with efficient machine production in which progress seems to be measured by making humanity generally less human in the cause of 'progress'. But ordinary people, at heart, wanted a 'civilisation in which "progress" is not defined as making the world safe for little fat men'.[74] They rejected the goals of Fabian socialism, said Orwell.

The task, then, was to see that the decency myth of socialism was not intellectualised but humanised. 'We have got to fight for justice and liberty, and Socialism does mean justice and liberty when the nonsense is stripped off it.'[75] These were the central objectives that must be put in the forefront. Cleaned, purified and restated, the decency myth of socialism would win the 'exploited' middle-class over, for they would come to realise that the real struggle was not between those who did or did not pronounce their aitches but, simply, between the exploiters and the exploited. To give the myth social and political salience meant to prune socialism of its 'nonsense'. But this was not enough. It was necessary also to jettison the nonsense-makers. In the rather unconvincing guise of Devil's Advocate,[76] Orwell unleashed a bitter attack not so much against the British Left in general as against left-wing intellectuals. Some were figures of fun, harmless eccentrics, often utopians, who simply gave socialism a bad image, turning working people away from it. Socialism would have to rid itself of them.

The working-class tended to see socialism as an ideology, not a value system, and they recoiled from it and from its ideologues. We are reminded of Robert Tressell's *The Ragged Trousered Philanthropists*, in which Owen's workmates recoiled from his uninspiring socialist lunchtime monologues. Far more important, though, was to rid socialism of its ideologists. It is widely known that Orwell came to despise Stalin and to believe that he was the greatest obstacle of all to the establishment of socialism. In 1936, however, it was British intellectuals who were the target of his ire, none more so than his erstwhile heroes, Bernard Shaw and H. G. Wells, many of his colleagues at *The Adelphi* and a substantial number of the members of the Left Book Club, who had indirectly financed his northern pilgrimage. The socialist movement ought not to be a league of dialectical materialists but rather a league of the oppressed against the oppressors. What socialism needed was a myth-maker who could speak out for its primal sanities: 'less about "class consciousness", "expropriation of the expropriators", "bourgeois ideology", and "proletarian solidarity", not to mention the sacred sisters, thesis, antithesis and synthesis; and more about justice, liberty, and the plight of the unemployed.'[77] This was to be the task that Orwell would set himself.

Orwell's call to arms did not receive unqualified support from the officer class in the legion of socialism, but we should not doubt that Orwell was determined to win over the bulk of what he called 'normal, decent people' to the socialist cause by proclaiming it to be their cause. If it were to be victorious, the movement would have to become not 'a league of dialectical materialists but a league of the oppressed against the oppressors'.[78] *Wigan Pier* was, unmistakably, not just an account of the working and living conditions of the poor and the tribulations of the unemployed: it was a call to arms to all people of good will.

Almost from the beginning of his writing career, then, Orwell had not only established a brand of socialism rooted in the myth of working-class decency, but had chosen a role for himself from which, as we shall see, he never entirely departed. To suggest, as many critics have done, that the myth needed to be elaborated into an ideology was, for Orwell, to miss the point entirely; the myth operated successfully in working-class life, at both the public and the private level. It is in this sense that Orwell's myth was concrete; it represented a way of living one's life. Orwell believed that socialism as a political system was possible only if it grew naturally out of the disposition of the ordinary people. A man who acted from ideology, wrote the theologian Dietrich Bonhoeffer, sought justification in his ideas, but for Bonhoeffer Christianity led away from abstractions and towards 'an ethic which is entirely concrete'.[79] For Orwell too, actions could be justified only by a 'concrete' ethic: the values of working-class decency.

In reviewing *The Freedom of the Streets* by his friend the working-class author Jack Common, Orwell suggested that Common's voice was that of the ordinary man 'who might infuse a new decency into the control of affairs' if he could ever get beyond the sweat-shop or the trenches. Common's book had little to say about socialism as a theory but a lot to say about it as 'a body of belief, one might almost say a way of life'.[80] The working-class socialist John McNair[81] claimed that his friend Orwell recognised that rigid ideology, with all that it implied in terms of Foucaultian intellectual domination, stood in the way of the growth of his moral system; recognised, in the words of the ethical socialist Robert Blatchford, quoted by McNair, that no economic or social change could transform humanity 'if the human heart is not sweet and sound'.

In seeking to articulate socialism as a way of life, a value system, rather than an ideology, Orwell was undertaking an immensely difficult and destructive enterprise, but not a totally obscure one. Vaclav Havel, Czechoslovakia's celebrated dissident author and later its first post-war democratically elected president, wrote an essay in 1978 entitled 'The Power of the Powerless'.[82] In it Havel, like Orwell, rejected rigid socialist ideology in Marxian terms, as 'the interpretation of reality by the power structure', yet amongst the ordinary people, he continued, there was to be found a potential, what Havel called a pre-political power, which made itself felt in 'the obscure area of being itself'. This potential power would eventually triumph over the existing order because the values it championed would inexorably change the political system. He called the system that would eventually emerge the post-political system, in which ordinary men and women would genuinely participate in decision-making. Havel's thesis can be said to support Orwell's, and yet in the comparative tightness of Havel's argument Orwell's own pronouncements are exposed as tensile, capable of being stretched to the point almost of shapelessness.

Might it not be the case, Havel's thesis notwithstanding, that Orwell's working-class decency was a myth only in the pejorative sense, that is, an untruth? Gissing, whom Orwell greatly admired and to whom he expressed an affinity,[83] had taken a very different line. He knew the poor well, far better than Orwell did, and he regarded the working-class as savages who should on no account be let anywhere near power. Gissing, Orwell knew, did not believe that the kind of social change he championed would be progressive at all.[84] And yet, as Orwell acknowledged, Gissing himself was a humane, intelligent and scholarly man who came from an ordinary home. In a review of Graham Greene's work,[85] Orwell himself exposed an inconsistency in the decency myth. In *Brighton Rock*, Pinkie, a small-time gangster, engaged in a moral dialogue with his 'still more limited' girlfriend about abortion, which both agreed to be clearly immoral. It is simply incredible, wrote Orwell (who, incidentally, would have shared their condemnation), that 'the most brutish, stupid person can, merely by having been brought up a Catholic' be capable of distinguishing between the moral categories of good and evil. Now, ordinary Catholics would at least have had the Catechism knocked into their heads, but Orwell was clear that they would nevertheless not be able to make moral distinctions. His worker, on the other hand, as we remember, though he may not be able to open his mouth without uttering a heresy, had the heart of the matter in him – simply by virtue of being working-class. If it is impossible for any religious group, however cohesive, to claim to instil a perspective on morality in individuals, then how could Orwell claim this power on behalf of a social class? Thanks to Orwell we have a phrase for this kind of reasoning: doublethink.

Finally, it might be argued that even if Orwell's myth of working-class decency had some substance at the time he created it, it has none now. Suppose the myth embodied nothing more than the defence mechanisms of a community under the pressure of poverty? One of Aldous Huxley's characters in the novel *Point Counter Point*, a working-class communist, observed that when you live on less than £4 per week you've 'dammed well got to behave like a Christian and love your neighbour'.[86] If Orwell wrote *Wigan Pier* to sensitise us to the hardships of working-class life and to prompt us to instruct our politicians to alleviate these hardships, what then would remain of the decency myth? Would it survive the accretion of greater personal wealth, or the post-1945 welfare state, with its health, housing, education, and income support and unemployment policies? We know that cumulatively better welfare provision has tended to erode working-class communities in a comprehensive manner. It is an open question whether Orwell's myth could have survived that transformation. Orwell was always clear about his opposition to 'progress' because of its impact on working-class life and values, but he did not, like G. K. Chesterton, go on to oppose the greater provision of welfare. Quite the opposite. Yet the welfare state took upon itself the role of the Christian 'good neighbour', and in so doing it may have laid the groundwork for the destruction of the very values Orwell cherished. We might also consider the effect that the growing impermanence of marriage in working-class, as well as middle-class, cultures during the last thirty years would have had upon Orwell's working-class families and their values, the bedrock of his decency myth.

Nowadays British working-class decency has to try to withstand not fascism so much as the ravages of unaccustomed prosperity, large-scale rehousing, drug-related urban crime, a system of education that is palpably failing it and nourishment from a people's press that for its devotion to voyeurism and corruption, its self-righteous jingoism and bellicosity is an affront to just about every value that Orwell prized. In a recent book on working-class South London, Michael Collins spoke movingly of a culture that had been destroyed by brutalist housing estates. 'We couldn't find words, couldn't articulate what the heart of it was – but . . . I get an inkling of the spirit of sociability, and trust, that was traditionally at the core of working-class communities . . . [touching] a point reached nowhere else . . . by instinct rather than as the result of exhortation and conscious virtue.'[87] That sociability and trust were lost when these old communities were sacrificed to progress.

During the period since Orwell's death, working-class culture, too, has been transformed, but it has not been submerged. Working-class accents, clothing and entertainment have come to dominate British culture. Modern role models are mostly drawn from the conspicuously working-class fields of soccer and pop music. C. B. Fry, that quintessentially upper-middle-class sporting hero of Orwell's boyhood Britain, has been replaced by the unmistakably working-class David Beckham. The middle-classes have, indeed, lost their aitches, but despite Orwell's assurance, that is not all that they have lost and it is not immediately easy to see what they have gained. If this constitutes a victory for the working-class, it is a Pyrrhic one; the post-industrial state has no need of the virtues of fellowship and equality that shaped the working-class communities of Orwell's day. Indeed, it has less and less need of the working-class itself. There is no better example of this than the demise of the miners, once the largest and most influential component of the labour force, now almost an endangered species.[88] In that popular picture of northern working-class life in the post-industrial state, *The Full Monty*, 'the working-class, backbone of the Labour Party and residue of Orwellian hope, weakened by affluence, broken by neoliberalism, [is seen] finally exiting stage left, naked, with a song. A more powerful narrative of the decline of working-class socialism would be difficult to imagine.'[89]

Orwell would certainly have been aware of the shortcomings in his decency myth. But we should remember how high the stakes in his game were. He recognised the crucial importance of making socialism, in Lukacs' phrase, man-centred, so that it could confront the growing threat of totalitarianism. In recognising that the way to achieve this was to strengthen the relationship between the simple human, egalitarian virtues of the working-class and the morality of socialism, Orwell had a message for socialist movements everywhere. It seems that it was not heeded; the neglect of those values to which Havel alluded, and which are represented in Orwell's myth of working-class socialism, was apparently fatal; socialism clearly failed to make itself man-centred, and eventually workers almost everywhere brought it down.

4

Orwell's early literary endeavours were, as we have seen, received somewhat differently by different people. But there can be little room for doubt concerning the reception of *Wigan Pier*: it caused a furore. It, or some of it, was disliked intensely by many who read it, but none would have doubted its persuasive power. Orwell maintained the role of observer and not participant in *Wigan Pier*. He kept his distance and thereby, he hoped, maintained his authorial impartiality and thus his right to speak for us all. His ability to create images that encapsulate a moral and political position from this standpoint of detachment is well illustrated by the description of the young woman cleaning out her drain-pipe. In the diary in which Orwell recorded his daily activities in the north, the entry for 15 February told of his walking up a 'horrible squalid' side alley where he saw a youngish woman, pale and exhausted, on her knees, poking a stick up a blocked waste-pipe. It was bitterly cold. Just at that moment she looked up and caught his eye, with an expression 'as desolate as I have ever seen'.[90] It struck him that she was thinking exactly the same thing as he himself was thinking. Now we note that in this extract, which we assume to be accurate, Orwell was involved, implicated even: he passed close by the woman and they exchanged glances. But compare this to the same story told in *Wigan Pier*. Here Orwell was on a train bearing him away from Wigan, a metaphor for context and comparison. This was March rather than February, but from the train window Orwell saw the woman, unmistakably the same woman, trying to unblock her drainpipe. But he was observing from the train, and not implicated in the scene: 'I was *almost* near enough to catch her eye.'[91] Now we discover that the woman was twenty-five but looked forty, or at least she 'had the face of the slum girl who is twenty-five and looks forty'[92] as a consequence of miscarriages and drudgery. She retained her desolate look and Orwell had time to reflect on the fallacy that slum-dwellers could imagine nothing but the slums and so did not feel that sense of desolation that 'we' would. 'She knew well enough what was happening to her – understood as well as I did how dreadful a destiny it was.'[93]

This is perhaps the best-known piece of description in the book and we can see here how carefully it has been built up. We are with Orwell on that train, observing things with the reserve that befits Albert Camus' good witnesses. But Orwell takes us well beyond simple observation. We feel that we know about the woman's life, the kind of conditions that would have given rise to frequent miscarriages, and above all we realise that as she watched the train pulling away to another world she knew that she was a prisoner, and would always be a prisoner of her own world. Orwell's skill was to regain the status as observer that he had abandoned in the original, to become our representative so to speak, and so to help us understand these bitter truths. Newsinger called Orwell's picture 'one of the most powerful images of social injustice in the English language'.[94]

The quality of Orwell's writing allows him to evoke in the reader a revulsion towards the squalor that characterised the north and incarcerated the people who lived amidst it, like that young woman:[95]

> I remember a winter afternoon in the dreadful environs of Wigan. All round was the lunar landscape of slag-heaps, and to the north, through the passes, as it were, between the mountains of slag, you could see the factory chimneys sending out their plumes of smoke. The canal path was a mixture of cinders and frozen mud, criss-crossed by the imprint of innumerable clogs, and all around, as far as the slag-heaps in the distance, stretched the 'flashes' – pools of stagnant water that had seeped into the hollows caused by the subsidence of ancient pits. It was horribly cold; the flashes were covered ice the colour of raw umber, the bargemen were muffled to the eyes in sacks, the lock gates wore beards of ice. It seemed a world from which vegetation had been banished; nothing existed except smoke, shale, ice, mud, ashes and foul water. But even Wigan is beautiful compared to Sheffield.

This represented a new mastery of the language on Orwell's part and a distinct development in his writing style. As Richard Rees noted at the time, it was as if a smouldering fire had suddenly burst into flames.[96] We feel the controlled power of Orwell's prose and especially the full force of the last, throw-away line in the extract. Dreadful as his picture is, Orwell tells us that this landscape does not represent the end of the world: Sheffield does. In Sheffield if, in rare moments, you stop smelling sulphur, it is only because you have begun smelling gas. You are truly in hell. It is difficult to disengage from these images, and in many respects all this was a great bonus for Gollancz and the members of the Left Book Club. But when Orwell brought his descriptive powers to bear on those enemies of his myth of working-class decency, in what Newsinger referred to, we recall, as his 'sustained, idiosyncratic diatribe', he stunned his audience.[97]

The 'enemies of socialism', which is really to say those not persuaded by Orwell's decency myth, were, he has told us, middle-class socialists. 'One sometimes gets the impression that the very words "socialism" and "communism" draw towards them with magnetic force every fruit juice drinker, nudist, sandal-wearer, sex maniac, Quaker, "Nature Cure" quack, pacifist and feminist in England.'[98] 'Real socialism' must rid itself of this motley group and send every 'vegetarian, teetotaller, and creeping Jesus' back to Welwyn Garden City to practise their yoga.[99]

More dangerous to the myth than these cranks, as we know, were the ideologues. He wrote: 'Sometimes I look at a Socialist – the intellectual, tract-writing type of Socialist, with his pullover, his fuzzy hair, and his Marxian quotations – and wonder what the devil his motive really *is*.'[100] Then he tells us what his motive is: simply a 'hypertrophied sense of order'. Listening to ideologues, Orwell gets the impression that for them socialism is 'a kind of exciting heresy hunt – a leaping to and fro of frenzied witch-doctors to the beat of the tom-toms and the tune of "Fee fi, fo, fum, I smell the blood of a right-wing deviationist!" '[101] But working-class decency, with its grasp of the nature of equality, decency and social justice as the central ideals of socialism, had almost been lost beneath innumerable layers of doctrinaire fastidiousness, internecine disputes and mindless progressivism until it had become 'like a diamond hidden under a mountain of dung'.[102] These caricatures of left-wing intellectuals, for that is what they are, stare out at us, like wantonly decapitated heads of enemies set on spikes around the walls of Orwell's citadel of decency, warnings of what can happen to the enemies of the decency myth – or at least to their reputations.

In *Wigan Pier* Orwell advanced a case for a new, different kind of socialism that drew its inspiration from ordinary people. I have suggested that this socialism was consciously built upon a myth of questionable authenticity. We shall have cause to return later to Orwell's decency myth, but at its heart lies the simple phrase that stayed with Orwell for life: any hope for the future lay with the proles. But let us be clear: whatever coherence and conviction the decency myth may have possessed came not from so much any closely formulated social or political reasoning but from the sheer vigour, vivacity and muscularity of Orwell's writing.

4 To the barricades and back

But the thing that I saw in your face
No power can disinherit:
No bomb that ever burst
Shatters the crystal spirit.
> George Orwell, 'Looking Back on the Spanish War', *The Penguin*
> *Essays* (Harmondsworth: Penguin, n.d., pp. 216–23).

Back from his pilgrimage to the north of England, Orwell managed to find time, whilst writing *Wigan Pier*, to get married, before setting off, in late December 1936, for Barcelona and the Spanish Civil War. It is sometimes forgotten that he went ostensibly as a war correspondent; forgotten no doubt because there is no indication that he seriously intended to do any such thing. He intended to fight fascism, though being Orwell he also intended to write about it. Although he was by this time comparatively widely read in socialist literature, had become emotionally attached to the cause of the working-class and, significantly, had acquired military training and experience through his days with the Imperial Police, nothing could have prepared him for the ideological and martial struggles of the Spanish Civil War or alerted him to the potential and problematic of revolution 'in action'.[1] Yet at the end of his time in Spain Orwell wrote that he had witnessed a nascent socialist society in Barcelona and had decided that, whatever his misgivings – and there were a number – this revolutionary socialism was 'worth fighting for'.[2] Only five years later, however, Orwell was working on his fable *Animal Farm* and, to say the least, seemed to have lost all hope in revolution, or at least in the expectation of a successful socialist revolution in his lifetime.

If revolutions can represent an instinctive collective response to inhuman treatment and conditions, rather like the French Revolution of 1789, or indeed the spontaneous uprising of the animals in Orwell's *Animal Farm*, then consideration of their legitimacy seems theoretical and even otiose. They happen! Almost invariably, however, such events are not entirely discrete: even though they appear to be unplanned, these events will have been discussed in principle beforehand and justified in advance, morally or ideologically and probably both, as indeed was the revolution on Animal Farm, and there have been many advocates of the general theory of the legitimacy and the efficacy of revolutions. One of the early modern champions of revolutionary legitimacy, Baboeuf, argued that, throughout history, classes and social groups had guaranteed their pre-eminence by controlling the mechanisms of state coercion.[3] No such group would yield up its power peacefully to a rival class or group and so would need to be overthrown violently by the superior force of those whom they had oppressed. There was no alternative. This argument, as one writer concluded, was 'always an apology for violence from within the precepts of rationalism and never a vindication of it'.[4] That is to say, revolution was to be regarded as an unfortunate but unavoidable necessity. Others, of whom Georges Sorel[5] can be taken as an early modern exemplar, argued differently. It was only through revolutionary struggle that a group could fully realise its own political potential. Violence was seen as a creative force and only through decisive action could the people discover their virtue (as well, others would add, as their consciousness).

Marx himself argued that the traumatic experience of revolutionary violence would rid the proletariat of the illusion that its interests and those of the bourgeoisie might be reconciled. As Harding has suggested, Marx believed that 'the violence of the revolution clarifies the issues, obliges millions to declare their positions, it enormously accelerates the growth of consciousness'.[6] These arguments were picked up later by neo-Marxist writers such as Frantz Fanon,[7] reacting to the collapse of capitalism's so-called final stage, imperialism. Fanon sought to persuade colonial subjects that it was legitimate to want to 'rise up and cut off the heads of the slave-masters, that it is a way to achieve their manhood'.[8]

The appeal of this message to men of violence is plain enough, but it has also been persuasive to many whom we might call 'ethical' socialists.[9] The revolution admits of no prevarication: it demands that one take sides – with the exploited. 'I have no particular love for the "idealised" worker as he appears in the bourgeois Communist's mind', said Orwell, 'but when I see an actual flesh-and-blood worker in conflict with his natural enemy, the policeman, I do not have to ask myself which side I am on.'[10] This uncomplicated, not to say simplistic, declaration bears further investigation. It can be assumed that Orwell did not wish to imply that in any particular incident the workers were necessarily right and the police necessarily wrong. If anything, he was hinting at the opposite: sometimes it will be impossible to establish rights and wrongs in a particular dispute and the workers might be in the wrong in any specific situation, but a violent confrontation admits of no calculation; only action (or inaction) is possible. Orwell's ideological position was that historically and in general the powerful were wrong and the powerless right. Instinctively, then, he will side with the workers – the people – because in the larger picture they are 'right'. Orwell thus legitimised the impulse to violence just as much as Sorel or Fanon. The justification for these writers rested on the historical expectation that revolution would unlock the virtue and the true consciousness of the exploited, and lead to a genuine transfer of power. Orwell too hoped for this, though it seems unlikely that he expected it. But in a way, success, measured in terms of the transfer of power, was secondary: Orwell considered himself morally and emotionally committed to the workers in a struggle that, for much of his life, he regarded as inevitable and just, whatever its outcome.

Those who argue in support of the principle of revolutions tend to make the quite unwarranted assumption that they will be victorious. Victory, however, might be a long time coming. The former British Foreign Secretary, Lord Home, told of a conversation with the then Chinese Prime Minister, Chou En-lai, in which Home had asserted that revolutions always tended to fail, and he quoted the French Revolution as an example. Chou En-lai, by way of reply, politely pointed out that it was really too early to say. Not only does history suggest that the odds are in reality against victory, but even victory itself does not always imply achieving what was intended: revolutionaries might win, but what will they win? 'A mob of desperate sufferers', said Bernard Shaw, 'abandoned to the leadership of exasperated sentimentalists and fanatic theorists [not an essential precondition of revolution it has to be said] may, at a vast cost of bloodshed and misery, succeed in removing no single evil except perhaps the existence of the human race'.[11] When he experienced the revolutionary society of Barcelona, Orwell did not allow himself any such misgivings: the barricades were up and needed to be manned. As he said, there was much about this society that he did not understand, or even like in some ways, but he recognised it immediately as a state of affairs worth fighting for.[12]

1

Homage to Catalonia bore the seeds both of Orwell's hope and his disillusion. The book, which takes the form of a documentary account of Orwell's experiences during the Spanish Civil War, opens with a symbolic meeting between the author and an Italian militiaman. The latter made an immediately favourable impression upon Orwell. They shook hands and it 'was as though his spirit and mine had momentarily succeeded in bridging the gulf of language and tradition'.[13] Yet he instinctively realised that to retain his first impression he must not see the Italian again and neither did he. Orwell recognised in the stranger's face a preparedness to murder or to throw away his own life for a friend, and hoped that the Italian recognised something similar in his own face. They were bound together, he wanted to believe, by a mutual commitment to a comradeship based upon a respect for freedom and equality. Yet at the same time, Orwell understood that if they were really to get to know each other the strength of their relationship would inevitably be weakened, the spontaneity of their mutual regard exposed as fragile. Forged *in extremis*, these bonds might not be broken by death but they might very well be eaten away by familiarity. Put another way, though they might survive failure in the revolutionary enterprise, they would be unlikely to survive success. We cannot leave this scene without remarking on an important development. Orwell was no longer now the observer, the detached witness of *Wigan Pier* days: he was fully involved. Here he carefully describes a face for us and we remember a similarly careful description of another face, from a train window. This time, however, he and the stranger connect; they shake hands, and Orwell finds himself hoping that the Italian 'liked me as well as I liked him'.[14]

Orwell's description of Barcelona provides a similar picture of an exhilarating commitment and sense of purpose, with the loudspeakers blasting out the latest revolutionary songs, all the comrades in blue overalls or militia uniform, and no obviously well-to-do people to be seen.[15] He was deeply touched by this town in which the working-class was, or appeared to be, in the saddle. But he recognised its fragility. When he wrote of illiterate militiamen buying ballad sheets about proletarian brotherhood, painstakingly spelling out and learning the words and then singing them, it would come as no surprise if the words of one turned out to be the Catalan equivalent of: 'four legs good, two legs bad'. In the streets of the town were posters telling prostitutes not to be prostitutes now that socialism had arrived, reminding the reader of the best intentions of the cats and rats on Animal Farm. Orwell anticipated our reaction: to anyone from the 'hard-boiled sneering civilisation of the English-speaking races', he said, all this was 'rather pathetic'.[16] And yet it seems clear enough from his writing that Orwell himself was not entirely convinced. The clinching justification for fighting was simply the essential decency of the Catalan working-class and their largeness of spirit.[17] If asked what he was fighting for, he said, he would have answered: 'Common Decency'.[18]

In *Homage to Catalonia*, Orwell provides us with a full and clear account of the conflicting tensions between means and ends, the principles which a revolution seeks to establish and the methods necessary actually to win the revolutionary struggle. It is not the longer-term concern over the relationship between means and ends so incisively analysed in the debate between Ivanov and Rubashov in Koestler's *Darkness at Noon*,[19] but rather the immediate concerns of revolutionary strategy. Orwell's early experiences with POUM, a largely Trotskyite militia,[20] uncovered a strong sense of purpose but a damaging lack of training. He came to see the militia as a 'temporary working model of the classless society' based upon a 'near approach' to perfect equality.[21] It took longer to instil revolutionary discipline because this discipline was based upon political consciousness, upon an understanding of the reasoning behind orders and not simply upon doing as one was told: theirs *was* to reason why. Orwell had enough military experience to make a judgement on the efficiency of these units. The revolutionary discipline was more reliable than might have been expected, he thought, and not the cause of their undoubted military failings: these were chiefly the result of a lack of weapons. He laconically remarked at one point that if, as is commonly supposed, it took a thousand bullets to kill an enemy then it was going to be twenty years before he accounted for his first fascist.[22]

Later Orwell was to meet men who had not acquired the necessary political consciousness for revolutionary discipline. His response to encountering a detachment of Andalusians was a telling one: 'Few if any of them could read, and they seemed not to know the one thing that everybody knows in Spain – which party they belonged to.'[23] The sheep, it seemed, had arrived. Moreover, although by Second-World-War standards the Spanish Civil War was primitive, it was always going to be won by efficiency, technical expertise and superior equipment, all advantages held by Franco's falangists. When battles had been decided by, among other things, the courage and tenacity of individual fighting men, then the principles which incited that courage and tenacity were of great importance. Battles won by technical superiority owe little to the personal values of the military technician.

This fundamental point had been seized on earlier by H. G. Wells, who had argued with typical foresight and candour that the politics of equality in war had no future after battles had ceased to be won by ordinary men (for example, by the English bowmen of Crécy or the Scottish pike men of Bannockburn). Even the ever-victorious Oliver Cromwell, who stressed the importance of the prayerfulness of his New Model Army, owed his successes more to his revolutionary cavalry tactics than to the piety of his troops. Orwell made the point in respect of the Spanish Civil War, arguing that hand grenades and so on were democratic because they gave 'claws to the weak'[24] whereas tanks, battleships and bombers were inherently tyrannical – and, it has to be said, much more likely to be victorious. Social justice, egalitarianism and democratic structures were not, in themselves, means sufficient or even appropriate to achieving the ends of revolutionary victory.

The relationship between means and ends can be viewed through a different prism. If it is argued that the 'end' for the republicans in Spain was the establishment of an egalitarian democracy then the Civil War can be seen as the means. Yet as soon as winning the war becomes the prime objective it assumes, *ipso facto*, the status of identifiable end, and then the republicans begin to discuss the best means to achieve that end. For the revolutionary militias the war was only part of the struggle against fascism in all its aspects on behalf of worker control of the state. So, for them, means and ends elided;[25] the war had to be fought and won on those terms, and the militia's chief weapon, the diffusion of revolutionary consciousness, represented the fruit of this elision.[26] For the communists, on the other hand, the more limited objective was simply to win the war. The Soviet Union which, from the late autumn of 1936, had begun to supply arms to the Spanish government, believed that establishing a bourgeois democracy in Spain would be more appropriate to their new strategy of achieving an understanding with the West than would the setting up of a workers' state. Accordingly collectivisation of the peasantry was halted, and local government by democratically elected committees began to be replaced by central government by the party. If winning the war was all, then, as Orwell pointed out, it was not being obtuse to conclude that: 'whoever tries to turn the civil war into a social revolution is playing into the hands of the fascists and is in effect, if not in intention, a traitor'.[27] The POUM argument was pretty much the opposite. Bourgeois democracy and fascism were two sides of the same coin and the only true alternative to fascism was worker control. For the POUM the war and revolution were inseparable.[28]

Orwell could see both points of view, though he freely acknowledged that, given the circumstances, the communists appeared to be the only people capable of winning the war on the republican side. 'The revolutionary purism of the POUM, though I saw its logic, seemed to me rather futile. After all, the one thing that mattered was to win the war.'[29] He concluded his analysis of the political situation by unambiguously declaring; 'the war was worth winning even if the revolution was lost'.[30] Then he immediately confused the issue by adding that he doubted whether, in the long run, the communist policy would lead to victory. Perhaps he saw some middle way between fighting the communists' anti-revolutionary war and the POUM-anarchist revolutionary war. What it was, was never made clear, but it must presumably have involved winning support from the international working-class.

Orwell's involvement with POUM owed its origins largely to accident and ignorance. He joined them because he happened (his word) to arrive in Barcelona with ILP papers and 'I did not realise that there were serious differences between the political parties'.[31] Orwell also told his friend Jack Common that had he understood the political situation better on his arrival in Spain, he would probably have joined the anarchists.[32] In a letter to Victor Gollancz, however, he wrote: 'Owing partly to an accident I joined the POUM militia instead of the International Brigade.'[33] From the beginning, it seems, Orwell's support for the revolution in Spain was ambiguous, not to say confused.

Orwell's strong support for POUM and its objectives after his return to Britain was in part a consequence of their getting 'no hearing in the capitalist press and nothing but libels in the left-wing press'.[34] In short, he wanted to ensure that they got a fair hearing. A noble and fair-minded objective but not the one that is usually thought to have motivated Orwell on this occasion, nor indeed the one that most readers would take away from *Homage to Catalonia*. Elsewhere he went even further and declared that he had given a more sympathetic account in *Homage to Catalonia* of POUM tactics than he actually felt appropriate. He had always told them they were wrong, he said, and had refused to join the party.[35]

We know that Orwell made strenuous attempts to join the communist-backed International Brigade.[36] Bowker quotes a young British communist whose job was to report on volunteers from the ILP, who wrote that Orwell showed little political understanding: 'He is not interested in party politics, and came to Spain ... to fight fascism.'[37] He noted that Orwell had grown to dislike the POUM and was anxious to fight on the Madrid front, a much more important theatre of the war. In the end, Orwell did not join the International Brigade because when he came back to Barcelona on leave, intending to make the change, the Catalan communists, the PSUC, had begun the process of centralising power and eliminating independent centres of worker control. Since a number of these were controlled by the POUM,[38] Orwell found himself, willy-nilly, opposing the PSUC. Transfer was no longer an option even had he still wished it.

Orwell considered the efforts of the communists to discredit and even liquidate their revolutionary comrades-in-arms to be despicable, and not only because his own life was at stake. Thus, although he acknowledged that in theory the communists' case was strong, their behaviour suggested that they were not advancing it in good faith. Let me repeat, this argument over means and ends was not a philosophical one: Orwell had witnessed the reality. He was pleased to get back to the front where one knew who and where the enemy was. But at Huesca ten days later, in May, Orwell was shot through the throat by a sniper and his war was over. Whilst he was waiting for his discharge, communist-led police began to disarm and arrest POUM and anarchist soldiers and supporters. The Orwells[39] were in real danger, but escaped, after several alarms, to France. A number of their friends were less fortunate. Shelden[40] referred to security police documentation that later came to light in the Madrid National Historical Archive in which the Orwells were described as '*trotskistas pronunciados*' and 'likely agents of the ILP and the POUM'. These were grounds for arrest at least. Davison shows that the liquidation of the POUM had been Soviet policy from before Orwell's arrival in Spain; not surprising, then, that Soviet apologists saw the POUM as 'the direct instrument of fascism'.[41]

Another tension thrown up by the revolutionary agenda that was real and not simply philosophical was that between the nobility of the revolutionary cause and the sordid reality of the war. Shaw had chided socialists for their self-confidence: they always assumed that they would win the class struggle, but perhaps their opponents had not studied Marx, and did not know the script. It had been long recognised by Marxists like William Morris, regarded by Marx himself as a sentimental utopian, that the socialist revolution might be bloody but it would be relatively quick, decisive and victorious. That is how he depicted it in *News from Nowhere*.[42] Although it has become common to confront nationalists and militarists with the dire consequences of their ambitions,[43] it has been far less common to question the socialist revolutionary's equally quixotic and equally dangerous ideas of the certain glories of the revolutionary agenda. Orwell's picture of the socialist revolution contained great heroism, but it also contained lies, treachery, confusion, boredom, brutality – and finally defeat.

Perhaps Orwell expected all this; it is hard to imagine that any of the illusions he took to Spain or generated in Barcelona would have lasted long. What he clearly did not expect, however, was the selective coverage of events in Spain subsequently by the left-wing British media. Selective in the sense that the media not only chose what to report and what not to report, but in the sense that what was reported bore a selective relation to the truth. In Spain Orwell saw newspaper reports that were completely unrelated to the facts as he had experienced them, not forming 'even the relationship which is implied in any ordinary lie'. In London, he said, eager intellectuals 'built emotional superstructures over events that had never happened'.[44] He found this development profoundly sinister. It portended the disappearance from the world of the 'very concept of objective truth', a possibility that consumed his thinking towards the end of his life. It was for this reason that Orwell defended the POUM so resolutely on his return to Britain.

Did Orwell leave Spain with any hope? A comment he made in a letter to Cyril Connolly on his return seems to suggest that he did: he had seen wonderful things in Spain and returned 'believing' in socialism, which he had never done before.[45] This quotation is often used (incorrectly, I would argue) to show that Orwell had not before considered himself to be a socialist. It is more likely that he was using the word 'believe' in a quasi-religious sense; that is, the full acceptance, emotional and spiritual as well as intellectual, of a given truth. Orwell had seen wonderful things! He had joined the militia to fight for common decency and, at the end of everything, his desire to see socialism established had been made 'much more actual than it had been before'. Spain confirmed Orwell's belief that only the working-class and not the intellectuals or the ideologues were the true enemies of fascism. Parenthetically, some feminist writers, especially Daphne Patai, have been dismissive of Orwell's Catalonian socialism because of its overt masculinity, its 'insistent adherence to a gender polarisation that assumes male ... superiority'.[46] There is no answer to Patai's basic charge: most accounts of fighting are, after all, likely to be masculine. Newsinger argues that Orwell came back from Spain knowing socialism to be feasible and determined to bring it about. If so, this could only have represented a triumph of hope over experience, but at least, as we shall see, the Second World War allowed him to hope for a re-run of the Civil War. The British working-class would take on Hitler, destroy its own latently fascist ruling class and establish an egalitarian socialist society. The revolution would triumph this time.

2

The development of Orwell's thought after his return from Spain, however, was not uniformly consistent. He claimed that the 'real' struggle in Spain had been between the revolutionaries and the counter-revolutionaries (amongst whom he included the communists).[47] His Spanish experiences forced upon him the conclusion that fascism could not be opposed successfully by capitalist democracy, for these were in reality, he said, Tweedledum and Tweedledee,[48] the former only a development of the latter. It was for this reason that capitalist democracy (including the British left-wing press, as far as Orwell was concerned)[49] recognised 'the revolution' (in this case the position adopted by the Spanish anarchists and Trotskyites) as its enemy. Socialists should not, he concluded from his Spanish experiences, collaborate with capitalist imperialism by fighting the fascists.[50] 'If one collaborates with a capitalist-imperialist government in a struggle "against Fascism", i.e. against a rival imperialism, one is simply letting Fascism in by the back door', he wrote.[51] In April of 1938, having attended its conference the previous year, Orwell joined the ILP,[52] which at the time was determinedly pacifist and, as O'Callaghan reminds us, contained a strong Trotskyite element.[53] He seemed absolutely clear at this time that the way forward was to mobilise the ordinary people's dislike of war and use it against their own ruling class.[54] If the British workers were to collude with their upper-class masters in a war against fascism, this would only provide that class with the opportunity to 'slip the noose of fascism' over their necks.

All the 'utterly irresponsible' intellectuals who advocated war were either singularly ill-informed about the way politics and international relations were conducted in the modern world or were under the sway of the Soviet Union – either pansies or gangsters.[55] In September of 1938, Orwell signed a manifesto published in *The New Leader* repudiating all appeals to the workers to support a war fought in the interests of maintaining the Empire. He firmly believed that British working men would never again fight a war to support capitalism.[56] Writing to a French correspondent, he expressed the conviction that they would simply refuse to do so.[57] And amidst these overtly political activities, Orwell was also working on a new novel, widely regarded as pacifist, *Coming Up for Air*.[58]

In September of 1939, war broke out and, after all, British workers took up arms for British capitalism. And so did Orwell, greatly to the dismay of his pacifist friends in the ILP. The previous month, on the night before the announcement of the Russo-German Pact, he had dreamt that war had begun and his response had been unambiguous: he was glad the waiting was over and would do all he could to support the war effort. But he had by no means lost his faith in a British revolution. Towards the end of 1940, when British fortunes were at their lowest ebb, Orwell wrote a major essay *The Lion and the Unicorn: Socialism and the English Genius.*[59] We shall be considering what Orwell had to say about the English genius in the next chapter; for the moment, we shall concentrate on socialism and more especially its revolutionary variety. Orwell's rather dubious contention was that revolution was completely compatible with British values. Not only this, but the fact that Britain was at war had transformed socialism from a 'text-book word' into a 'realisable policy'. Socialism was more than possible; it was essential because the war could not be won without socialism. Shades of Spain and the POUM! It was necessary to harness Englishness to socialism or neither would stand against fascism. In a perceptive short essay, 'Wells, Hitler and the World State',[60] Orwell had criticised socialists like Wells for rejecting patriotism. The forces that shape the world, he said, spring from emotions, a fact that liberals who believed in reason and 'whose heart does not leap at the sound of bugles' could not grasp. Unfortunately, said Orwell, the liberal rationalists' equation of science with common sense did not hold. In the fascist states science was fighting on the side of nationalism and bigotry. Wells and his like were too sane to understand these 'creatures out of the dark ages' that, in Yeats' words, were slouching towards Bethlehem.[61] Only a socialism that dressed up in the Union Flag, a socialism that expressed that true spirit of Englishness, could hope to triumph. These arguments embodied Orwell's reflections on his Spanish experiences, but the introduction of English (or more correctly British) values adds a new dimension.

Orwell's task had been to establish that there was no fundamental dichotomy between the English genius and socialist revolution; in fact to establish the opposite. Ever since Dunkirk the government had been taking increasing powers upon itself; socialism had become synonymous with the war effort. He described the equality of war sacrifice as 'war-communism'. As we shall see in Chapter 5, Orwell managed to picture the socialist revolution as, on the one hand, a clear expression of British decency, and on the other, as a political system concerned to optimise the efficient use of resources through central planning. The socialist revolution was not about destroying the national 'family' but about replacing those in control of the family fortunes. And it had already begun. Orwell had changed his mind fundamentally. Britain's ruling class did not, after all, comprise cynical scoundrels out to drop the noose of fascism over the workers' necks and British socialists could legitimately join in the war against continental fascism because that war would inevitably bring about revolution, and that revolution would be true to British traditions by seeking to combine social and political change with cultural stability.

This represented a watering down of Orwell's earlier revolutionary hopes, and although it should be remembered that it was written with a clear war-propaganda aim in mind, it is also apparent that he was beginning to recognise the radical impact that the war was having upon British society. He believed that Britain could reasonably expect what would amount to a fundamental social transformation as the war progressed. He recognised revolutionary elements within the Labour Party. As late as mid-1942 he was expecting Sir Stafford Cripps to leave the government that he had recently joined and proclaim a revolutionary policy.[62] He was not alone: Borkenau, the historian of the Spanish Civil War whose judgement Orwell valued, had also spoken of Britain being in the first stage of revolution.[63] This was the same Orwell who had written less than two years earlier that he had nothing but contempt for 'the fools who think they can first drive the nation into a war for democracy and then turn round and say "Now we'll have the revolution" '.[64] It is transparently clear from his wartime writings that Orwell came to take exactly this position himself. Whilst he still accepted that the gutters of London might have to run with blood,[65] the 'possibility of building a Socialist on the bones of a Blimp' was genuine. This much was obvious to all but the 'boiled rabbits of the left'. More damaging to his consistency perhaps, Orwell had also written earlier that any genuine threat to British national interests would 'turn nine out of ten British Socialists into Jingoes'.[66] To say the least, there seems to be no good grounds for identifying Orwell as the tenth; the smell of boiled rabbit must surely have hung in the air in Orwell's London flat.

By the following year, Orwell had modified his views again: the 'old-fashioned' idea of the proletarian revolution, of 'red flags and street fighting' (and presumably the blood in the gutters) had gone. The opportunities of Dunkirk and Singapore had been missed.[67] Indeed, by the end of the war Orwell had become embarrassed by his earlier expectations and predictions. Writing to *Partisan Review*,[68] he admitted having fallen into the trap of believing that 'the war and the revolution were inseparable'. He accepted that he had made a major error of judgement, for 'after all, we have not lost the war and we have not introduced socialism'. He admitted, too, that he had over-emphasised the anti-fascist nature of the war and exaggerated the extent of the 'inevitable' social changes. As for the revolution, Orwell had come to the conclusion that theories of its efficacy were simply wrong. He wrote: 'throughout history one revolution after another – although producing a temporary relief, such as a sick man gets by turning over in bed – has simply led to a change of masters'.[69] Anyone who has experienced this unfortunate condition will know what a destructive metaphor this is for revolution. The sick person turns only out of sheer desperation, for the turning movement is of itself likely to be painful and is undertaken in the full knowledge that its benefits will be marginal and short term.

Orwell's thinking had indeed undergone major changes. He had, after all, been a supporter of pacifism, writing in August 1937 that war only happened when it was in the interests of capital and that fascism was only a rival form of imperialism. 'Any capitalist nation fighting a war against fascism would itself quickly become fascist.'[70] This argument had been proved false and he had abandoned it, arguing instead that revolution would come naturally and inevitably from the war itself (an argument, we have seen, that he had himself roundly dismissed earlier). Now he felt obliged to admit, and to be fair he admitted it with complete candour, there was no British fascism and no British revolution. He now held that to suggest that Nazism and capitalism were Tweedledum and Tweedledee was absurd, though, as we have seen, he had himself suggested exactly this – twice. He blamed the Left for being unprepared for war in 1939, declaring that 'many intellectuals of the left were flabbily pacifist up to 1935–9, and then promptly cooled off when the war started'.[71] He himself had been just such a pacifist; now he held that pacifism was 'such nonsense that no one who has ever been in contact with the realities would ever consider it . . . a child of six would be able to see that'.[72] Earlier he had attacked as a 'vulgar lie' the claim that communism and fascism were more or less the same thing.[73] In important respects this vulgar lie became central to his own thinking. In short, Orwell had been continually and comprehensively wrong. His 1942 declaration that Churchill's position was very insecure and that he would not be around for long was one of his least memorable predictions.[74] 'How could I write such things?' he asked, no doubt on behalf of all his readers. But even with this outpouring of *mea culpa* came the proviso that he had, after all, often been right when the leftist intellectuals were wrong. The evidence he provided for this claim, however, was less convincing.[75]

After the war the democratic socialism that he had championed, and in which he still claimed to believe, had at least survived as a future possibility, but by this time it inhabited a world of demons, chief amongst which was the USSR, which had the effrontery to claim to be its foremost exponent, and its allies amongst the Western intelligentsia. Socialists had to be made to understand who their real enemies were, and this new battle was not so much for the victory as for the survival of democratic socialism.

3

'How many . . . will wallow in the mire like pigs,
Leaving behind them nothing but infamous horrors.'
                              Dante, *The Divine Comedy*

Animal Farm[76] constituted a full-frontal assault on the 'real enemy' of democratic socialism, which Orwell had first identified in Spain: Stalin's Russia. At the time, Stalin's Russia was Britain's ally in the last stages of a brutal war, and T. S. Eliot (and Faber and Faber) turned the original manuscript down because they were convinced that the time was not right for 'this . . . point of view from which to criticise the political situation. . . .'[77] Interestingly, when the book was finally published, it was so immediately popular that Queen Elizabeth, later the Queen Mother, sent out for a copy. Warburg had sold out so the royal messenger had to go down to George Woodcock's Anarchist Bookshop to pick up her copy.[78] Woodcock's shop, ironically, was located in the former London home of the revolutionary socialist and scourge of the establishment, William Morris. While the book does not slavishly, or indeed sequentially, follow the events of the Russian Revolution, the parallels are clear: Marx, Stalin, Trotsky and the poet Mayakovsky are clearly represented. Events such as the 1917 revolution itself, the Kronstadt naval rebellion, the Treaty of Rapallo, the German invasion of Russia, the Teheran conference, are all unmistakable. So are four definable periods in Soviet history: collectivisation, the purges, the alliance with Germany, and finally the rapprochement with the West. The story of *Animal Farm* is, in short, an allegory of the Russian Revolution and post-Revolution.

Though Orwell identified his target unambiguously, it can be argued that *Animal Farm* hit not so much the Soviet bull's-eye as the sacred cow of revolution itself. When he attacked Stalin's revolution, he attacked the whole enterprise of revolution with it. Orwell showed that the kind of revolution undertaken by the animals (violent, conspiratorial, and led by a consciously power-hungry élite) could only result in one group of leaders replacing another. T. S. Eliot, though recommending its rejection, compared the work to Orwell's favourite book, *Gulliver's Travels*,[79] which is no mean praise. Swift's satire had been aimed at specific contemporary targets which any reader of the period would have been easily able to identify. Nevertheless, his stories had a universal reference and were to prove able subsequently to hit targets of which Swift could have had no inkling. Similarly, in a hundred years and more, people will read and learn from *Animal Farm*, though the names and events of the Russian Revolution may mean very little to them. What they will learn is that in Orwell's view revolutions tend to fail, and why.

Animal Farm is an account of a revolution on Manor Farm. This revolution occurred some time after a speech, delivered by Major, an old and respected boar. The speech, modelled on the concluding section of *The Communist Manifesto*, declared that all animals were equal and all men enemies; only by continuing to eschew the customs of humankind could the animals maintain their condition of equality. Major set the chief task of the days ahead: to create a true political consciousness. This task fell to the pigs, as the cleverest of the animals, with the most prominent parts being taken by Snowball, Napoleon and Squealer (Trotsky, Stalin and Mayakovsky). Major died before the revolution dawned, but dawn it unquestionably did, and sooner than any had expected. One Midsummer's Eve, Jones the farmer got drunk and forgot to put out food for the animals next morning, or indeed all the next day. So they took it for themselves and successfully resisted the farmer's subsequent attempts to drive them out of the food stores. The rebellion, unplanned, had been successful 'almost before they knew what was happening';[80] now the task at hand was to establish a revolutionary society.

The majority of the animals, says Orwell, were blissfully happy at the departure of their masters. As the revolution developed, a number of the animals adopted a cynical approach. The cat, for example, 'purred so affectionately that it was impossible not to believe in her good intentions' as she sought to persuade the birds of her solidarity with her winged comrades.[81] As for the other animals, they 'rolled in the dew, they cropped mouthfuls of the sweet summer grass, they kicked up clods of the black earth and snuffed its rich scent',[82] and in their bliss they had not the least idea of what was to become of them. Indeed. But Snowball and Napoleon had. During the previous three months the pigs had taught themselves to read and write – not forbidden by Major – and they wrote the Seven Commandments of Animalism on the big barn wall. These stipulated that all animals were friends, all humans were enemies, and that no animal should indulge in any of the activities that defined humanity, such as smoking, drinking, sleeping in beds, wearing clothes. And crucially, it was stipulated that all animals were equal.

Thereafter the pigs organised the other animals for the benefit of all. We should note two developments in these early days of the revolution. First, the pigs kept the milk and apples for their own use, because these particular foods were so important to brainworkers. 'This has been proved by Science, comrades', Squealer explained.[83] All the pigs were in full agreement on this point. They did not actually like the milk, but needed to preserve their health and brainpower for the good of the whole animal community: a noble sacrifice. Second, the pigs did not actually do any work but directed and supervised the other animals. With their superior knowledge, says Orwell, it was 'natural that they should assume the leadership'.[84] From the very beginning, then, a division of labour came naturally into being. Animals were not equal after all, in this most fundamental of senses. It was natural for the more intelligent to take control and, as far as Orwell was concerned, to assume privileges.

There seems to be an inevitability about the sequence of events on Animal Farm thereafter. Formal Meetings were held on each Sunday and at each meeting resolutions were agreed upon concerning the work. But these resolutions always came from the pigs. Snowball was assiduous in organising the animals to increase productivity: the Whiter Wool Movement for the sheep, the Egg Production Committee for the hens, and even the Wild Comrades' Re-education Committee to make the rabbits and rats more responsible comrades. (The cat joined this committee to assist in this pioneering work.) And always in the background the sheep chanted Snowball's maxim: 'four legs good, two legs bad'.

As time wore on, it became apparent that though the pigs were unchallenged in their authority, there was increasing tension between Snowball and Napoleon, and that although the former often seemed to get the better of the arguments, the latter was adept at drumming up support for his position, especially with the sheep, who would frequently interrupt Snowball with their bleating of 'four legs good, two legs bad'. There were ideological differences between the two: Snowball-Trotsky wanted to stir up insurrection on other farms and thus spread the revolution, whereas Napoleon-Stalin wanted to concentrate on homeland defence and to come to some *modus vivendi* with local farmers. Finally, they collided on policy. The former's reading habits had taken on a technical flavour and he had mastered theories of bricklaying, electricity and so on. He then produced a scheme that would transform Animal Farm – the building of a wind-mill (industrialisation). It would demand a huge amount of work on the part of all the animals to complete. He set the plans of the building out on the floor for the animals to study, though they hardly under-stood them. Napoleon, however, understood them and he did not like them. He could have argued against them on practical grounds; it was an immensely ambitious and problematic project. He could certainly have objected to them on ideological grounds; after all, Old Major had specifically warned them against engaging in trade,[85] and in order to build the windmill they would clearly have to do this. In fact, he did neither: he cocked a leg and urinated on them.[86] And when the final decision was to be made by the animals, Napoleon produced his strongest argument: nine enormous dogs with brass-studded collars who made straight for Snowball. Snowball escaped with his life – just – but was never to be seen again. From now on, said Napoleon, the charade of Sunday morning meetings of all the animals would be replaced by a committee of the pigs.

A few weeks later, the animals were surprised to learn that the windmill was to be built anyway (Stalin had been suddenly converted to industrialisation and economic planning). Orwell writes: 'All that year the animals worked like slaves', though their food rations were no better than they had been under Jones. Napoleon meanwhile courted local farmers, trading produce for the tools and materials they needed for the windmill. And the pigs moved into the farmhouse. Strange to relate, although some of the animals seemed to remember that the laws of animalism forbade sleeping on beds, they were reassured to have the relevant commandment read out to them: no animal was to sleep on a bed with sheets. The descent into privilege and tyranny seems inescapable.

Only occasionally do we catch a glimpse of possible alternative developments, for example when Boxer the carthorse expressed slight doubts about some of Napoleon's policies and was attacked by some of the dogs. He beat them off easily and could have killed them. It was within his power at that point to challenge Napoleon's leader-ship. But Boxer was, in fact, one of the latter's strongest supporters and was oblivious of the reality that the animalism to which he wholeheartedly subscribed was being betrayed. Boxer did not seize his chance and his subsequent fate at the hands of the duplicitous Napoleon becomes all the more poignant. Having worked himself nearly to death in the cause of animalism, Boxer was rewarded by being taken off to the knacker's yard and not, as he and the other animals had been led to believe, to the local veterinary hospital.

When the animals, and indeed Boxer himself, realised this treachery there was nothing they could do but weep.

Animal Farm became a tyranny. Its enemies within were purged and their punishment ferocious. Napoleon's rule was based upon the cult of his own personality. The animals' great anthem 'Beasts of England' was replaced by the hagiographic 'Comrade Napoleon', and every failure to achieve a target was blamed upon the activities of the treacherous Snowball and his secret acolytes. With the passing of time, all the pigs came more and more to resemble human beings and the commandments of animalism were amended accordingly. So when the pigs began to consume alcohol the relevant commandment, it was discovered, quite clearly forbade drinking only to excess. Unlike Jones the farmer, who had been only intermittently cruel and generally careless of the animals' welfare, the pigs used terror systematically as a means of social control. Finally came the greatest of treacheries. One evening after work Clover, Boxer's mare, set up a terrified neighing. She had seen a pig walking on two legs. It was Squealer, the spin doctor. He carried a whip in his trotter. 'But just at that moment, as though at a signal, all the sheep burst out into a tremendous bleating of – "Four legs good, two legs *better*. Four legs good, two legs *better* ..." '.[87] The book ends with Napoleon and the leading pigs entertaining the local farmers one evening and the animals, drawn to the farmhouse by the raucous laughter, found it quite impossible to distinguish the pigs from the humans any more. And of all the commandments of animalism on the barn wall only one remained, a simple explosive oxymoron whose warped logic and unmistakable stench of doublethink has lodged it for ever in the modern consciousness:

> All animals are equal
> But some animals are more
> Equal than others.

The revolution on Animal Farm was now completed, from slavery through revolt and through freedom and back again to slavery. It could be argued that failure was a consequence of the fact that the animals had been catapulted into revolution before they had become sufficiently politically conscious. Marx had said that the violence of revolution would accelerate the growth of consciousness, and yet the most numerous of the animals on the farm were sheep. Who could have roused their political consciousness? Moreover, we should remember in whose 'hands' the task of consciousness-raising was placed: the pigs. Animal Farm can only provide a loose analogy for human society, yet the British Marxist Hyndman had written: 'a slave class cannot free itself. The leadership, the initiative, the teaching, the organisation, must come from those comrades who are in a different position and who are trained to use their faculties in early life.'[88] This Marxist would-be revolutionary had a plain message: leadership must *always* come from the pigs.

Alternatively, it could be argued that the revolution on Animal Farm failed because the leadership forsook the principles of the revolution and lost contact with the mass movement: more public-spirited pigs, T. S. Eliot had suggested. This was to assume that the pigs had ever subscribed to the principles of animalism, which is itself open to question. It also suggests that as leaders of the revolution the pigs might have worked closer with the mass movement. Yet in the early days of the revolution the only aspiration that the mass movement could put into effect was to crop mouthfuls of the sweet summer grass. The objectification of the principles of animalism was the task of a leadership which would, seemingly inevitably, become divided but which even collectively would be unlikely to countenance the canvassing of alternatives. And from the beginning, this class united unanimously behind a willingness to take privileges to itself. In the days of the early Christian Church, when principles not unlike those of animalism were being expounded, St Paul wrote reminding the Thessalonians that when he and Timothy were with them, they had 'wrought with labour and travail, night and day . . . to make an example unto you to follow us'. But after their departure there had arisen a group of leaders who did no work but were 'busybodies'. St Paul's approach was quite different to Napoleon's and Snowball's and he commanded: 'If any would not work, neither shall he eat.'[89] Control of Animal Farm passed from a social élite to a political élite, from the farmer and his family to the pigs. The gains in this transfer for the other animals were minimal. True, they were always dubious of Squealer's production statistics: 'there were days when they felt they would sooner have had less figures and more food',[90] but for a long time they accepted their sufferings because the farm 'belonged to them'. Almost to the end, the animals never gave up hope,[91] but the fact was that the tyranny of pigs proved more efficient than the misrule of the farmer, and so the animals could be said to have been worse off than before.

From the beginning, the pigs intended to replace the traditional capitalism of Manor Farm not with democratic socialism but with another form of centralised control, and this intention was clearly shared by Snowball. Napoleon ruled through fear. Snowball took the trouble to seem to include the animals in his decisions, but they were, all the same, palpably his decisions. The windmill was his idea; the process of rapid industrialisation which that process invoked implied that the ordinary animals would be excluded more and more from decision-making: increasingly, this would become a job for the experts. In short, whichever course it adopted, the process of revolution led inescapably to the enthronement of a new, in this case totalitarian, élite, and the only safeguard against such a development that Orwell had invoked throughout his career, the value system of the working-class, finished up in the hands of Alfred Simmonds, Horse Slaughterer and Glue Boiler. Boxer tried to kick his way out of the knacker's van, but by then his great strength was spent. 'The time had been when a few kicks from Boxer's hoofs (sic) would have smashed the van to matchwood.'[92] Always susceptible to Napoleon's exhortations, as Orwell had noted working-class audiences to be susceptible to Mosley's,[93] Boxer had given everything to Napoleon, believing he was thereby giving it to animalism. The poignancy of his death shakes us; with Boxer die hope and decency.

One last point. The final scene in the story shows the pigs and the local farmers drinking and playing cards together, an allusion to the Teheran Conference towards the end of World War Two. Although from the animals' perspective their leadership was indistinguishable from the leadership of the other farms, we should not be lulled into imagining that pigs and humans were reconciled.[94] Far from it. All that had happened was that an experiment in democratic farming, encapsulated in the theory of animalism, had failed, and Manor Farm had become like others farms (only more efficient) and would jostle with them in the world of competitive agriculture.

Revolution seemed at first sight to offer socialists a prompt and effective way of redressing the many profound ills of their unequal societies. However, as we recall, Bernard Shaw pointed to an assumption that is both hidden and unwarranted: that the forces of revolution would inevitably be victorious. He went on to suggest the contrary: 'demolishing a Bastille with seven prisoners is one thing; demolishing one with fourteen million prisoners is quite another'.[95] Shaw was right: to manage a successful socialist revolution in any modern industrial state would prove immeasurably difficult. To some revolutionaries this hardly signified: they were concerned with (or consumed by) vengeance. Hemmelreich, for example, in André Malraux's *Man's Estate*, wished only 'to requite by no matter what violence, to avenge with bombs the unspeakable horror of the existence which had poisoned him since the day of his birth, and which would poison his children in the same way'.[96] Yet for socialists concerned with victory not vengeance, the storming of the barricades, however difficult, however dramatic, would prove to be the easier part. It was the establishment and administration of a revolutionary society that has always constituted the major problem. In the words of Aldous Huxley's revolutionary Mark Staithes: 'Revolution's delightful in the preliminary stages. So long as it's a question of getting rid of the people at the top. But afterwards, if the thing's a success – what then? More wireless sets, more chocolates, more beauty parlours, more girls with better contraceptives.'[97] Ironically, in light of the events on Animal Farm, Staithes goes on: 'The moment you give the people the chance to be piggish, they take it thankfully.' Through Orwell we come to understand that the pigs, given only half a chance, will become people-ish.

4

In this chapter, we have dealt with three quite different genres of writing: reportage in Spain, essays and journalism in respect of war and revolution in 1939–45, and imaginative literature in *Animal Farm*. *Homage to Catalonia* constitutes an attempt to deal with very complex ideological issues and to tell an exciting story. It was one of Orwell's dying wishes that the overtly political chapters should be omitted from future editions of the book, and finally this wish was granted by Peter Davison in his *Complete Works* edition (volume six). Perhaps Orwell feared that, like many of his contemporaries, he had outgrown some of the political views he held at the time. Perhaps he was aware of the inconsistencies we have noticed in his treatment of the ideological themes. Certainly, he was advised that as a piece of literature the book was simply better without them.[98] Perhaps all three considerations weighed on him. But in truth, these chapters form part of the historical record of Orwell in Spain and the book is surely the poorer for their omission. *Homage to Catalonia* stands as Orwell's finest work of reportage, but this does not mean that we should regard it as historically accurate. Indeed, he says so himself:[99]

> It is very difficult to write accurately about the Spanish war, because of the lack of non-propagandist documents. I warn everyone against my bias, and I warn everyone against my mistakes. Still, I have done my best to be honest.

No doubt he did. But Orwell was not particularly fluent in Spanish. Skilled linguist though he certainly was, Orwell tried to teach himself the language from a dictionary *en route* to Barcelona,[100] and he arrived there with no Catalan at all. He spent only a few days in Barcelona, where he was shown around by a local POUM militiaman who found it difficult to make any real contact with his ward, describing him much later as unsympathetic. 'He was a silent, taciturn person. I didn't get the impression he was interesting.'[101] They conversed in French. It was Walter Lippmann who spoke of observers seeing things through the habits of their eyes. Orwell was in no position even to attempt a dispassionate analysis of what was happening in Barcelona; he saw pretty much what his eyes wanted to see. Altogether he was in Spain for five months or so, and he spent nearly all that time on the Aragon front where very little of military or political significance happened. To those who complain that *Homage to Catalonia* was about as unbiased as an account of the English Civil War by one of John Lilburne's Levellers would have been, there can be no effective riposte except this: we should take the title of this work of literature seriously. Orwell wrote a moving tribute to the people of Catalonia, portraying both their aspirations for a fairer future (which he honoured) and their desperate sense of betrayal (which he shared). He tried, with consummate skill, to communicate a set of experiences based upon those hopes and despairs. 'I happened to know, what very few people in England had been allowed to know, that innocent men were being falsely accused. If I had not been angry about that, I should never have written the book.'[102] If he was biased, well, he told us as much. *Homage to Catalonia* is widely regarded as one of Orwell's greatest literary achievements, but it would not pass muster as a history and neither did it seek to do so.

Less successful as literature and certainly as polemic, are Orwell's wartime essays in which he wrote about the linkage between war and revolution. I have suggested that Orwell passionately wanted a re-run of the Spanish Civil War. This time, revolutionary expectations would not be decoupled from the effort to win the war. Indeed, quite the opposite. As we read these essays and journalism, however, we realise that Orwell's prejudices lead him time and again to misread events. As I suggested in Chapter 1, the quality of this literary genre will inevit-ably be measured in large part by the accuracy and insight of its portrayal of events and the sagacity of its prognostications. Orwell was simply wrong too often.

By contrast, *Animal Farm*, in the eyes of many, was Orwell's great-est literary and political achievement. He wrote it because he wanted to waken the world to the threat of totalitarianism, and especially to its Soviet form. After returning from Spain, he sought to expose the

Soviet myth 'in a story that could be easily understood by almost everyone and which could easily be translated into other languages'.[103] He believed – and who would dispute it – that he had produced a work that would speak for itself. The philosopher Richard Rorty was unstinting in his praise of *Animal Farm*. In depicting the events of the failed revolution, wrote Rorty, Orwell 'attacks the incredibly complicated and sophisticated character of leftist political discussion ... by retelling the history of the [twentieth] century in terms suitable for children'.[104] The story of the twentieth century was one of revolution betrayed: in Russia (and Soviet-style systems everywhere), in Spain and on Animal Farm.

We noted at the beginning of the chapter that Orwell took from Spain both hope and a sense of disillusion. He expressed his hope in the final triumph of the values of ordinary people, which constituted the defining characteristic of his democratic socialism, his decency myth. Hope, that is to say, still lay with the proles. But his disillusion fed off a growing belief that there appeared to be no possibility of these values coming to dominate the polity in the foreseeable future. His experience showed him that the socialist revolution, as exemplified by Barcelona in 1936, might be not only transitory but also chimerical.

5 Family and nation

> It's easy to die if the things you care about are going to survive. . . . that's how people used to see it. Individually they were finished, but their way of life would continue. Their good and evil would remain good and evil. They didn't feel the ground they stood on shifting under their feet.
>
> George Orwell, *Coming Up for Air* (Harmondsworth: Penguin, 1990, p. 111).

Many commentators have described Orwell as quintessentially English,[1] and there is no doubt that his patriotism was an important, perhaps even a defining, characteristic of the man if not always the writer. It is equally clear that, whatever the shortcomings of his own childhood, he considered family life to be of great consequence, not only for the individuals concerned but also more broadly for the polity. It is also clear that in Orwell's mind family and general cultural values were mutually supportive. This chapter will be concerned with Orwell's writings on these subjects, and on their interrelationship.

This elision of family and general cultural values is enshrined in Orwell's patriotic essay *The Lion and the Unicorn*, written in 1940, in which Orwell famously wrote that England:[2]

> resembles a family, a rather stuffy Victorian family, with not many black sheep in it but with all its cupboards bursting with skeletons. It has rich relations that have to be kow-towed to and poor relations who are horribly sat upon, and there is a deep conspiracy of silence about the source of the family income . . . Still, it is a family. It has its private language and its common memories, and at the approach of an enemy it closes its ranks. A family with the wrong members in control – that, perhaps, is as near as one can come to describing England in a phrase.

This metaphor provides a key to understanding the nature of Orwell's patriotism, and we will need to analyse it with some care if we are to come to grips with what was, after all, a major strand in Orwell's thinking. But what did Orwell mean by family, and in what sense might England be said to resemble one? Before considering these questions, though, it is appropriate to clear up the prior matter of what constitutes England; that is to say, the small matter of Englishness and Britishness.

Nowadays Englishness, to coin a phrase, is a contested concept. Those who write on nationality and national consciousness tell us that it is only when these concepts are in doubt that a people seeks to discover itself and its values.[3] Jeremy Paxman, in his popular study,[4] shows that England and Englishness are now perhaps for the first time subjects for debate,[5] almost certainly as a consequence of two developments: multiculturalism and devolution. Paxman notes that when A. S. Byatt was editing a collection of English short stories, she looked at a series of essays, *Studying British Culture*, and found 55 references to Scottishness, 20 to Caribbean culture, 27 to the Welsh and 28 to the Irish. The only mention of Englishness or English culture that she was able to locate was in the preface: there were three brief references challenging 'the hegemony of England'. She concluded: 'You got the feeling that the English only exist to be discarded and challenged.'[6] On the other hand, as George Mikes observed half a century ago, 'When people say England they sometimes mean Great Britain, sometimes the United Kingdom, sometimes the British Isles – but never England.'[7]

This was not how things were in Orwell's day; Englishness was not a contested concept, in fact it was a concept perhaps too readily taken for granted. Orwell himself used Englishness and Britishness to mean much the same thing. Although he readily admits that Scotsmen, Irishmen and Welshmen, and indeed Cockneys and Yorkshiremen, might be offended by his shorthand, he tells them that to the outside world they are all much of a muchness. This would not have been generally regarded as contentious until comparatively recently. That quintessentially Scots missionary David Livingstone, for example, in his copious correspondence, used 'English' in a narrow and often waspishly critical sense as referring to someone or something from south of the Tweed, but he also frequently used it as synonymous with British and actually frequently applied it to himself.[8] The elision of English into British, then, was not simply an English imperial conspiracy. All the same, Orwell was said to have had one of the best noses of his generation.[9] It is reasonable to expect that he would have been sensitive to this confusion and would have had something to say about it.

1

Orwell's family came originally from Scotland, though he would have to go back beyond his great-great-grandfather, who was from Dorset, to discover his Caledonian heritage. That great-great-grandfather was the absentee owner of tropical plantations in the West Indies and was married to the daughter of the eighth Earl of Westmoreland. If Orwell's deepest roots, along with the name Blair, were indubitably Scottish, he nevertheless affected a strong disdain for both roots and name. In his essay on his school days, 'Such, Such Were the Joys', Orwell talked scathingly about the 'cult of Scottishness', though when we dig deeper we discover that this cult was indulged in by Englishmen as much as Scots, and in fact what Orwell had really taken a dislike to was 'toffs' taking off to the Highlands for their summer 'hols' and disseminating this information widely and loudly.[10] One of the reasons Orwell gave for taking a pseudonym was his distaste for his family name Blair, because it was 'Scotch', and aristocratically 'Scotch' at that (he used this form of the word because, as he told Anthony Powell, it annoyed Scotsmen[11]). Crick informs us that Orwell once refused to attend a meeting of the PEN Club which was to be held at the home of a couple called Muir, because he believed them to be Scots.[12]

Orwell's police service in Burma reinforced his antipathy to the Scots. He saw that they played a disproportionately large part in the business of empire. 'The British Empire', he said, 'is simply a device for giving trade monopolies to the English – or rather to gangs of Jews and Scotchmen'.[13] One of the first men to instruct Flory in the ways of the *pukka sahib*, the *sahiblog*, was 'an old Scotch gin soaker who ran a crooked pony racing business'.[14] The chief Scots character in *Burmese Days*, Deputy Commissioner Macgregor, however, can be seen as a man who, though no more liberal than other members of the club, was nevertheless trustworthy and respected by the local Burmese.

Later on, Orwell, writing about the reception of US troops in Britain during the war, declared – on what kind of evidence it is totally unclear – that in Scotland relations between the locals and the billeted troops were better because 'the people are certainly more hospitable than in England'.[15] Nevertheless, when he was editor of *Tribune* he published a hostile review of the first edition of *Poetry Scotland* and seems to have taken a rather schoolboy satisfaction from the antagonism the review generated north of the border.[16] He saw Celtic nationalism as racially prejudiced, as assuming the moral superiority of the Celtic peoples over others, especially the Anglo-Saxons, and on these grounds he was happy to see it and its poetry traduced.

In late 1945, Orwell went to live on the Hebridean island of Jura. Before he set out he had had no knowledge at all of Scottish nationalism as an ideology or as a political movement and, though he never became an expert, he did come to recognise the economic argument for nationalism, admitting: 'in this country [England] I don't think it is enough realised – I myself had no idea of it until a few years ago – that Scotland has a case against England'.[17] He went on to observe that the Scottish upper class was Anglicised in speech and custom so that in some areas Scotland appeared to the native working-class almost to be an occupied country. The working-class spoke with a markedly different accent, indeed in some cases even used a different language. Orwell recognised this as a more dangerous kind of class division than any existing in England.

Living on Jura sensitised Orwell to the language issue, to the decline in the use of Gaelic, and he became a strong supporter of measures to strengthen the language. Once upon a time, he mused, he would have thought it absurd to keep minority languages alive, but now he recognised the importance of the language in protecting the indigenous culture and saw bilingualism as a value in its own right. But although Orwell became sympathetic to Scotland's distinctive economic and cultural identity, he remained opposed to the thrust of nationalism and especially, not surprisingly, its anti-Englishness.

One of Orwell's qualities was a readiness to admit mistakes. Ignorance seldom made him reticent, but knowledge, usually gained through experience, never prevented him from recanting. When he first went to Yorkshire he hated its tribalism. Yet by the time he left the north of England, Orwell had become a champion of the northern working-class and its values. Much the same happened when he went to Scotland: old prejudices were soon sloughed off. Not long before he died, Orwell spent several months in Hairmyres Hospital in East Kilbryde, where he hardly ever heard an upper-class English accent. He grew accustomed to working-class and lower-middle-class Scottish voices. Back in the southwest of England, in Gloucestershire, he heard those upper-class English accents again:[18]

And what voices! A sort of over-fedness, a fatuous self-confidence, a constant bah-bahing of laughter about nothing, above all a sort of heaviness and richness combined with a fundamental ill-will – people who, one instinctively thinks, are the enemies of anything intelligent or sensitive or beautiful. No wonder everyone hates us so.

An altogether sweeping criticism, just as sweeping, in fact, as his earlier criticism of the Scots had been, but it suggested that Orwell's views of Englishness and Britishness were no longer one-dimensional. He wrote very little about the Welsh or Welsh nationalism and was hostile to what he considered to be the excesses of Irish nationalism, but he was sympathetic to these patriotisms and noted, for example, that the Scots, quite understandably so he felt, did not like to be called English.

Nevertheless, as we have observed, in composing *The Lion and the Unicorn*, Orwell made the powerful but contrasting point that the differences between the peoples of Britain fade away the moment that any two Britons are confronted by a European. We may be sure, then, that in writing this essay extolling the virtues of 'the English', Orwell really meant the British. He did not even address the question of the extent to which Gaelic and Welsh-speaking cultures incorporated his Englishness, but as we shall see later he was very well aware that even in the north of England social values predominated that appeared to run counter to his Englishness. It is a frustrating shortcoming of *The Lion and the Unicorn* that these issues were barely discussed at all, and certainly not resolved. Had he lived in Jura before writing the essay, perhaps Orwell would have pursued these themes more assiduously. On the other hand, he is right to conclude that, seen from the outside, most British people share very similar social and political values. One further point: most socialists would want to propose that the real differences between peoples concerned social class, not nationality, and it cannot be denied that Orwell had a lot to say about class difference. However, as to national differences in Britain, when Orwell said English he almost certainly meant British. He wanted to speak to and on behalf of the whole nation. He wrote, for example, that the one positive gain to emerge from the dreadful summer of 1940 was 'the integrity of British national feeling'.[19] Nevertheless, for the sake of convenience and consistency I shall reluctantly stick to Orwell's usage in the following discussion of Orwell's patriotism and refer generally to England and the English.

2

When he was Prime Minister, John Major sought to define Englishness. Significantly, he did so in a speech to the Conservative Group for

Europe,[20] seeking to identify what would not be lost as Britain became more integrated into Europe. He spoke of warm beer, cricket on the village green and, referring back to Orwell, the spinster cycling home from church. He was not the first prime minister to paint such a picture,[21] but the key point in Major's homily was this: England will still be the same country fifty years from now. This notion of the permanence of England is a beguiling one; as the song says, there will always be an England, 'wherever there's a cottage small beside a field of grain'. Although the nineteenth century had witnessed a major shift in the balance of economic and, to a lesser extent, political power from the landed aristocracy to the industrial bourgeoisie, the new guardians of power did not seek to cast a new England in their own image: rather, they aped their betters, taking on their values,[22] remaining what D. H. Lawrence called 'pseudo-cottagey'.[23] Even some socialists expressed a strong sentiment for such an England, William Morris for example favouring a landscape in which 'all is measured, mingled, varied, gliding easily one thing into another, little rivers, little plains . . . little hills, little mountains'.[24] But where was the small cottage beside the field of grain? Certainly not in Scotland's Central Belt, nor for that matter in the Highlands and Islands. Not in Yorkshire, or indeed anywhere in the industrial north (only remember Engels' descriptions of industrial Lancashire,[25] or Dickens' Coketown!([26]). This pseudo-cottagey version of England has always been essentially southern, rural and Anglican, and the picture that has been painted is indeed still there to be seen, though whether it can be considered, or could ever have been considered, typical is another matter.

This traditional England may not, in the strictest sense, be or have ever been real; yet to call it a fantasy would be to misunderstand its nature. It is better understood as an imagined world, standing as a symbol for certain social and political values. Myths have their force; reality is different because of them. It was this rural myth that Rupert Brooke conjured up when considering the possibility of death in the First World War. He contemplated:[27]

Her sights and sound; dreams happy as her day.
And laughter, learnt of friends; and gentleness
In hearts at peace, under an English heaven.

And what did George Orwell have to contribute to the myth of Englishness? We might expect a man with his reputation for general iconoclasm and apparent hatred of the 'Pox Britannica' to be scathing about notions of England and Englishness, to be anxious to lay these concepts finally to rest with a few surgically incisive phrases, showing them to be nothing more than cloaks for the cynical exploitation of the working-class. He did no such thing, and although much of his patriotic writing represented a conscious attempt to strengthen the nation's resolve in a time of dire threat, we can sense that he was drawing on deeply held feelings, which he was able to deploy without sacrificing any basic principles.

Orwell's first and unsocialist observation in *The Lion and the Unicorn* was that brothers and sisters though we may be in this world, we are certainly not all the same. For Orwell, the whole nation of England had a 'single identifiable character' and culture – 'instinctively we know that such things as national character exist', he wrote;[28] things that happen in one country, he added, simply do not happen in some others. He proceeded to sketch that character, beginning, in true Orwellian style, with some generalisations 'that would be accepted by almost all observers'.[29] First, the English are not musical like the Germans and Italians. There is no evidence that Orwell himself had any interest in or knowledge of music. Did he carefully weigh and then reject the traditional music that so enriched the lives of the regions of Britain? Was he really dismissive of the magnificent English choral tradition with its reverence for polyphonic harmony, encompassing the work of Purcell or Byrd or Dowland or Tallis?[30] Did he believe that the naturalising of Handel and the lionising of Haydn signified nothing? How did he rate the work of his contemporaries, broadly speaking, like Vaughan Williams, Walton, Delius, Elgar, Holst or Benjamin Britten? Or did he simply not know much about any of these?[31] Second, we are reliably informed that painting and sculpture have never flourished in Britain as they have in France. Did Orwell discount the work of Constable, Gainsborough, Reynolds and, above all, Turner,[32] or his contemporaries like Henry Moore and Barbara Hepworth? He wrote nothing about these. Third, we learn that the English have a horror of abstract thought. Put so baldly, this would surely have come as a revelation to the English logical positivists and their friends, in particular Bertrand Russell and A. J. Ayer (both of whom Orwell knew: indeed in a letter to his [and Ayer's] old Eton tutor S. F. Gow he wrote of Freddie Ayer as 'a great friend of mine'[33]). Hobbes, Locke and Hume, to mention only the most obvious, might also have felt they had grounds for lodging an objection. Fourth, what the English did possess was a distinctive love of flowers, apparently the first thing one notices when coming to England from abroad. A day trip to Holland or to any of the Scandinavian countries, just a sight of the *villages fleuris* of France and their equivalents across the

European continent, might have given Orwell cause to reflect on this claim.

I certainly do not wish to propose that it would be impossible, though perhaps unlikely, for an expert in any of these cultural fields to make some comparative generalisations along the lines that Orwell advanced, especially regarding philosophical traditions, and maybe even arriving at conclusions somewhat similar to his. But their conclusions would certainly be balanced and hemmed in by caveats and exceptions. What I do want to propose, however, is that Orwell was not anything remotely like an expert in any of these fields and that his generalisations were entirely ill considered. What I would further like to propose is that what Orwell was really telling us about was himself and not England at all. Margaret Thatcher did something similar much later when she claimed that she knew instinctively what the people of Britain felt about issues. She felt it in her heart. Orwell's grasp of Englishness was no more plausible than hers turned out to be. He failed here in these opening passages to provide us with anything solid that might serve as a model of English personal and social values that could link to, and help to explain, their political values. But he was not finished yet.

There was something distinctive he went on unabashed, about the culture based upon these characteristics. Though they were not musical or creative or given to philosophy, the English were addicted to an individual liberty in which each was king in his own Chestertonian castle. Above all, the English were a gentle people with an anti-militaristic sentiment. Their great war poems celebrated not victories but defeats. Such hypocrisy, the continental European might charge: what about the British Empire? Orwell acknowledged the sharpness of this barb, but countered that few Western nations did not seek to establish empires, and at least the British Empire was run by a relatively incorruptible bureaucracy and a relatively small imperial military presence. Moreover, as we have seen, the British had a sense of responsibility. We observed that in *Wigan Pier* Orwell had written, recalling his experiences in Burma, that the convicted criminal was superior to any hanging judge.[34] Here, fourteen years later, in *The Lion and the Unicorn*, he referred again to 'that evil old man in scarlet robes and horsehair wig', but significantly adds now that he will always 'interpret the law according to the book and will in no circumstances take a money bribe'. All in all, he concluded, British democracy, empire notwithstanding, was much less of a fraud than it sometimes appeared.

Regarding its social structure, earlier taken to be another form of

imperialism, Orwell accepted that England was still divided fundamentally by a class system so intense that the common people had to
live 'to some extent against the existing order'.[35] Even so, members
of the ruling class were part of the nation and certainly not the
'cynical scoundrels they are sometimes declared to be'.[36] Moreover, he
observed that, quite contrary to Marx's prediction, the middle-class
was growing and the working-class, much better off, coming increasingly to resemble it. Although no-one could claim Orwell as a pro-
ponent of the Thatcherite trickle-down theory of wealth creation, he
came dangerously close when he declared: 'A millionaire cannot, for
example, light the streets for himself and darken them for other
people.'[37] This analogy is part of a broader picture of beneficial social
change, the symbol of which was Betjeman's detested new town,
Slough.[38] Orwell called towns like it the future of England. He specifically praised the labour-saving homes and the tinned food so despised by Betjeman. (And as we shall see later, by George Bowling.)
He had misgivings, it is true, but they were not Betjeman's. Whilst
the latter was concerned that the young men of Slough could not
distinguish the bird song from the radio, Orwell was more concerned
that they would know much more about magnetos than the Bible.
Nevertheless, he was, or claimed to be, as confident as John Major
that, despite future changes, including this apparent decline in class
differentiation, England would always be England, 'an everlasting
animal stretching into the future and the past and, like all living
things, having the power to change out of recognition and yet remain
the same'.[39]

This was Orwell's version of Englishness. Did he believe it? Knowing what we do of his earlier writing, it is somehow hard to convince
oneself that he did. Then what was Orwell's game? Perhaps in truth
this Englishness was nothing more than a Trojan horse, inside which
were Orwellian socialists waiting to spring out. The English have been
told how superior their civilisation is, and softened up to the prob-
ability of social and political change, though a change that will
strengthen and not destroy England. Now the horse disgorges and we
discover: 'It is only by revolution that the native genius of the English
people can be set free',[40] and later 'by revolution we become more
ourselves, not less'.[41] Socialism was more than possible however;
it was necessary, because 'we cannot win the war without introducing socialism'.[42] Now it was necessary to harness Englishness to
socialism. The gentle, inartistic, unmusical, flower-loving English, it
seems, needed a socialist revolution to express their true national consciousness. But what about that other version of Englishness that we

encountered in *Wigan Pier*? Did it not contrast with the picture painted above? Orwell briefly draws our attention to this alternative 'northern' Englishness in *The Lion and the Unicorn*, but hastens to assure us that, in the prevailing international confrontation between good and evil, differences of region and class and Englishness were not of consequence (though he had firmly held the opposite view between 1936 and 1940). That enduring metaphor of England as a family with which we began clearly indicated that, at this time and in these circumstances, Orwell thought the two versions of Englishness, like the social classes generally, had sufficient in common to be considered as one. Both were to be harnessed in the name of socialism.

It is difficult to accept that Orwell illuminated the concept of Englishness in any way, except in the literal sense that more light tends either to bring into focus, in all their confusion, the inherent complexities and ambiguities of a subject, or to submerge everything in such a brilliant light as to render individual details indistinguishable. Orwell's illumination was of the latter variety. In neither case does it help. I have suggested that Orwell's Englishness was chiefly created as a disguise for socialism, or perhaps two separate disguises. Yet these disguises should not obscure what Orwell took to be an underlying reality, and one which others have recognised. If the myth of Englishness offered the English some sense of who they thought they were, then it had some political importance. In a later essay, *The English People*,[43] Orwell recited the social and political virtues of the English again, concluding: the English should not listen to those who tell them that their country is finished. If they can come to terms with the realities of the post-war world, they could give an example to others. 'The world is sick of chaos and it is sick of dictatorship. Of all peoples the English are likeliest to find a way of avoiding both.'[44] But the English can only accomplish this immeasurably important task if 'the ordinary English in the street can somehow get their hands on power'.[45] That represented an enormously difficult task, but an impossible one if the values Orwell associated with Englishness did not have the symbolic resonance that he claimed for them. What Orwell completely failed to do was to indicate convincingly how these essentially private values that enshrined gentleness, pragmatism and love of liberty, even if as widespread as he believed, might become the dominant political values in his changing England. But before we become too maudlin about the gentle English, a quotation from that quintessentially English character actress Joyce Grenfell, niece of Lady Astor and practising Christian Scientist, might inject a sense of balance. Writing to her American mother about the carpet bombing of German cities, she declared: 'I'd like to see every single German mown down and exterminated – every bloody one of them!'[46]

When Cecil Rhodes remarked that to be born an Englishman was to have won first prize in the lottery of life, he was not referring to country cottages or grim northern industrial landscapes but to Britain's constitution and the values that it was supposed to represent. As Dickens' Mr Podsnap patronisingly explained to the foreign gentleman: 'We Englishmen are very proud of our constitution, Sir. It was bestowed upon us by providence. No other country is so favoured as this country.'[47] The Conservative constitutionalist Sir Ernest Barker[48] fleshed out the kinds of values that underpinned the much envied constitution: amateurism, the idea of the gentleman, eccentricity, humour, social homogeneity and the voluntary habit. Together these values produced a robust individualism that rejected collectivism and indeed all ideologies. We might want to add respect for the rights of others to this list. Who but the British would have continued to pay Hitler royalties every time the BBC used excerpts from *Mein Kampf* during its war-time broadcasts?[49] Paxman drew an important, if provisional, distinction between English and continental European values: 'It is tempting to conclude the French believe that the state is the people, while in England, the state is something else – "them".'[50] What these examples show is that it is possible even in popular as opposed to academic analysis to forge a connection between private and public values, which shows how the former may shape the latter. Though it was crucial to his own argument, Orwell simply failed in this patriotic essay on Englishness to link private and political values causally even in the short-hand way that Barker and Paxman attempted in such a clear manner.

3

I should like now to return to the notion of family. It is intriguing to wonder what picture Orwell might have had in his own mind when he used the analogy of England as a family. The first port of call in any tour of Orwell's portrayal of the family is *Wigan Pier*. Here, we discover the virtues of working-class family life. A working-class family, as we have seen, hangs together and does not go to pieces as a result of poverty. A working-class home has 'a warm, decent, deeply human atmosphere which is not so easy to find elsewhere'.[51] The memory of such interiors, especially those he claimed to have seen in his childhood, was positive enough to lead Orwell to conclude that his age had not been altogether a bad one to live in. Given that Orwell, almost immediately after writing this, informed the reader that he had been forbidden to play with working-class children from an early age, let alone go to their houses, it is more likely that this image was cast in Wigan, and not, as he claimed, during his childhood. Indeed, we might remember that Orwell's 'shabby genteel' childhood left him with only one opinion about the lower classes – they smelled.

Orwell did not analyse the structure of the working-class family in *Wigan Pier*. He did no more than touch on the role differentiation structured on gender, pointing out that workmen, even when unemployed, would not assist their wives with the housework for fear of being thought to be 'Mary-Anns'.[52] Nor did he paint a fuller picture of the working-class family in any other of his works. In fact, the only detailed account of the structure and values of family life is to be found in the novel *Coming Up for Air*, published in 1939, and here the subject was not the industrial proletariat but the small-town *petite bourgeoisie*. However, although the familial virtues that he extolled were primarily to be found in his descriptions of working-class communities, Orwell frequently used the phrases 'working-class' and 'ordinary people' almost synonymously.[53] This would scarcely have passed muster in a sociological work and remains problematical in any serious analysis, but as far as Orwell was concerned, the chief characteristic of those whom he called ordinary was what we might call their negative relation to power – they had none. It was this crucial characteristic of economic and political powerlessness that they shared with working-class families. In *Coming Up for Air* Orwell gave the fullest picture of the family lives of ordinary people; it is there that he dealt with ordinary life 'in the flesh', as it were, rather than symbolically. If we wish to examine his assessment of the family values of ordinary English people, we cannot do better than consider this work.

George Bowling, the novel's central character, was a lost soul. He was transfixed both by the fear of approaching war and its consequences and by the crisis in his own life. Bowling, shaving with his bluntish razor, looked out onto his garden, the ten yards by five of grass, with a privet hedge around it and a bare patch, worn by his children, in the middle. He reflected that the same back garden, same privets, same grass, was to be found behind every house in Ellesmere Road. 'Do you know the road I live in? . . . even if you don't you know fifty others like it . . . Long, long rows of little semi-detached houses . . . the stucco front, the creosoted gate, the privet hedge, the green front door . . . [and] in every one of those little stucco boxes there's some poor bastard who's never been free except when he's fast asleep.'[54]

Chief amongst George Bowling's sources of dissatisfaction was his wife, Hilda. Why did he marry her? For no good reason, he concluded, and then challenged: 'but why did you marry yours? These things happen to us.' Sometimes, he tells us, he lays on his bed wondering about women: 'why they're like that, how they get like that, whether they're doing it on purpose . . .'[55] But Bowling's discontents played on a larger stage and he fantasised about erecting a huge statue to the building society that made Ellesmere Road and his lifestyle possible: in one hand it would hold an enormous key, to the workhouse, and in the other, a 'whole cornucopia out of which would be pouring radios, life-insurance policies, false teeth, aspirins, French letters and concrete garden rollers'.[56] Bowling detested his lifestyle and the world that framed it. He hated its modernity, its slickness, its enamel and its chromium-platedness, characteristics he collectively called its 'stream-linedness'. The modern world was symbolised for Bowling by the hamburger he bought in a milk bar. Naturally he assumed it comprised meat, but discovered, after his first mouthful, that he had 'bitten into the modern world and found out what it was really made of . . . rotten fish in a rubber skin. Bombs of filth bursting inside your mouth.'[57] It was in this state of mind that Bowling, through a chance word connection in a newspaper headline, became suddenly mentally transported to his childhood home in the small Home Counties town of Lower Binfield. We soon discover that it was family life in pre-1914 Lower Binfield that provided Bowling with his point of reference from which he judged his own world. Lower Binfield was a community of ordinary people whose life was built around the family unit.

Lower Binfield lay in a valley near the Thames; a small market town dominated by Binfield House, The Hall, as it was commonly called, home of the local aristocratic family. Orwell offers over seventy pages of nostalgic description of the life of the young George Bowling. He evoked the particular sounds, sights, tastes and, above all, smells of Bowling's country childhood. What he sought to do was to recreate the sense of family life in a small-town community. Life was not easy for them, but it was, says Bowling, good. Pivotal to the good life of the family was Bowling's mother: 'When you saw her cooking you knew that she was in a world where she belonged, among things she really understood.'[58] His father, a seed merchant, meanwhile, busied himself with 'men's work'.

Lower Binfield was not a society of equals but of 'big social distinc-tions' (and even bigger gender distinctions, about which the author had nothing whatever to say), and yet it represented a true community. To be a boy was to be bound up with 'breaking rules and killing things . . . the hot sweaty feeling of one's clothes . . . the sour stink of the rubbish dump ... the stamping on young birds, the feel of the fish straining on the line – it was all part of it'.[59] Better than anything, even the blowing up of toads with bicycle pumps, was the fishing. Fishing, says Bowling, was the archetypal activity of that civilisation. Even the names of the course fish had a poetic ring; they were made up by men who had never heard of machine guns. Fishing was everything. 'If you gave me the choice of having any woman you care to name', Bowling concluded, 'but I mean any woman, or catching a ten pound carp, the carp would win every time'.[60] This imagined choice signified the unmistakable masculinity of Bowling's preferred world. Women do not fish. They never experience the intensity of the almost primeval sensation of hooking a fish. 'Thank God I am a man', said Bowling, 'because no woman ever has that feeling'.[61] Not in pre-war Lower Binfield at least.[62]

Why was life really better in Lower Binfield, for it certainly was not softer? Because of the continuity of community values; because you could accept even death when you knew that the things your community cared about would continue after your death. Your sense of good and evil would remain good and evil. You did not feel that the moral ground was shifting beneath your feet. And the foundation of that security and certainty was thoroughly gendered. 'For ever and ever decent God-fearing women would cook Yorkshire pudding and apple dumplings on enormous coal ranges, wear woollen underwear and sleep on feathers.'[63] Eventually, George Bowling decided that he must pay a secret visit to Lower Binfield simply to snatch a draught or two from the cask of those traditional values.

But Lower Binfield, when he finally plucked up the courage to take a few days off and visit it, had become simply unrecognisable. 'Oh yes', Bowling tells us conspiratorially, 'you knew what was coming. But I didn't.' He could not find his bearings because the small market town had been engulfed by new buildings and become dominated by two new factories. He had to ask his way around, but his respondent was unable to help. She answered in an accent you could 'cut with a spade': Lancashire. Bowling was nonplussed, feeling that a 'kind of enemy invasion had happened behind my back'.[64] Everything seemed to have changed, including his father's shop, which had been converted into a teashop. Only the church was the same: the same pews, the same smells, even the same vicar. Worse followed as Bowling explored the area more carefully. Going to his favourite river where he had fished in solitude as a boy, for example, he found caravans, teashops, ice cream stalls – a riverside Margate. Men were fishing every five yards of the river, having to compete with canoes, rowing boats and motor launches, all making a fearful noise. It was the working-class at play and Bowling's judgement was crisp: 'crowds of bloody aliens'.[65] All in all, his Lower Binfield had degenerated, swollen, he said bitterly, 'into a kind of Dagenham'. He had come looking for something that did not exist in the 'streamlined milk-bars with the radio playing' of his own world and found that it no longer existed even in Lower Binfield. One last, desperate effort to rescue the past remained: he had to visit the secret pool behind The Hall, where the largest carp were to be found; surely its remoteness and seclusion would have saved it. Its fate, in fact, had been even worse: it had been drained and was being used as a refuse tip. The Hall, moreover, had been sold and had become Binfield House: as Bowling despairingly exclaimed, it has become a 'loony bin'. No, the good life was finished and the bad times were coming. And the 'streamlined' men were coming too. George Bowling motored back to Ellesmere Road deflated, defeated and despairing.

What Lower Binfield represented was a family-centred, timeless tradition; just the kind of society so roundly detested by Wells' Alfred Polly.[66] Orwell was very fond of *Mr. Polly* and there are many points of comparison between the two novels:[67] it is hardly coincidental that Orwell reversed the thrust of Wells' story, with the hero running to the solid, small-town, lower-middle-class kingdom from which Polly fled. Moreover, Bowling sought to escape from the very kind of modernity which Orwell associated with Wells. It is true that Orwell juxtaposed Lower Binfield's timelessness and security with Bowling's fears of the uncertainties of war and the horrors of fascism, true that images of warplanes were everywhere, but fundamentally the comparison was with the modern age; Bowling's great rage was against modernity. If only he could have persuaded one of the bombers to release its friendly bombs (made in one of the new factories in Lower Binfield) to fall on West Bletchley! Was this the same Orwell who was to champion these very towns in *The Lion and the Unicorn* a few years later? In forsaking the traditional life that Polly had hated, Bowling, far from being liberated, had become encaged; by his wife, by his family, by his house and by his job – just like everybody else. In West Bletchley he had lost contact with the purely sensory pleasures of the country, with what Whitman had called the primal sanities. As we have noted, the word that Bowling used to conjure up the intensity of his dislike of modernity was streamlined. (How Polly, or George in *Tono Bungay*, would have loved that word and all it signified.) Though he looked more like Parsons, Bowling was a precursor of Winston Smith; he could not love the big brother of modernity, which circumscribed his life at every level, but unlike Winston he lacked the courage to revolt.

I have dealt with *Coming Up for Air* in some detail because it provides Orwell's only detailed picture of the family and community life of the ordinary people he claimed to admire. Unlike the snap-shots of Wigan and Sheffield with their 'symmetrical' working-class lives and their air of equality, the reality of Lower Binfield is based on social inequality and the ravages of competitive commerce. From time immemorial it had been dominated by The Hall, symbolically overlooking all. Orwell said nothing about it or its owners, itself an interesting omission. When the aristocratic dominance it represented had finally gone, it had been replaced by a lunatic asylum, the very antithesis of the kind of transformation wrought in Morris' *Nowhere*, in which the Houses of Parliament, an even greater symbol of aristocratic domination, became a useful and productive dung market.[68] The prevailing social norm of the community had been Smilesean self-help, each family looking after itself, with neighbours helping each other, but only to a point. Above all, it had been a man's world.

The world of Lower Binfield was exclusive. When Bowling railed against the riverside scene he witnessed on his return, for being just another Margate, when he referred dismissively to the Lancastrian invasion, and when he characterised working people enjoying themselves noisily as a crowd of aliens, we feel the true weight of this prejudice. Like many communities, Lower Binfield was enclosed, bound closely together by its dislike of outsiders. If we were to seek a parallel in literature to Bowling's depiction of his birthplace and its subsequent development, it would surely be Gissing's picture of New Wanley in *Demos*,[69] the symbol of Gissing's devastating attack on modernisation, and indeed on socialism.

And what, finally, are we to make of Bowling's passion for fishing? Of all activities fishing *à la* Bowling is the least social. We would expect to find good working-class socialists in a Sheffield angling club but Bowling's fishing is not of this order. It is solitary, we might say even antisocial, and traditional. It is a sport for countrymen, for Tories of any class.[70] On the night of his death, George Orwell had a newly acquired fishing rod across the bottom of his bed.

The passion that fired Bowling's image of Lower Binfield was a vision of a society where everyone knew his or her place. Especially her place. We should observe that this world, with its moral certainties that can even take the sting out of death, is centred upon the mother. The ordinary social values that Orwell prized, such as the class solidarity of the industrial proletariat and the family solidarity of ordinary people, were unmistakably based upon women remaining in the world they belonged to and understood. It was because these women were there 'for ever and ever' that men could be men. In that popular cinematic portrayal of a modern Orwellian mining community, *Brassed Off*, much of the film's tension was provided by the fact that women were no longer willing to play the role defined by Orwell. Family life was in the process of redefining itself in Grimley. A few years later, in the Sheffield of *The Full Monty*, the transformation was complete. Economic power had transferred to women, and Yorkshire puddings, if they were still being cooked at all, would have been bought frozen from Tesco's, not 'stirred wi' love' at home, as in the traditional recipe that Mrs. Bowling senior would doubtless have followed.

Bowling gave no indication of any kind of community life in the streamlined world of West Bletchley. Objectively, George Bowling was no worse off than Alfred Polly. Indeed, as he made clear, had his parents been able to see him they would have thought how well he had done for himself. But his wife was liberated and the buckle that fastened the traditional family together and held in its traditional values had broken open. What took its place was, for Bowling, almost by definition dysfunctional. 'There've been times when I've thought of separation or divorce, but in our walk of life you don't do those things. You can't afford to. And time goes on, and you kind of give up struggling.'[71] And for Bowling, whose world seemed to be disintegrating, there was no alternative form of family or community. 'We're all on the burning deck and nobody knows it except me.'[72]

Before leaving the Orwellian family, we should note that it appears vestigially in both *Animal Farm* and *Nineteen Eighty Four*. In the former, the carthorses Boxer and Clover symbolise the working-class, and early in the story we find an example of their familial status when a brood of orphaned ducklings come to one of the meetings addressed by Major. 'Clover made a sort of wall round them with her great foreleg, and the ducklings nestled down inside it, and promptly fell asleep.'[73] Thereafter, Boxer and Clover became the pigs' most faithful disciples and, despite occasional misgivings, they acted as bellwethers for Napoleon's many schemes. Even when Snowball was declared to have acted treacherously at the Battle of the Cowshed, it was enough for Boxer to learn that, despite the evidence of his own eyes, Napoleon had declared this to be so. What the carthorses gave to animalism was unflinching loyalty, and to the movement unquestioning solidarity. And this was simply a reflection in the public arena of their private values. But they had been duped. When Napoleon set up his bloody show trials, 'the animals huddled round Clover, not speaking'.[74] They began to sing 'Beasts of England', but 'slowly and mournfully, in a way they had never sung it before'.[75] With the death of Boxer, their betrayal was complete.

Nineteen Eighty Four depicted a society almost devoid of normal human values; it is also a society in which the proles play no part. When, near the beginning of the novel, Winston attended a cinema, he saw on the newsreel an attack by an Oceanian helicopter on a lifeboat full of enemy women and children. The audience were able to see clearly a mother doing her best to protect her terrified child against the coming bombs. As the bombs fell, applause broke out from the party seats, but down amongst the proles a woman shouted: 'they didn't oughter of showed it not in front of kids they didnt it aint right not in front of kids'.[76] She was applying a set of values that were rooted in a traditional conception of family life; the police threw her out.

Winston himself had no immediate family and the only picture the novel provides of family life amongst outer Party members is of the Parsons. On the walls of their flat were the scarlet banners of the Youth League and the Spies, and a full-sized photograph of Big Brother. Winston described the Parsons' children as like tiger cubs, soon to grow up into man-eaters. They were disappointed, when Winston first encountered them, because they had not been allowed to go to the public hanging. As Winston left the Parsons' flat, the boy hit him with a stone from a catapult, yelling 'Goldstein!' after him. Winston was seized, as he turned to face the boy, with the 'look of helpless fright' on his mother's face. Within a few years, he ruminated, the children would be watching their parents night and day for signs of unorthodoxy. 'It was almost normal', he concluded, 'for people over thirty to be frightened of their children'.[77] Sure enough, when Winston was taken into custody by the Thought Police, he shared his cell briefly with Parsons, pulled in for thoughtcrime. Winston asked Parsons whether he was guilty and was told that, indeed, he was guilty. He had been caught denouncing Big Brother in his sleep. And who had denounced him? 'It was my little daughter . . . pretty smart for a nipper of seven eh?'[78] But this loyalty to the Party was not new. Parsons' children had earlier set fire to an old woman's skirt in the market because they saw her wrapping up sausages in a poster of Big Brother.[79]

Though he had no family of his own, Winston frequently dreamed of his mother and the dream was of a sinking ship and of his mother sacrificing herself and his little sister so that Winston could live. Such a tragedy belonged to a time long ago 'when there was still privacy, love and friendship, and when the members of a family stood by one another without needing to know the reason'.[80] In custody Winston met 'an enormous wreck of a woman with great tumbling breasts' who was heaved into his cell. Having thrown up over the cell floor, she introduced herself and they discovered that they shared a surname. 'Thass funny. . . . I might be your mother', she said.[81]

A final example of the oblique way in which the concept of family is brought in as a counterpoint to the main theme of a dehumanised society is provided by the picture of the prole woman singing in the yard outside the junk shop in which Winston and Julia used to meet secretly. She was pegging nappies on a clothes line. Was she a washerwoman or just washing for her many grandchildren? She was beautiful, Winston concluded, in the way of a rosehip: 'why should the fruit be held inferior to the flower?'[82] To how many children had she given birth? How much laundering, scrubbing, mending had she done, for children and then for grandchildren? Yet there she stood, a 'solid, unconquerable figure, made monstrous by work and childbearing, toiling from birth to death, and still singing. Out of those mighty loins a race of conscious beings must one day come.'[83] If there was hope, it lay with the proles. It is no wonder that Orwell used the family as a metaphor in seeking to characterise England, or more correctly Britain: at bottom family and nation were held together by the same values. But how successful was the metaphor?

4

Orwell's project, set out unequivocally in *The Lion and the Unicorn*, was to link his characterisation of English virtues with those of the traditional family. Like all his projects, this was both aesthetic and political in nature, and it was a particularly important project because it embodied Orwell's hopes for the establishment of democratic socialism within the context of the traditional moral values of the British people. The continuity of these values was bound up within and protected by the traditional family structure, which was thus a *sina qua non* for the establishment of Orwell's decency myth. However, it has to be said that the notion that the contemporary family might provide a repository for the ark of the socialist covenant was savagely challenged by Orwell's own forensic dissection of the Bowlings in *Coming Up for Air*. The sense of continuity of values – what is held to be good and evil today is just the same as it was yesterday and will be tomorrow – explodes like George Bowling's hamburger. The moral ground on which we stand shudders and we fear for the future of our world.

What was so different about the world of Lower Binfield? We should note that its very cosiness was a function of a rigid hierarchical structure. Orwell's family was built upon and around the mother:

Orwell's ordinary woman was, he said, as solid as a Norman pillar. We noted in a previous chapter that he had described the miners as caryatids, but now we discover that for miners to be miners women have to cook Yorkshire puddings and wash nappies endlessly. We have already observed how, in his short book *Orwell's Victory*, Christopher Hitchens attempted stubbornly to defend Orwell against the principal charge of misogyny by a number of feminist writers,[84] but finally all even he can say is that Orwell had 'participated' in the unending conflict over what is 'natural' in sexual relations with – weasel words – 'a decent minimum of hypocrisy'.[85] Well, let us be as minimally hypocritical as Hitchens says Orwell was: Orwell's model family and its values would fall down if women were not in a subservient place. Orwell attacked Lawrence Woolf's book *The Reilly Plan*[86] which discussed liberating women through the concept of kitchenless houses. Meals would be delivered by thermos containers and taken at community centres. This would clearly destroy family life, and even worse (for Orwell) you would have to use other people's crockery. Woolf replied by attacking Orwell as a 'cataleptic conservative', and he had every right to be annoyed; Orwell had himself written in favour of similar changes, though not communal eating, only a year before. He envisaged a municipal van taking one's dirty crockery away in the morning and bringing it back clean in the evening.[87] The only possible defence against the charge of misogyny in *Coming Up for Air* would be to suggest that the whole novel constituted a clever parody of male chauvinism. Not surprisingly, nobody has advanced such a case. When George Bowling thanked his god for being a man, he meant it. (In Orwell's own life, he could not have achieved what he did without the active support of Eileen, who put her own career in abeyance by giving up work on the dissertation she was writing for her MA at University College London – she was pursuing research on creativity in children under Cyril Burt – mainly because she believed in her husband's art and chose to support him.[88]) But the family he pictured was already becoming part of history even as Orwell painted it, and he knew this. In *Coming Up for Air*, Bowling's own, modern family was dysfunctional; he looked back to the families of his childhood with nostalgia and envy in search of a model.

It seems clear to me that Orwell's family offered no serviceable metaphor for the England of his day and its values, still less of our day and its values. We have also to bear in mind, though, that England was not simply a family but a family with the wrong people in charge. The young were thwarted, Orwell tells us by 'irresponsible uncles and bedridden aunts'.[89] But even families with the right people in charge are still hierarchies, and they are clearly not, except by accident, merito-cratic. How could an avowed egalitarian see the traditional family as a model for his preferred society?[90]

But the project was more ambitious even than to save the tradi-tional family. It was to link the family to those values that Orwell enumerated later in *The Lion and the Unicorn*. Now, to claim that the most marked characteristic of English civilisation was its comparative gentleness was not of itself naïve. After all, Yossarian, in *Catch 22*, as he set out on his Roman bacchanalia, reflected: 'Mobs . . . mobs of policemen – everywhere but England was in the hands of mobs, mobs, mobs. Mobs with clubs were in control everywhere.'[91] He offered no evidence, but he clearly agreed with Orwell. Orwell, how-ever, needed to be much more explicit if he wished to show how private values could be invested in political culture. This is no easy task. The periodical *Prospect* published a debate on national values entitled 'Rediscovering Britain' in 2005, involving the Chancellor of the Exchequer Gordon Brown (whose speech on the subject some months earlier had sparked the debate), the philosopher Roger Scruton (author of *England: An Elegy*[92]), and several other prominent figures, which failed to establish whether characteristic national values existed at all, and if they did, how they could be incorporated into political culture. Gordon Brown concluded that the National Health Service provided an example of the embodiment of national values in a polit-ical structure. Scruton concentrated on a key component of national culture that Orwell had alluded to briefly but not developed at all: the nature of common law. Despite the wide divergence of views in the debate, more matters of substance were covered in the six-page report[93] than are to be found in Orwell's fifty-page essay. Moreover, others had written about the incorporation of private values into polit-ical structures before Orwell. G. K. Chesterton, for example, managed to establish a vibrant connection between private and public values with his own version of Englishness in such works as *The Flying Inn* and *The Napoleon of Notting Hill*.[94] The US scholar Robert Benewick studied Mosley's British Union of Fascists and concluded that the reason Mosley failed to attain the prominence of his continental coun-terparts was, essentially, this same native gentleness and love of liberty to which Orwell referred.[95] But Benewick developed a far more sinu-ous argument than did Orwell with his cat's cradle of generalities. Orwell's case for the political consequences of the alleged gentleness of the English in *The Lion and the Unicorn* simply did not get beyond the status of assertion. All in all, it is not difficult to sympathise with his own wish to see the essay suppressed.

Why, then, is *The Lion and the Unicorn* still widely read? Why do readers still take some comfort from these values that might not really exist, might not ever have existed, and are, anyway, according to Orwell, going down, along with the traditional family? Surely it is only because Orwell was skilful enough as a writer to stroke his English and Anglophile readers into a mild patriotic self-congratulatory stupor. English patriotism is 'bound up with solid breakfasts and gloomy Sundays, smoky towns and winding roads, green fields and red pillar-boxes'[96] he tells us. Addressing his fellow countrymen, Orwell says: 'this is *your* civilisation, it is *you*. However much you hate it or laugh at it, you will never be happy away from it for any length of time. The suet puddings and the red pillar-boxes have entered into your soul.'[97] Who could fail to succumb to such a deftly constructed soft-focus picture of oneself and one's countrymen, to a picture of patriotism that seems to go beyond standard stereotypes and definitions, evoking a sense almost beyond patriotism, perhaps articulating that missing quality that Edith Cavell sought when, in 1915, she faced the firing squad and declared that simple patriotism was not enough?

6   Two plus two equals four

'Freedom is the freedom to say that two plus two equals four. If that is granted, all else follows.'

George Orwell, *Nineteen Eighty Four* (Harmondsworth: Penguin, 1960, p. 68).

Few books have had a greater public impact on their readers than *Nineteen Eighty Four*. When Frederick Warburg read it before publication, he wrote: 'This is amongst the most terrifying books I have ever read. The savagery of Swift has passed to a successor who looks upon life and finds it becoming even more intolerable . . . It is a great book, but I pray I may be spared from reading another like it for years to come.'[1] The second publisher's reader, David Farrer, agreed: 'In emotive power and craftsmanship this novel towers above the average. Orwell has done what Wells never did, created a fantasy world which yet is horribly real so that you mind what happens to the characters which inhabit it.'[2] Warburg's report was a long one, yet he admitted that it gave no sense of the 'giant movement of thought' that he believed Orwell had set in motion. *Nineteen Eighty Four* has generated a vast amount of critical comment, so varied in its nature that it becomes necessary to start with Orwell's categorical statement about the book's intention. 'My recent novel is NOT intended as an attack upon socialism, or on the British Labor (sic) party (of which I am a supporter) but as a show-up of the perversions to which a centralised economy is liable and which have already been partly realised in Communism and Fascism.'[3]

Although he argued consistently that hope for a better world lay with the proles, it is clear that Orwell had always recognised the political significance of what he called the middling people who felt themselves excluded in a system that was still largely paternalistic, and were anxious to share power.[4] It was primarily for such people that Orwell wrote, as he made clear in *Wigan Pier*.[5] He later identified these middling people as scientists, technicians, teachers, journalists, broadcasters, bureaucrats and professional politicians. This middling class was the one that James Burham had called the managerial class,[6] and Orwell considered that it had to be won over to democratic socialism if this was to succeed; it had to be convinced that it had nothing to lose in the process but its aitches. It was principally to the managerial class that *The Lion and the Unicorn* had been directed. What particularly began to concern Orwell was the perception that some of these middling people, especially the intellectuals, appeared to be overly impressed by power. His attacks in *Wigan Pier* on intellectuals, whom he thought to be more susceptible to totalitarianism than the workers, were an early indication of this preoccupation.[7] In reviewing Hayek's *Road to Serfdom*,[8] Orwell found the author's assertion, that British intellectuals were more totalitarian-minded than the ordinary people, persuasive, and agreed that the creation of a strong central state would be likely to give power to an inner ring of bureaucrats (some of the middling people) who would be tempted to use that power for its own sake. Around the same time, in an unpublished review of Laski's *Faith, Reason and Civilisation*, Orwell attacked the author for equating socialism with Stalin's Russia. Laski had used the establishment of Christianity as an analogue for the worldwide establishment of socialism via Russia, but Orwell argued that the Christians had been a persecuted sect whereas almost one-sixth of the world already lived under the domination of Soviet communism. Moreover, Christian doctrine was constant, whereas Soviet communism was constantly changing. A despotism based upon power rather than inherited wealth, such as the Soviet one, represented a substantial threat to democratic socialism, and it was 'vitally necessary that [this] should be foreseen in advance'.[9] Laski, a leading British socialist intellectual, perceived no such threat. This concerned Orwell.

What turned Orwell's world on its head was the German invasion of Russia, which he had failed to foresee, writing only a week before the event that such an invasion was by that time unlikely, for it entailed the inescapable consequence of producing an alliance between Stalin and Churchill. 'This disgusting murderer is now on our side and so the purges, etc., are suddenly forgotten.'[10] Remarkably, six months later, he wrote: 'I never thought I should live to say "Good luck to Comrade Stalin" but so I do.'[11] Though understandable in the circumstances, this *volte face* on a central issue surely constituted an example of Orwell tacitly doing what he accused the Russians of doing: accepting that desired ends sometimes justified unpalatable means. Before long, however, he had resumed his customary anti-Russian stance with a renewed bellicosity.[12] In a 1941 lecture to the Fabian Society, entitled 'Culture and Democracy', Orwell advanced the case against totalitarianism as a threat to the very existence of the individual as a morally autonomous agent. It is not clear whether this was the individual as citizen or as writer, as defender of what Orwell called objective truth, though for Orwell these were almost certainly interdependent. His conclusion could not be plainer: we must defend ourselves against totalitarianism 'as we should defend ourselves against an invasion from Mars'.[13] In using this simile, he would have had in mind Wells' *War of the Worlds*.[14] To describe the confrontation between the Earthmen and the invaders as a fight to the death hardly does justice to the feral ferocity of the struggle that Wells depicted.

It is undeniably true that the writing of *Nineteen Eighty Four* was greatly influenced by Orwell's physical and mental state when he completed it; he was a very sick man. Moreover, Anthony West's assertion that the novel was largely the product of the author's neuroses, that Oceania was St. Cyprian's on a global scale,[15] clearly also has some validity; indeed, how could things have been otherwise? Alan Sandison has argued at length, and persuasively,[16] that the novel is really about Orwell's relationship with the Roman Catholic Church, and indeed it is impossible to avoid allusions to the Church and its dogma in the work. But the greatest influence on *Nineteen Eighty Four* was the obvious one; Orwell believed, from experience as much from reasoning, that totalitarianism threatened the very survival of Western values, and that the embodiment of that threat was Stalin's Russia. He believed this with such a passion as to astound those readers who had lived in Stalin's Russia with the depth of his empathetic understanding of how things were. And finally, we should remember that *Nineteen Eighty Four* did not come out of the blue; it was preceded by an earlier onslaught on Stalin, *Animal Farm*, and by a great deal else.

Was this totalitarian threat to the West real? After all, Hitler would be defeated soon and Stalin was an ally. Yet since 1936 Orwell had been certain of it. In 'Looking Back on the Spanish War', written in 1942, he asked whether it was childish or morbid to terrify oneself with visions of a totalitarian future, as Bowling had, for example, in *Coming Up for Air*. Well, he replied, who, twenty years ago, would have imagined the return of slavery to Europe? 'Just remember that in 1925 the world of today would have seemed a nightmare that could not come true.'[17] Imagine a ruler who could change the past, and you will understand, he wrote, why he and Arthur Koestler had agreed that history, a 'true' account of events, had ended in 1936. So let us be clear: when Orwell said that *Nineteen Eighty Four* was not an attack on the Attlee government, he was speaking the plain truth, even though Warburg erroneously believed that the book would be worth a 'cool million' votes to the Conservative Party at the next general election (1950)[18] and even though the editor of the London *Evening Standard* thought it should be required reading (as a corrective) for all Labour MPs.[19] Orwell was determined to shake Western socialists into a realisation of the totalitarian peril and to that extent, but only to that extent, he aimed the book at his fellow socialists in Britain.

There were other literary antecedents to the novel. When Orwell wrote *Nineteen Eighty Four* he was influenced principally, though not exclusively, by two books, one an account, already referred to, of the rise of a new social order embodied at the time in the totalitarian states of Germany, the USSR and to a lesser extent Italy, James Burham's *The Managerial Revolution*.[20] This book helped Orwell to theorise the state structure of Oceania. Orwell was convinced by Burnham's picture of historical change being fuelled by new élites seeking to replace old élites in the name of fraternity or equality or democracy. But as the Puritans in England, the Jacobins in France and the Bolsheviks in Russia showed, it is largely naked ambition that drives these new élites on. Burnham foresaw capitalism being replaced not by socialism but by a new more efficient form of a centralised, planned economic structure. Burnham also predicted that the USSR would split in two. The more westerly parts would be added to a Europe dominated by Germany, forming Eurasia; Siberia would be taken from the USSR and added to Eastasia. The third power block of the new world would be based upon North America, Oceania.

But a second book, Yefgeny Zamyatin's *We*, which Orwell reviewed in 1946,[21] was even more useful in terms of plot. This novel, which was first published in French in 1929, had originally been written in late 1921 at the time when the Bolsheviks were consolidating their hold on power and human perfectibility was a political goal. Taylorism, the optimal organisation and employment of people as a resource, was being championed by influential leaders such as Lenin's consort Krupskaya, and Zamyatin concerned himself with the regimentation of society. In *We*, The Benefactor was the absolute ruler of OneState and, uniting the characteristics of Lenin and Dostoevsky's Grand Inquisitor, ruled over a society that had almost achieved perfection, having abjured the 'messy inconvenience' of freedom. The Great Operation, the surgical removal of the imagination, represented the culmination of the search for perfection. The Taylorised citizenry were identified not by names but by numbers; indeed, they were referred to collectively not as the people but as the Numbers and they were overseen by the Guardians. They lived in transparent buildings and did everything in unison, and by number: 'like one body with a million hands, at one and the same second according to the Table, we lift our spoons to our lips'.[22] They were allowed some time to themselves, 'personal hours', though it was hoped to be able eventually to do away with these, for they were a sign of inefficiency. Numbers also had sex days, in which they were allowed to draw their blinds and have sex with partners to whom they had been allotted.

Although it has been argued that the novel concerns the clash between energy and entropy,[23] it also concerns the clash between individual liberty and collective identity, between imagination and reason. D-503 was a loyal Number and although, like Winston Smith, he became embroiled in a revolutionary movement, he did so largely at the behest of the movement's spectacularly beautiful leader I-330, with whom he had become besotted. Yet D-503 never quite forsook the collective subconscious, was never won over to the Orwellian shibboleth that identity was personal and the product of reason and experience. For D-503 the primitives who lived beyond the wall that encompassed OneState were to be feared and despised: they suffered from freedom and imagination. OneState believed that since love and hunger ruled the world then it was necessary to save humanity by conquering both. In the traditional world, there was not enough love to go round; in OneState 'any Number has the right to any other Number as sexual product'.[24] As a citizen of Aldous Huxley's brave new world would have said: everyone belongs to everyone else. In the traditional world, there was not enough food to go round. In OneState all numbers were well fed on a petroleum-based, artificially produced foodstuff. In short, OneState was the conscious embodiment of the application of mathematical principles to human affairs. The book ends with D-503 happy that those Numbers who had betrayed reason, the revolutionary Mephi, whom he had betrayed, were to die. He remained certain that, whatever the immediate difficulties, OneState would triumph because reason has to win. This was the background against which Orwell's novel was written: now for *Nineteen Eighty Four* itself.

1

'But it was alright, everything was alright, the struggle was finished. He had won the victory over himself. He loved Big Brother.'[25] Orwell had contemplated entitling his last novel *The Last Man in Europe*, for such was Winston Smith's role and status. By the end of the novel, humanity as Orwell represented it had ceased to exist. The novel concerns the process of its destruction at the hands of the centralised (in this case totalitarian) state, and so Orwell can be understood to be seeking to establish what being human entailed and how the necessary values could be constricted and eventually strangled to death by a self-seeking totalitarian élite. *Nineteen Eighty Four* is Orwell's longest, most complex and, in many ways, most ambitious book. Its basic premise appears at first glance to be that the only constraint upon a totalitarian regime is provided by liberal man, the individual acting as an autonomous moral agent capable of passing judgements upon the nature of external reality and by extension upon the actions of the state. (Autonomy here means simply a sense of moral and intellectual independence from monolithic institutions, especially the church or, more recently, the state.) For its part, the state will seek to crush the individual by controlling every aspect of his life, thereby undermining his autonomy and rendering him incapable of making independent judgements upon the actions of the state, indeed upon anything. Reduced to this condition, the individual needs the state to tell him what to think. Sandison, I have said, saw this as an allegorical representation of the relationship between the individual and the Roman Catholic Church and for Sandison, if Winston Smith was the last man in Europe, then Martin Luther was the first. This is not strictly so: Orwell was doing what he said, writing about the relationship between man and the modern totalitarian state, though his analysis was informed by that deep suspicion of the Church that he carried throughout his life. *Nineteen Eighty Four* also deals with the nature of power itself, but I propose to examine this issue in another chapter. For the present we need to consider three separate but related aspects if we are to make intellectual sense of Orwell's portrayal of the destruction by the state of man as an autonomous moral agent. First, we need to establish the prerequisites for the individual to act as an autonomous moral agent, to discover in which values that autonomy is rooted, and parenthetically to what extent Winston himself possessed these values. Second, we must explore Orwell's view of the nature of man's reason, the mainspring of his being able to act autonomously, in order to assess its durability as a bulwark against tyranny. Third, we need to analyse Orwell's very notion of objective truth, of an external world about which 'true' statements can be made. If truth exists, we need to understand the extent to which it is accessible to ordinary common sense. If we can shed light on these three issues, we might better understand the nature of Orwell's chilling warning. First then, the roots of autonomy.

2

Winston Smith was not a good example of a morally autonomous agent, not what we might call a whole man. When he confronted his persecutor O'Brien, he did so armed only by a partial moral autonomy rooted in sensory perception authenticated by reason. He possessed no belief that might have furnished some religious or transcendental dimension to his autonomy. What he represented, in fact, was a kind of secularised Protestantism, a priesthood of all non-believers, in which each of us is connected by reason and experience to unmediated reality. As autonomous individuals we can both make and recognise true statements about that reality. Irving Howe pointed out that the autonomous individual was socially constructed, what he called a 'cultural idea'.[26] But this moral autonomy had to be nurtured by a value system if it was to be strong enough to withstand the Party, and Orwell realised this. Winston's was not.

Crucially, moral autonomy needed the medium of a full family life in which to grow. In Oceania, we know, family life among Party members had broken down entirely. Inner Party members simply had no family. As for the Outer Party, the family had become simply an extension of the Thought Police, so that everyone could be surrounded night and day by informers who knew them intimately.[27] The model of Oceanian family life is provided by Winston's near neighbours in Victory Mansions, the Parsons. Parsons himself, than whom a more stalwart and hearty Party member could not be imagined, was eventually betrayed to the Thought Police by his own daughter. But Parsons' predicament was far from unique. 'It was almost normal for people over thirty to be frightened of their children.'[28] The Party had destroyed love and family loyalties and thus deprived the individual of the sustenance that these could provide. As a focus for loyalty, love and broader social values, and as a bastion of privacy, the family was an institution that the totalitarian state had needed to smash, and it had done so. We know the importance that Orwell attached to family life. When reviewing a book on rehousing programmes in 1946, he noted that, however radical their plans, the planners sought to preserve family life as a priority: a deep-seated feeling alerted them to the importance of the family, 'which had become the only real refuge from the state'.[29]

The autonomous moral agent needs more than a full family life, however. He needs to be part of a system of traditional values that he has inherited and has good expectations of passing on to his children. Orwell had a writer's sensitivity towards issues of language and his horror of the abuse of language, especially by politicians, led him to appreciate the importance of the cultural habits locked into the traditional structure of syntax and idiom. No wonder that the leaders of Oceania were so resolute in their ambition to modernise and sanitise the language. Newspeak encompassed all moral judgements within composites based upon the unit word 'good'. Thus: good, ungood, doublegood, doubleplusungood and so on, were the only available expressions of moral judgement, rendering the making of all but the crudest moral distinctions impossible. If this were not enough, the system of thought known as 'doublethink' (to which we shall be returning shortly), by which two contradictory opinions may be held simultaneously, made it practically impossible for any individual to perceive, let alone articulate, any moral truth.

Language was not the only significant conduit of these traditional values. 'The first step in liquidating a people,' said Milan Kundera's Hubl, 'is to erase its memory. Destroy its books, its culture, its history. Then have someone write new books, manufacture a new culture, invent a new history. Before long the nation will begin to forget what it is and what it was.'[30] In *Nineteen Eighty Four* Winston attempted to re-establish connections with a vanished culture and history so as to erect a barrier between himself and the Party. The book he bought as a diary was an elegant old one with smooth, creamy paper. Its value did not reside in its functionality; quite the opposite, it resided in its status as part of a non-utilitarian past. He bought it in Charrington's junk shop,[31] to which he had been instinctively drawn. Then he bought himself a paperweight, a beautiful piece of crystal but without any real function. 'If it [the lifestyle and hence the values of the past] survives anywhere, it's in a few solid objects, with no words attached to them, like that lump of glass there', Winston remarked.[32] The paperweight 'was the room he was in, and the coral was his lover Julia's life and his own, fixed in a sort of eternity at the heart of the crystal'. The room above the junk shop which Winston and Julia rented from Charrington was described as 'a world, a pocket of the past where extinct animals could walk'.[33] In such a world Winston became physically healthy again, his nagging leg-ulcer and his cough briefly cured. Predictably enough, when the Thought Police finally broke into the room, one of them smashed the paperweight on the hearthstone, symbolically shattering the crystal spirit which epitomised those values (and which, in Spain, Orwell had believed unbreakable[34]). The fragment of coral that had symbolised their relationship rolled across the mat. 'How small', thought Winston, 'how small it always was!'[35] Winston's recognition of the need for a cultural heritage was exemplified by his toast in O'Brien's flat when he mistakenly believed that he was being recruited into the Brotherhood: 'To the Past!' His first diary entry, a dedication, had also been 'to the future, or to the past, to a time when thought is free, when men are different from one another and do not live alone – to a time when truth exists and what is done cannot be undone.'[36] It was the quest for this now-dead culture which called to Winston through the half-remembered nursery rhyme 'Oranges and Lemons'. Charrington was able to complete the rhyme; it was he who lit a candle to light them to bed. It was the Party, anxious to halt this quest for the authentic past in its tracks, which wielded the chopper to chop off their heads. Franz Kafka's was also a world whose anchor chain to a past culture and its values had been deliberately severed, a world which 'has lost all continuity . . . a humanity that no longer knows anything, that lives in nameless cities with nameless streets or streets with names different from the ones they had yesterday, because a name means continuity with the past and people without a past are people without a name'.[37] Kafka's world, like Oceania, was a world of totalitarian nightmare.

Orwell's next precondition for moral autonomy was a full emotional life. He believed that a totalitarian élite would, sooner or later, seek to control even human emotions: indeed, we discover that, in Oceania, the Party's biologists were already at work on abolishing the orgasm.[38] All feelings of passion would henceforth be directed towards the Party and used by the Party. Already the love of Big Brother encapsulated a hatred directed to those external threats, Eastasia or Eurasia, and to the internal threat of Goldstein and the Brotherhood. Julia's great attraction, as far as Winston was concerned, was her vaunted promiscuity, her simple, unconstrained love of carnal pleasures. When they were first alone in the hazel grove, Winston described Julia quickly unzipping her clothing and flinging it aside as a gesture which seemed to be annihilating a whole civilisation based upon the Party's values. He was fully aware of, indeed rejoiced in, the treasonable nature of sexual pleasure. 'Listen,' he said to Julia, 'the more men you've had, the more I love you . . . I hate purity, I hate goodness! I don't want any virtue to exist anywhere. I want everybody to be corrupt to the bone.'[39] Promiscuity, Winston recognised, would provide 'a force that would tear the Party to pieces'. Irving Howe argued that it is eroticism not love that is the enemy of the state in *Nineteen Eighty Four*, but he is only partly right.[40] In Room 101 Orwell intended us to believe that it was love that was cleansed from Winston, not simply carnality.

Orwell also claimed material sufficiency as a precondition for a full life for the individual. Winston possessed some ancestral memory which caused him to reject as unnatural the discomfort, the dirt and the scarcities of life in Oceania. He felt 'cheated of something you had a right to'.[41] Man had a right to something better than Victory Mansions with its 'lifts that never work, the cold water, the cigarettes that came to pieces, the food with its strange, evil tastes';[42] a right to something better than a world in which 'nearly everyone was ugly, and would have been ugly even if dressed otherwise than in the uniform blue overalls'. It was deliberate Party policy to maintain a condition of scarcity for all except members of the Inner Party, so as to enhance the importance of even minor privileges. The dire struggle for day-to-day necessities wore down the human spirit and denied individuality.

Last, though by no means least, Orwell argued for the importance of individual privacy, for the existence of a private world into which a person could securely retire. We know that Orwell cherished the privateness of the British way of life; a home of your own to do what you like in. That was why 'the most hateful of all names in an English ear is Nosey Parker'.[43] But Oceania's telescreens made privacy impossible, and because Big Brother might be watching, people were obliged to walk about with an expression of quiet optimism; the portrayal of any other emotion could be construed as treason. The temple of privacy, as the tramp Bozo had told Orwell when he was down and out in London,[44] was inside the skull, and Orwell wanted to make it plain that the Party had desecrated that temple. By taking away freedom of speech and the possibility of creative socialisation, the space inside the skull so prized by Bozo had become not a temple of private autonomy but a void, and as the Party knew, nature abhors a vacuum.

A rich and sustaining family life, cultural continuity, based upon a vibrant language, a full emotional life, a life of reasonable material sufficiency, and finally a completely private world into which one could retire: these were the prerequisites for the full moral autonomy of which Winston Smith is recognised as a champion, even though he did not himself possess them. Unfortunately for humanity, he was the very last champion. But note: what limits Winston's power to act autonomously is the very absoluteness of his autonomy. He is truly alone.

3

Whilst he was no epistemologist, Orwell had a firm idea of the nature of knowledge and man's proper relationship to knowledge. Like the empiricist he was, he held knowledge to be the result of our comprehension of the world based on our capacity for observation and reflection. He rejected completely any approach that suggested that knowledge might be relative, and still more that it might actually be socially constructed. For Orwell reality, the external world, could be discerned by the undeceived intelligence (the phrase that Trilling used to describe Orwell himself) of the ordinary individual by means of sensory perception interpreted and codified by reason. That this ordinary individual, ready to do battle with the collective state over the issue of truth, might itself be a socially constructed myth was not a possibility that Orwell consciously entertained. He was, himself, a solitary man. Man's very humanity and identity, he believed, were rooted in his capacity to apply reason to sensory experience, and his capacity for reason leads him to grasp the nature of objective truth. In some respects, Winston's claim on behalf of the individual reflected Martin Luther's claim on behalf of all people, that they could achieve salvation, through God's grace, only by their own agency as individuals and not by the intercession of any collective identity such as the Church[45] (or the Party, as far as Winston was concerned). The Catholic Church, on the other hand, has traditionally believed that salvation could be attained only through its good offices.[46] O'Brien argued that truth about the external world can only be gained through the Party. Winston Smith fought to sustain his autonomous capacity to grasp and hold on to truth, and the story follows his endeavours to do this, first via the acquisition of a diary by means of which he could record and interpret reality, then by his affair with Julia, in which he explored his individuality through sensually experienced reality, and finally by his putative anti-state terrorism, with O'Brien acting as *agent provocateur*, in which he attempted to change reality. It is our certain knowledge of the world gained through experience mediated by reason, Winston maintained, that guarantees our freedom and allows us to act in an intelligible and meaningful way. If we can retain our confidence that two plus two makes four, he says, then 'all else follows'.[47]

Orwell was fishing in deep waters here. Where did his faith in man's reason come from? There is no evidence that he ever read Descartes or Kant on the nature of the relationship between sense and reason. He was unfamiliar with Mills' work, though naturally sympathetic to his emphasis – or what Berlin called his over-emphasis[48] – on rationality. Although towards the end of his life Orwell included amongst his acquaintances both A. J. Ayer and Bertrand Russell, he was simply not interested in schools of philosophy and had no great capacity for philosophical thought. Neither Ayer nor Russell records discussing philosophical issues with Orwell.[49] Indeed, in a letter to Richard Rees in which he referred to a philosophical argument of Bertrand Russell, Orwell wrote: 'But I never can follow that kind of thing. It is the sort of thing that makes me feel that philosophy should be forbidden by law.'[50] We could be sure that, if he had understood them, Orwell would have been offended by the relativistic tendencies of existentialism, the philosophy that had influenced so many of his contemporaries. Indeed, he wrote of one of Sartre's books, 'I doubt whether it would be possible to pack more nonsense into so short a space', and of Sartre himself (to whom, incidentally, he had sent a copy of *Animal Farm*) he wrote: 'I have maintained from the start that Sartre is a bag of wind, though possibly when it comes to existentialism, which I don't profess to understand, it may not be so.'[51] Orwell would have been unaware of the distinction, essential to our understanding of empiricism, that Leibniz had first drawn between analytical and synthetic knowledge,[52] a distinction that had persuaded Hume to counsel diffidence about what we think we know from experience about the world.[53] Only analytical knowledge is certain, but since it inhabits the world of mathematics and formal logic, it has no relevance to the world of experience and value. As Crick says of Orwell (or does he?), 'The very image he came to exhibit or establish is complex for such a simple man (so it is said).'[54]

Orwell's contention that if we can be certain that two plus two equals four, 'all else follows' constitutes a truism, some have even argued a tautology;[55] it is an analytical statement and thus one that simply could not be perverted even under the conditions of absolute human isolation, or indeed under the ravages of brutal torture. Hannah Arendt showed the limitations of Orwell's argument when she wrote that two plus two equals four was the only absolutely reliable truth human beings could fall back on. 'However,' she added significantly, 'this "truth" is empty or rather no truth at all because it does not reveal anything'.[56] Outside of mathematics and logic, what follows from the statement that two plus two equals four is – nothing. A. J. Ayer argued that it was an error to suppose that we can deduce any information at all about matters of fact, let alone value, from such analytical propositions.[57] Unfortunately, he does not appear to have told his friend. It follows that to suggest, as Orwell did, that it was inevitable that the Party would one day feel obliged to announce that two plus two equals five, that the logic of its position would require this,[58] and that it would be necessary for everybody to believe it (to accept it would not be enough), is simply misguided. When Winston himself felt no longer certain that two plus two equals four, we recognise that he was signalling not that he had been mistaken but that he had been broken. The laws of mathematics are independent even of Big Brother and will stand despite the fact that the last man in Europe has temporarily lost faith in them. This symbolic use of two plus two equals four as a guarantee of individual autonomy represented some confusion concerning the nature of statements of value. Nevertheless, it stood, if awkwardly, as a badge of man's undeceived intelligence, his 'common sense',[59] his ability to reach out confidently to objective truth and so to stand against the Party. For Orwell, to deny that two plus two equals four was to deny not merely the validity of experience but the very existence of a knowable external reality. What Orwell was saying was that the Party declared itself, not the individual, to be the only source of truth. That is why, according to Goldstein, the state was the enemy of empiricism, why it denounced common sense as the 'heresy of heresies'.[60]

Let us grant Orwell's dubious argument for the time being, and let us see where it leads. Our confidence in our individual reason, as exemplified by our certainty that two plus two equals four, is a guarantee of liberty. But why? Orwell was not the first writer to commission the laws of mathematics to the ranks of political writing. Zamyatin, whose influence on Orwell we have already noted, wrote about a society based upon numbers. His Numbers were bound together by the song of reason, which went:[61]

Forever enamoured are two plus two,
Forever conjoined in blissful four
The hottest of lovers in the entire world:
The permanent weld of two plus two

Zamyatin's OneState was the embodiment of reason expressed mathematically and yet its purpose was the very opposite to increasing individual moral autonomy; indeed, it represented the tyranny of reason expressed in numbers. Zamyatin was not alone in empowering numbers. Nineteenth-century British utilitarianism brought together a belief in the liberating power of reason and society's capacity to employ reason mathematically in the form of the felicific calculus. It was this combination that brought forth the notorious system of indoor poor relief based upon the workhouse. Zamyatin's fellow countryman Chernyshevsky wrote the influential novel *What is to be Done?*[62] – an excellent example of what Orwell was to call a 'good bad book'[63] – to argue the case that reason, organised as socialism, would save Russia; and just in case he was right, the authorities sent him to Siberia for nearly twenty years. Chernyshevsky, like Orwell, believed in man's innate capacity for reason; he saw reason as an essential, and indeed a sufficient, precondition for liberty and progress. But faith in the reason of the autonomous individual led Chernyshevsky to champion a rigid, moralistic, utilitarian state, not at all the kind of state in which Winston Smith would have flourished. In *Nineteen Eighty Four*, by contrast, the state embodied not reason but unreason,[64] and so reason itself was its enemy. In Zamyatin as in Chernyshevsky, conversely, reason was embodied in the state: what then was the guarantee of individual autonomy? To answer this question we must refer to the foremost opponent of reason's enthronement, Dostoevsky. For him reason was only one critical faculty, whereas individual volition was a 'manifestation of the whole of life'.[65] Dostoevsky savaged Chernyshevsky's faith in reason: 'What a baby!' he exclaimed:[66]

> We have something inside us which is stronger than self interest ... Isn't there something that is dearer to almost every man than his own best interests ... and for the sake of which man is prepared, if necessary, to go against all the laws – that is, against reason ... [namely] one's own free and unfettered volition, one's own caprice, however wild ... that is the one best and greatest good.

It is reason, said Dostoevsky, that tells us that two plus two equals four, but his Underground Man set little store by this as a safeguard of anything at all, and certainly not autonomy. ' "I agree", he said, "that two and two make four is an excellent thing: but to give everything its dues, two plus two make five is also a very fine thing".'[67] For Dostoevsky it was in *rejecting* rationality that man safeguarded his autonomy. It was only by pursuing one's own 'free and unfettered volition, one's own caprice', that one became truly oneself. In becoming truly himself, in attaining the moral autonomy that Winston Smith claimed as his intellectual birthright, man 'sends all systems and theories to the devil'.[68] Orwell was not influenced by Dostoevsky; in fact, in the entire corpus of his writing we find only a few very brief references to Dostoevsky. Surprising then to hear that it is sometimes suggested that the Underground Man was a prototype for Winston Smith.[69] Nothing could be further from the truth. In some respects, he did indeed represent a prototype, not for Winston but for Julia. It is clear that it was love for Winston and not any desire to overthrow the regime that drove her to join the brotherhood. Julia was concerned only with little victories, with defeating the Party every time she made love, drank real coffee or used make-up. Julia, not Winston, was concerned with pursuing her own 'free and unfettered volition'. When it suited, she accepted the Party's truth because 'the difference between truth and falsehood did not seem important to her'.[70] She had said apropos Winston's newspaper report, his 'concrete, unmistakable evidence' of the Party's falsification of reality, whose discovery made him the sole guardian of the truth, 'I'm quite ready to take risks, but only for something worth while, not for bits of old newspaper'.[71] We can believe O'Brien when he reported to Winston how quickly she had recanted in the Ministry of Love. Winston had noted earlier of her that 'the standards she obeyed were private ones. Her feelings were her own, and could not be altered from the outside.'[72] And ultimately, Winston dismissed her as a rebel only from the waist downwards. Winston Smith was not the last truly autonomous individual in Europe; Julia was.

4

Having considered Winston's claim to individual moral autonomy through the exercise of reason, we need now to consider Orwell's notion of objective truth, or to rephrase the task, to ascertain the extent to which there exists a reality about which objectively true statements can be made. Orwell told the apocryphal story of Sir Walter Raleigh's attempt to write a history of the world whilst imprisoned in the Tower of London.[73] Having begun work on volume two, Raleigh's attention was taken by a scuffle in the yard outside and he witnessed at first hand a murder taking place. When he came to write an accurate account of this event later, he realised that he simply could not manage to do so to his own satisfaction. He abandoned his world history, burning the completed first volume in despair. Orwell was critical of this decision. Whilst complete accuracy might not be feasible, he acknowledged, it was possible for an individual, if he attempted it dispassionately, to write history that approximated to the truth. Each of us has a sufficient grasp of reality to be able to attempt this. But when Winston Smith's interrogator O'Brien challenged him on the nature of reality and of truth, he did so by arguing that no individual could hope to have a grasp of reality, of the external world.[74] Indeed, he seemed to annihilate Winston's argument. But his victory was not the consequence of his intellectual superiority, undoubted though this was, nor even the strength of his argument. Rather, it was his ability to cause Winston physical pain. Winston believed in reality as 'something objective', whereas, said O'Brien, it was the creation of the human mind. Not the individual human mind, for individuals were only minorities of one – lunatics – but in the 'collective and immortal' mind of the Party. It follows, he continued, that no reality existed before the advent of humanity. The flaw in this argument is obvious even on O'Brien's own terms. Humanity existed before the Party, and so reality existed before the Party. Then where was it to be found? When Winston advanced a Cartesian case to prove his own existence and therefore, by extension, to prove the existence of a wider external reality – he thinks he exists therefore he exists, and added to it a version of G. E. Moore's evidence for an external reality, his own hands when he waved them about[75] – for Winston it was the observable reality of his own arms and legs – O'Brien did not attempt to counter his argument philosophically. When Winston sought to push home his point by establishing the inherent logical absurdity of O'Brien's claim 'You do not exist', it was not Winston's argument that was destroyed, it was Winston's person. Winston won an intellectual victory here, but only a minor one: individuals may indeed possess autonomous knowledge but only, on this evidence, of the world of which they have immediate and direct experience.

From the perspective of a broader reality, however, it might be said that Winston had already defeated his own argument concerning autonomous understanding. One of the key passages in *Nineteen Eighty Four* tells of Winston gaining 'concrete, unmistakable evidence' of the Party's falsification of reality.[76] Amongst the few survivors of the original revolutionary leadership were three men: Jones, Aaronson and Rutherford. Each had been arrested in 1965 and tried for embezzlement and intrigues against Big Brother. After confessing, they were pardoned, and Winston had actually seen them at the infamous Chestnut Tree Café, noticing that two of the men had broken noses. Later the men were re-arrested, they had been discovered still up to their old tricks, and were executed. Some time later, in fact in 1973, Winston found himself, as part of his job in the Ministry of Truth, required to destroy a copy of *The Times* from about ten years earlier. His eyes had inadvertently taken in details of a photograph of a Party function in New York. In the middle of a group of prominent Party members were, unmistakably, none other than Jones, Aaronson and Rutherford. Yet at their trial each had confessed to having been in Eurasia, passing on important military information to the enemy, on that very day. This, thought Winston, was a fragment of reality, a fossil bone from the abolished past. This knowledge made him, Winston Smith, the sole guardian of the truth.

But did it? Suppose the photograph in question had itself been a forgery, a manipulation of some earlier and long-forgotten truth, and that the three had never been to New York at all. Why pick on one particular bone and declare it, without any adequate means of verification, to be a genuine fossil? Nobody knew better than Winston about the falsification of evidence. Had not he himself invented the past when he created Comrade Ogilvy? Ogilvy was brought into existence to cover up the disappearance of one Smithers, a prominent member of the Inner Party, who had fallen foul of a change in Party policy and consequently, in the fullest sense of the phrase, descended from Party hero to Party zero: he had become an unperson. Indeed, he had never existed. It was Winston's task to recast *The Times* report, Big Brother's earlier speech extolling Smithers' virtues, into something quite different. Instead of simply trying to reverse the tendency of Big Brother's speech, however, Winston decided totally to replace it with a speech extolling the virtues of a fictional Comrade Ogilvy, a hero killed in battle. Winston created a whole history and persona for Ogilvy. And thereafter Ogilvy, who had never existed in any present, came to exist in the past, 'just as authentically, and upon the same evidence, as Charlemagne or Julius Caesar'.[77] All history was like this, a palimpsest 'scraped clean and reinscribed as often as was necessary'. In *The Book of Laughter and Forgetting*, Kundera, giving an example of the kind of work in which Winston himself was involved, the airbrushing out from old photographs of discredited influential figures, argued that it is our past that gives us weight and substance, that provides a shape and consistency to our self-conceit. 'The struggle of man against power is the struggle of memory against forgetting', said Kundera. But the memory of the individual was just as selective, and indeed creative, as the memory of the Party,[78] he went on, just as capable of rewriting history. Winston may not have been engaged in creating Comrade Ogilvies all the hours of his day but he was certainly involved in creating and recreating Winston Smith; and we too will airbrush the Smithers out of our past and replace them with our own glorious Comrade Ogilvies.

Just as he failed to disprove Winston's argument for autonomy in regard to the individual's immediate experience, so O'Brien failed to establish a convincing philosophical case for the Party's monopoly in understanding and commenting on broader external reality. He claimed, for example, that the stars were near or distant according to the needs of the Party; if it found it necessary or useful the Party would invent a dual system of astronomy – 'Do you suppose our mathematicians are unequal to that? Have you forgotten doublethink?'[79] O'Brien's oxymoronic characterisation of the relationship between the Party and external reality as 'collective solipsism' is arresting but not persuasive. Galileo might have been obliged by the Church formally to acknowledge his errors and to give way to Ptolemy, but it was his vision and not the Church's collective solipsism that has governed modern man's understanding of astronomy. It was Brecht's Galileo who longed for a day 'when we no longer have to look over our shoulder like criminals when we say that twice two is four'. In fact, O'Brien established only the reality and decisiveness of power, where power consisted in winning arguments by inflicting pain. And it has always been so. J. S. Mill once noted that the dictum that truth will overcome falsehood was refuted by experience. Persecution, he said, had always succeeded. 'It is a piece of idle sentimentality that truth, merely as truth, has any inherent power ... of prevailing against the dungeon and the stake.'[80] But he added significantly that dungeons do not last forever; truths might.

Though Winston successfully defended a common-sense view of man's relationship to external reality – physical facts are independent of mental facts – he did so only in a limited and, indeed, selective sense. As science developed following Galileo's discoveries, it became apparent to thinkers like Descartes that truth and reality no longer surrendered to contemplation. Common sense, the sharing of human experiences and perspectives, no longer led necessarily to an understanding of concepts or to an accurate account of past events. To hold on to the belief that truisms are true, that the 'solid world exists; its laws do not change. Stones are hard, water is wet ...'[81] is not to establish a convincing case for encouraging Walter Raleigh to pursue his attempted history of the world. In Oceania the Party pronounced *ex cathedra* on the nature of the external world and the only ground that Winston had for standing against its version of reality was the common sense of an individual whose moral autonomy was seriously compromised but who obstinately believed in the indefatigable 'spirit of man'.[82] But as O'Brien pointed out, Winston Smith was, after all, the last man.

A major factor, already alluded to, that assisted in establishing the Party's monopoly in deciding what constituted reality was the concept of doublethink. Doublethink entailed holding simultaneously two contradictory ideas and believing in both. The concept is not a new one. It was used in biblical times when believers were advised, 'let not thy left hand know what thy right hand doeth'.[83] Orwellian doublethink is not basically different, requiring us to 'use logic against logic'.[84] Some theorists have invested this concept with considerable philosophical significance.[85] David Rudrum has linked the apparent contradiction of doublethink to the kinds of ambiguity inherent in Wittgenstein's exploration of the differences between the statements 'I know' and 'I believe'.[86] It is true that Wittgenstein's last major work, *On Certainty*, was concerned with the relationship between knowledge of the external world and subjective phenomena like belief. Orwell had not read Wittgenstein but he had written before about the power of holding mutually contradictory ideas, though then he called it schizophrenia, a vice that flourished, he said, in politics.[87] Orwell's elaborate structure of doublethink: believing two contradictory principles at the same time; simultaneously repudiating and claiming morality; 'consciously to induce unconsciousness, and then, once again, to become unconscious of the act of hypnosis that you had just performed' was not as substantial as it seems: in fact he brought it down himself. As Winston made clear 'the subtlest practitioners of doublethink are those who invented doublethink and know that it is a vast system of mental cheating'.[88] The rhetoricians and metaphysicians of the Inner Party did not hold ideas mysteriously incorporating seemingly contradictory articles of knowledge and belief simultaneously: they only pretended to. This was an idea that Orwell had entertained for some time, writing in 1939, for example: 'It is quite easy to imagine a state in which the ruling caste deceive their followers without deceiving themselves.'[89] Rudrum gives the example of meat-eating as doublethink – I hate the mistreatment of animals but I enjoy a good steak, and so I simply refuse to confront the contradiction. This mental state is surely better understood as an example of what psychologists call cognitive dissonance. We all have to come to terms with the fact that we are naturally inconsistent. It was cognitive dissonance that allowed the Outer Party members, with the help of the Party, to make some sense of their bewildering world. But it is ingenuous to imagine that Inner Party members needed the same crutch. They recognised doublethink for what it was: a sophisticated and sophistical method of social control through which war may be represented as peace and slavery as freedom.

Another area of social control that Orwell explored, fitting hand in glove with doublethink, was language, that 'repository of forgotten experience' as Margaret Canovan called it,[90] and its Oceanian variety Newspeak. Whilst they were lunching together, Winston's 'friend' Syme, who was working on the eleventh edition of the Newspeak dictionary, explained the nature of his work. Its object was to narrow the range of thought by paring vocabulary to its irreducible minimum. 'In the end we shall make thoughtcrime literally impossible, because there will be no words in which to express it.' The Revolution will only then have been completed: 'Newspeak is Ingsoc and Ingsoc is Newspeak.'[91] This process, he went on, involved the destruction of the entire literary heritage and with it all the old ways of thinking that had created that heritage and then become embedded in it. Winston found himself listening to a man at a nearby table, an important figure from the Fiction Department. He was speaking about the 'complete and final elimination of Goldsteinism', but Winston found himself imagining that it was not a human brain that was speaking but only a larynx. This was not speech in any real sense: it was a noise, a simple repetition of meaningless phrases 'like the quacking of a duck'.[92] Orwell's analysis of the importance of language in social transformation was prescient. Koestler wrote that it was possible to recognise Communists, for example, by the words they used: the word 'concrete' was enough to give away a young KPD member being questioned by the Nazis.[93]

Since the time of Engels, communists have been notorious for duckspeak. But they have been far from alone. Military spokesmen, perhaps more than any other group, have developed vocabularies specifically designed to anaesthetise and mislead the public upon whose support they rely through the use of grotesque euphemisms. They have developed a particularly obnoxious form of ungood duckspeak. 'Friendly fire' and 'collateral damage' are only the most obvious examples but from the Vietnam War came 'ambient non-combatant personnel' for refugees, 'pacification programmes' for the widespread destruction of villages, and the chilling 'pre-emptive defensive strike' for acts of unprovoked aggression. In 1984 in the USA the National Council of Teachers of English gave Doublespeak Awards to the Pentagon for its rendering of peace as 'permanent pre-hostility' and its description of the invasion of Grenada in 1983 as 'predawn vertical insertion'.[94] Even more recently, in 2005 the US administration referred to the alleged transportation of suspected terrorists to countries with a record of interrogating through torture as 'extraordinary rendition'. On a more everyday level, the institutional reforms initiated by the Thatcher and Blair governments in the United Kingdom as part of the general process of liberalising state structures, were accompanied by a new vocabulary that had to be learned as much by the opponents of reform as by its supporters.[95] Foucault and Marcuse have famously written about the undemocratic nature of dominant discourses, the latter referring to a one-dimensional language that restricted thought and debate to the terms and interests of the establishment. Marcuse referred to this as 'Orwellian language'. A debate in a university over a programme of 'voluntary' redundancies centred around the timing of these redundancies: could they not be left to natural wastages, pleaded the opponents of reform? No, the Principal declared to the university's governing body: what was needed was 'a front-loaded programme scenario'. Doubleplusungood duckspeak!

To acknowledge the importance of the relationship between language and politics is one thing; to believe that a state can actually manipulate not merely the perception but the behaviour of all citizens is quite another. In the Appendix to *The Principles of Newspeak*, Orwell gave the example of the effect of the invention of the word 'sexcrime' on sexual behaviour. It covered all sexual misdeeds, from normal sexual intercourse indulged in for pleasure and not procreation to all forms of sexual perversion, which might include raping a minor. Orwell argued that because only one word was available to describe all of these misdeeds, they would in time become recognised as equally culpable and deserving of the same punishment. It is unlikely that sensitivity towards human suffering, as in the case of rape, would become so dulled that it would be regarded as no more reprehensible than having sex for pleasure – but it is not impossible. As a writer, Orwell was particularly sensitive to the significance of language and its abuse. The rest of us should be warned.

In summary, Orwell can be said to have failed to convince us either that the state can truly pronounce *ex cathedra* on the nature of external reality or that the autonomous individual – even one who works in the Ministry of Truth – can do so. But at the same time, he depicted techniques of social control that the state could employ when claiming to know reality that were so decisive that we become convinced that the state knew best. Philosophical debate would be otiose.

5

Nineteen Eighty Four, Orwell claimed, was intended as a satire. Now historically speaking the purpose of satire was to expose vices through irony, so as to subject their perpetrators to ridicule and opprobrium, and thus to limit their influence. Orwell explicitly wrote that whilst he did not envisage a state like Oceania, or a world system such as the one managed by the three superpowers of Oceania, Eurasia and Eastasia coming into being, he did think them feasible if not vigorously fought against. We misunderstand Orwell if we do not attach full weight to his detestation of the Soviet Union. 'In the name of Socialism', he fumed, 'the Russian regime has committed almost every crime that can be imagined.'[96] Moreover, the systemic evil, he pointed out, was not accidental. It had been present from the beginning and nothing would have been different if Lenin or Trotsky had remained in their positions of power. Although he conceded that central control was a necessary precondition for the emergence even of democratic socialism, it was clearly not of itself a sufficient precondition, and in fact was particularly susceptible to perversions such as the Soviet Union. We have already seen that allies of the Soviets had sought to imprison Orwell and Eileen in Barcelona, and that later Orwell himself carried a fear of assassination with him. This made him all the more determined to fight against the perversions of centralisation, especially though by no means exclusively the Soviet variety. In short, we should not read the word 'satire' as implying that *Nineteen Eighty Four* was not to be taken with the utmost seriousness.

Within thirty years of the book's publication, a so-called socialist regime in Cambodia acted against its citizens with a brutality every bit as obscene as that depicted in Room 101. Pol Pot's favoured title, a coincidental amalgam of Orwell's and Koestler's socialist leaders, was Brother Number One.[97] Pol Pot claimed to act from ideological motives and he seems to have convinced himself that the brutality of Stalin's programme of collectivisation in the Ukraine and Mao's Cultural Revolution in China had both been highly successful in the long run in furthering the cause of socialism. In Cambodia, like Russia, every crime that could be imagined, and many that are simply unimaginable, was committed in the name of socialism. He sought to eliminate his people's intellectual, cultural and religious heritage, to liquidate its entire intelligentsia and to destroy the institution of the family (in a society that revered its ancestors). In truth, his regime was the very embodiment of Orwell's nightmare.

Much as the political right may lionise Winston as a champion of individual moral autonomy, and Orwell gave sufficient emphasis to this aspect of Winston's struggle with the state to make this a reasonable reading, there is more to be said on the matter. Hannah Arendt suggested that at his very birth Enlightenment Man, the supreme individual, the paradigm of reason – and Winston Smith's direct ancestor – having freed himself from the enfolding bosom of the Church, promptly recreated himself a social being in order to be able to defend his newly discovered inalienable rights. Hardly had he appeared as an emancipated, autonomous moral being 'who carried his dignity within himself' than he disappeared again, to become a member of the people. The German Enlightenment thinkers, especially Hegel, sought the creation of a collective body that would truly represent the individual, optimising not subjugating his identity.[98] They found it in a special form of the state. Rousseau, too, urged man to become conscious only of the common, collective life.[99] For liberals, however, the state occupied a far more limited place than it did for Hegelians. It allowed, indeed encouraged, a plurality of institutions in which individuals, in

Arendt's words, could recreate themselves as social beings. That is why Bakunin, certainly no lover of the state, nevertheless cried from his heart that he did not want to be 'I'; he wanted to be 'We'. Orwell himself, elsewhere, recognised this social dimension of autonomy. The human being, he wrote in 1944, is not truly autonomous. Defoe, he said, could never actually have written *Robinson Crusoe* on a desert island, nor could any philosopher, scientist or artist function in isolation; 'they need constant stimulation from other people, it is about impossible to think without talking'.[100] J. S. Mill, who, like Orwell, sought to champion the cause of individual moral autonomy, and whose discussion on the issue in part resembles Winston's, was also certain about the social dimension of that autonomy. Truth was to be nailed not by individual experience alone, but by discussion, by 'the steady habit of correcting and completing his own opinion by collating it with those of others . . .'.[101]

Winston's cry was not, after all, the cry of the 'I' who wants to remain 'I', the champion of individual moral autonomy, but the cry of the 'I' who craves to be 'We'. Not the 'We' of the state, but the 'We' of some collective agency for which he would be willing to sacrifice his autonomy. It ought never to be overlooked that Winston Smith was prepared to commit himself to undertake the most heinous of crimes against ordinary innocent civilians to further the cause of a movement or agency about which he knew almost nothing.[102] Sandison, we recall, likened Winston Smith to Martin Luther, the last and the first men in Europe. The comparison stands better if we remember that Luther's attack on the Church led not to an entirely new relationship between God and millions of morally autonomous men and women but to a rival institution demanding a similar kind of loyalty. Left to his own devices, as Mill had established so clearly almost one hundred years before Orwell's novel appeared, individual man can provide no safeguard of liberty or autonomy. Even his ability to reason, and thus to recognise the truth, clumsily exemplified here by the equation two plus two equals four, is just as likely to prove to be an emblem of tyranny as of autonomy. Reference to Dostoevsky reminds us that two plus two equals four leads us away from that champion of individual identity, the Underground Man, and straight towards that other memorable fruit of Dostoevsky's imaginative powers, the Grand Inquisitor. Far from a searcher for the truth, a bloodied champion of the individual as an autonomous moral agent, Winston Smith turned out to have been a closet collectivist, and indeed a potential terrorist. Can we seriously consider a man who was prepared, even anxious, to undertake savage acts which, of their nature, would necessarily deprive many unknown individuals of their own truths, indeed of their own lives, to be a talisman for individual moral autonomy? Winston Smith was just as willing as Rousseau to force people to be free.

Orwell portrayed the struggle for individual liberty as being bound up in a struggle over the nature of reality fought out between the state and the autonomous individual, with only one possible winner. Moreover, he depicted this dispute being conducted, at considerable length, through the medium of torture. Orwell's story allows us to lose focus on the crucial importance in the debate of civil society and its institutions. Civil society has no place in *Nineteen Eighty Four*, though it would be unfair to characterise the novel as *Hamlet* without the Prince of Denmark; rather it is, say, *Macbeth* without the Prince of Denmark, for there was never intended to be a picture of civil society in the book. What Orwell wrote about in *Nineteen Eighty Four* was a state in which civil society had been utterly crushed. And yet the problem remains: without the endorsement of the institutions that make up civil society, the autonomous individual simply cannot build any safeguard against the all-powerful state. As Arendt suggested in respect of Enlightenment Man, individual autonomy can only be defended by sacrificing part of it to civil society, by becoming 'the people'. Orwell would have been happy to endorse that idea; indeed, it was central to his politics that we become truly autonomous only by sacrificing some autonomy. However, it was just such a surrender that Orwell himself found impossible. But his primary intention in *Nineteen Eighty Four* was to scare us by depicting the world devoid of civil society. Arendt wrote that only by founding civil institutions that represent our aspirations as human beings could we rescue ourselves from the 'holes of oblivion' into which totalitarianism had sought to cast us.[103] Indeed, Edmund Burke's opposition to the French Revolution was precisely that, if its ideas spread to England, it would bring about the demise of the institutions of civil society whose 'parts are so made for one another' that to change them would destroy them and thus the constitution.[104] Burke gave us the analogy of civil society being like a clock, which functions effectively because of the successful interaction between many constituent parts. For Burke and for Orwell, reason had, in a Hobbesian kind of way, become the servant of unreason and of passion, producing tyranny. It would not be appropriate to take the discussion further,[105] but it can safely be asserted that the importance of civil society to the democratic polity is widely recognised.[106] The only kinds of institutions and organisations that might make up a civil society in Oceania were to be found in the underground world of the proles. And like the animals, the proles did not matter.

There is another aspect in which, for liberals, Winston Smith could be said to lack real autonomy: he possessed no private property. When we consider those aspects that comprise the values necessary for individual autonomy, as outlined by Winston, most could be said to be associated with, if not characteristic of, property ownership: a rich and sustaining family life, cultural continuity, based upon a vibrant language, a full emotional life and perhaps, above all, a completely private world into which one could retire. Orwell had established the importance of private property earlier, in *The Lion and Unicorn*.[107] A life of reasonable material sufficiency, it could be said, is not necessarily associated with property ownership, though property would enhance the capacity to choose in which goods one aspired to be sufficient. Orwell did not address the matter of property ownership or raise the notion of private property as a principle, but we need not be so reticent. Lack of property and the choices that tend to accompany it are central to Winston's lack of autonomy.

Woodcock described *Nineteen Eighty Four* as the culmination of twenty years of writing, and 'an authentic product, not of the tortured body registered at various sanatoria under the name of Eric Blair, but of the imaginative being who bore the name of George Orwell'.[108] I have suggested that the book contains deficiencies, some, Woodcock's view notwithstanding, are no doubt the consequence of Orwell's mental and physical state as he completed the final version. The book represented a towering achievement and is the book for which Orwell is best remembered. Perhaps it does not match up to *Animal Farm* as a work of literature, but its sheer intensity of purpose, its relentless pessimism, its surgical dissection of the nature of totalitarian regimes, make it an exceptionally powerful book, indeed powerful enough to have helped shape the modern world. Isaac Deutcher recounted the story of the blind news vendor thrusting a copy into his hands and saying, 'You must read it, sir. Then you will know why we must drop the atom bomb on the bolshies.'[109]

Deutscher himself was guarded in his assessment of the novel's qualities, judging that although Orwell's imagination was ferocious and penetrating, his book lacked 'width, suppleness and originality'.[110] It is reported that when the BBC broadcast a production of *Nineteen Eighty Four* on Sunday, 12 December 1954, the man whose face was used on posters to represent Big Brother, a cameraman, was abused by members of the public after the showing, so great was the film's impact. Thousands protested at the production, hundreds phoned the BBC to criticise the play because it was 'sadistic', and 'barbaric' and not a single caller supported it.[111] Five Conservative MPs sponsored an

Early Day Motion in the House of Commons deploring the BBC's tendency to 'pander to sexual and sadistic tastes'. One correspondent referred to the BBC's 'opening the floodgates of Hell' – and he was an ex-soldier. One housewife is reported to have died of a heart attack after the torture scenes.[112] The *New York Times* reported that the broadcast had become 'the subject of the sharpest controversy in the annals of British television'.[113] Orwell had indeed captured for all time the essence of a 'world of rabbits ruled by stoats', a world that he had earlier considered to be exclusively fascist.[114]

Although it is frequently said to represent only a nightmare, *Nineteen Eighty Four* is no more 'only' a nightmare than Stalin's Soviet or Hitler's Nazi regimes, the Khmer Rouge regime in Cambodia between 1975 and 1979, a range of South American and African dictatorships or Saddam's regime in Iraq, to mention only the more obvious. At its centre lies the argument that if the individual can strive to hold on to certain fundamental truths, of which the certainty that two plus two equals four is held erroneously to be emblematic, then his autonomy will be assured and tyranny can be withstood. But what the book actually shows is that individual autonomy is as much a myth as O'Brien claims. Our capacity to recognise truths is social, and the truths we recognise are social, nothing more (nor less) than a by-product of our loyalty to the social agencies of civil society to which we happen to belong. But no matter: the potent threat that *Nineteen Eighty Four* exposed was what would follow from the destruction of civil society. Small reminds us[115] that the Nazis' final solution to the Jewish 'problem', as nightmarish as anything, had already been parodied over two hundred and fifty years before, by Orwell's literary hero, Swift. The Houyhnhmns debated the final solution of the Yahoo problem and their decision was, we remember, to expel them from the 'arse-hole of the world'. Though he called it satirical, Orwell's great novel was not, like Swift's, allegorical. Orwell confronted his life's enemy directly and deliberately, but indirectly he confronted a similar potentiality in all modern collectivist governments and, insofar as he located a tendency to totalitarianism in man generally (including Winston Smith), his last book was a powerful warning to us all, and as Patrick Reilly succinctly asked: 'Who writes a warning against an impossibility?'[116]

7 Orwell, socialism and the soul of man

> For she perceived that for all that happens in church, however cowardly
> and absurd its purpose may be, there is something of decency, of spir-
> itual; comeliness – that is not easily found in the world outside. It
> seemed to her that even though you no longer believe . . . it is better to
> follow in the ancient ways, than to drift in rootless freedom.
>
> George Orwell, *A Clergyman's Daughter* (Harmondsworth:
> Penguin, 1964, p. 220).

So far in this analysis of Orwell's social and political thought we have
been considering Orwell's principal writings. I argued that Orwell was,
above all else, a great writer and so if we wished to come to understand
his political thinking, this is where we should start looking. Now I have
to come clean and admit that there is one element of his thinking that
cannot be explored through the principal agency of a major work: that
is Orwell's moral perspective. In fact, to come completely clean I
should also admit that in my opinion this one element in his thinking is
the most significant. This is not the customary view of Orwell, or
indeed one that he himself held, but it is nevertheless the position that I
will try to advance. It is true that one of his early novels, *A Clergyman's
Daughter*,[1] was chiefly concerned with advancing a distinctive moral
perspective, but this novel is generally regarded as Orwell's least successful and one of which he claimed to have been ashamed.[2] We shall
not ignore the novel, even so, but neither will we be dealing with it
exclusively by any means. Whatever its literary shortcomings, it provides important insights into Orwell's moral thinking and gives us a
lead into understanding how Orwell linked his moral and political
thought, enabling us perhaps to classify his version of socialism. Let me
start, however, by considering Orwellian socialism in relation to more
conventional currents of contemporary socialist thought.

1

'George Orwell was a sick, counter-revolutionary fink. It was good he died when he did.'[3] Without a second thought, the young radical of the 1960s from Saul Bellow's *Mr Sammler's Planet* dismissed one of the most widely read socialist writers of the twentieth century; consigned to irrelevance a partisan who had fought for the revolution in Spain and been almost fatally wounded; ignored as inconsequential a humanitarian who, though himself consumptive, passed on some of his wartime food rations to the poor; rejected as a class enemy a comrade who declared that every line he had written was to advance the cause of democratic socialism. Why the anger?

Was it no more than an example of the contempt that the young (and the not so young) of some groups on the Left tend to nurse for those in other groups on the Left? Yes, it was more: Bellow's young radical was in fact denouncing Orwell for his alleged desertion from the colours to become a lackey of British imperialism. He was by no means alone in doing so. In fact, for a writer whose career was relatively short and whose output comparatively meagre, Orwell contrived to evoke a bewildering array of responses, and by no means all of them favourable. His friend and mentor Richard Rees described him as a democratic socialist;[4] others called him a Tory radical[5] or a sentimental liberal,[6] whereas Isaac Deutscher[7] and George Woodcock[8] considered him to be an unsophisticated anarchist. It is well known that the publication of his last novel, *Nineteen Eighty Four*, earned Orwell the accolade from one Communist magazine of 'maggot of the month'.

A more commonly held attitude, however, is that Orwell developed as a political thinker from a generalised socialistic standpoint to a clear and unequivocal revolutionary socialism and finally to an intensely anti-revolutionary and largely anti-socialist individualism. This development, the argument runs, is clearly evident in his major works. In his early work Orwell expressed sympathy for and solidarity with the powerless and the oppressed. Our discussion of *Down and Out, Burmese Days, Keep the Aspidistra Flying* and *Wigan Pier* bears this line of argument out. Then came the committed socialism of *Homage to Catalonia* when Orwell became intoxicated by the experience of what he took to be, in Barcelona, the first stage of a socialist society. Again: no argument here. When war came to Britain but socialism did not, Orwell became increasingly pessimistic and the apparent rise and rise of Soviet communism in the eyes of the Western intelligentsia evoked the brilliant anti-Soviet fable *Animal Farm*. Finally, as his own health deteriorated, Orwell wrote his desperately apocalyptic dystopia *Nineteen Eighty Four*, based on a future British socialist state. To those who accept the basic stages in this chronology, and our own enquiries tend to support it, Orwell did indeed appear to have deserted the flag; or worse, to have proved to be nothing more than a sentimental and confused bourgeois who flirted with an economic and social theory he barely understood and finally abandoned to return to his roots and become a famous Cold Warrior.

I want to try to argue to the contrary: that there *is* a consistent, if not always unambiguous, pattern of thinking in Orwell: in short, to save Orwell from his opponents. This will require some preliminary explanation as to why Orwell was so vehemently criticised by many on the Left, not just Sammler's young radical student. Second, I want to expose Orwell's thought to a rather different line of criticism which will seek not to criticise as such, but to re-categorise that pattern of thinking in terms of its relationship to socialism: to save Orwell from his friends, so to speak. Finally, I shall propose a reappraisal of Orwell's political thought, linked to the notion of Orwell as an imaginative writer, which shows Orwellian socialism in a different and, I think, new light: to save Orwell, to be presumptuous, from himself.

First, then, why was Orwell so roundly disliked by many on the Left? To understand this state of affairs, we need only to reflect on Orwell's career as we have seen it develop. Let us consider *Wigan Pier*. Although the first half provided just the kind of systematic analysis of the lives of the poor in Yorkshire and Lancashire that Gollancz had expected, much of the second half constituted a savage attack on the very kind of people who had indirectly financed his journey north, the Left Book Clubbers. He castigated ordinary middle-class socialists in the most outrageously sweeping terms. At best figures of fun – like Red Indians, said Orwell[9] – their prominence in the socialist movement made it unattractive to potential working-class adherents. At worst they were potential totalitarians.

Before he completed *Wigan Pier* the Civil War had broken out in Spain, that touchstone of the Left's ambition as McNiece called it, and Orwell set off to fight for 'common decency'. When finally he got his political bearings in Spain, he was dismayed to discover that not all socialists were on the same side. Indeed, the communists were intent upon imprisoning him, and in the end Orwell was lucky to escape with his life. On his return to Britain Orwell openly championed the cause of proletarian revolution, coupled with pacifism, and equally openly attacked British imperialism, Western capitalism generally, but above all the Soviet Union. When war broke out in 1939 he turned to attack his former pacifist allies whilst continuing to champion the cause of revolution. But the war ended without a British revolution, and Orwell began to concentrate on attacking the notion that the Soviet Union was truly socialist. In *Animal Farm*, however, he was widely thought to have rejected revolution itself as a way to achieve socialism. In rejecting pacifism, the Soviet model and revolution as ways to achieve socialism, just as he had rejected middle-class libertarianism, Orwell again cut himself off from the mainstream of socialist thinking and antagonised its many adherents.

Orwell's Spanish experiences caused him to refocus on the role of intellectuals,[10] particularly ideologists, in achieving socialism. In his Eton days, we remember, Orwell had presented himself to his peers as the new Bernard Shaw. But intellectual socialists such as the Fabians were, he was later to discover, avowedly élitist: 'socialism without experts is as impossible as ... dentistry without experts', Shaw once declared.[11] Socialism for them was not about empowering the proletariat. No Fabian would do that, said Shaw, unless he wished to achieve a *reductio ad absurdum* of democracy.[12] For the ideologues, said Orwell, power was both the end and the means. Ideology, socialism as much as any other, was no more than a spurious justification, a mask behind which these intellectuals could hide their natural totalitarian instincts. In this savage attack on socialist intellectuals, Orwell cut himself off from the Fabian tradition of state socialism, thereby turning his back on yet another mainstream of socialist thought.

Last, Orwell showed no enthusiasm for parliamentary socialism. Even though he became the literary editor of *Tribune*, he wrote surprisingly little about the Labour Party or its major figures. Only towards the end of his career, when he was concerned about the influence within the parliamentary party of the pro-Soviet left, the fellow travellers, did Orwell devote much time to writing about the politics of the Labour Party. An early reference in *Wigan Pier* to Labour backstairs crawlers[13] seemed to suggest little sympathy with the cause of parliamentary socialism as such.[14] His view was that Labour candidates were selected for their docility, most of them elderly trade union officials who slavishly followed the party line.[15] Even when Aneurin Bevan became general editor of *Tribune*, Orwell devoted only a very small part of his time to considering the man and his politics, though we might have assumed this working-class politician would have ignited Orwell's interest.[16] As for the trade union movement and its political aspirations, Orwell had almost nothing to say.[17]

Small wonder, considering this catalogue of animosity and disdain, that many on the Left considered Orwell to be either at best an unreliable ally or more simply their enemy. Indeed, even a neutral observer might wonder whether any soil remained that might prove suitably rich for the development of Orwell's professed socialism.

2

We know that there was. We know that he rooted it in the values and lives of ordinary people: this was his decency myth. The decency myth incorporated a form of socialism that was non-libertarian, non-ideological, non-utopian, non-progressive and non- (probably anti-) intellectual. It could not be systematised into an ideology or even a programme for action, because it represented less a set of philosophical premises or policy goals than a way of living.

This way of living was shaped by the Judaeo-Christian heritage, that 'ineradicable belief in decency' that ordinary people cherish. 'Everywhere, under the surface, the common man sticks obstinately to the belief that he derives from the Christian culture.'[18] When he wrote at length about Dickens,[19] Orwell commented that although formal religion played no part in his life, Dickens was a Christian because he naturally sided with the oppressed. He was a Christian, Orwell said, in the sense that he became 'the standard bearer of common decency'.

But the celebrated essay on Dickens began with an admonition: Dickens was not a revolutionary writer. Macaulay was said to have refused to review Dickens' *Hard Times* because of its 'sullen socialism'. What nonsense, says Orwell: 'there is not a line in the book that can properly be called Socialistic'.[20] Quite the reverse, the book was pro-capitalist and its moral seemed to be that capitalists ought to be kinder. 'His whole message is one that at first glance looks like an enormous platitude: If men would behave decently the world would be decent.'[21] This apparent shallowness was the consequence of Dickens' lack of grasp of social and economic relations; he failed to understand that given the nature and shape of capitalist society certain evils could be said to be structural and therefore irremediable. And yet half way through the essay Orwell began to shift his ground. When Dickens attacked institutions he was more concerned with changing their spirit than the structure, but this was because he believed that changing institutions without changing their spirit was a waste of time.[22] Now we are told that although Dickens might not be a revolutionary writer in the accepted sense, it is perfectly feasible to argue that a *moral* critique of a society or an institution might not be equally as revolutionary as the 'politico-economic criticism which is fashionable at this moment';[23] so fashionable, in fact, that Orwell had himself begun by employing it to criticise Dickens. And so the axiom that the world would be a decent place if man behaved decently is not such a platitude as it sounds. Marx may have blown the moralists' position sky high, but the sappers of moralism were soon at work themselves undermining Marx's position just as comprehensively. Dickens, he repeated, had no clear grasp of the society that he was attacking and no suggestions to make for its improvement. What Dickens opposed, then, was not a society or an institution but what G. K. Chesterton identified as 'an expression on a human face'.[24]

Orwell identified Dickens as a Christian moralist, though he knew Dickens could hardly have been described as a religious man. He quoted a letter that Dickens had written to his youngest son, urging on him the recognition of 'the truth and beauty of the Christian Religion, as it came from Christ himself'.[25] Significantly, Orwell went on to say that this kind of Dickensian moral stance was to be found in the history of working-class socialism. Whereas just about every modern intellectual had gone over to totalitarianism, he argued, the common man was still living out Christian values. Dickens' great skill was to be able to express in a simplified manner the 'native decency of the common man'. Orwell's great skill, on the other hand, was to be able to characterise Dickens' art memorably: Tolstoy's characters might cross frontiers, he said, but Dickens' characters could be captured on a cigarette card.[26] Orwell concluded this essay by suggesting that when we read Dickens' work we see a face : 'the face of a man who is generously angry – in other words, of a nineteenth-century liberal, a free intelligence, a type hated with equal hatred by all the smelly little orthodoxies that are now contending for our souls'.[27] With this explosive conclusion, Orwell appeared not simply to be carving out a niche for moralism in the revolutionary agenda but actually granting it a superior status to that of ideology.

I referred briefly to Orwell having connected his decency myth to traditional Christian values in *Wigan Pier*. It was this connection, we remember, that Chaplin made explicit in his cinematic characterisations. Now we find Orwell suggesting that Dickens too was able to appeal to his audience through the medium of Christian morality. Bearing in mind the moral basis of his decency myth, we might well be prompted to ask, as others have: was Orwell himself a closet Christian?

3

At Eton Orwell was confirmed into the Anglican Communion by the well-known Christian Socialist Bishop Charles Gore. Later he was married according to the rites of the Church of England. Knowing Orwell as we think we do, could we really believe that he would have done this thing for convention, or in response to some momentary whim? He told an Eton contemporary, Denys King-Farlow, that before his wedding he spent days consulting the *Prayer Book*.[28] It is typical of Orwell that he portrayed this as an attempt to fortify himself against 'the obscenities of the wedding service'. But there were no pressures upon him to marry in church: he, certainly not Eileen, consciously chose to heap those obscenities upon himself. Moreover, we know that earlier Orwell, then a young teacher, not only attended Communion at the local church but also served at the altar. Once again Orwell took pains to report this to a friend, Eleanor Jacques.[29] He did these things, he told her, to support his only friend in the area, a young curate (coincidentally another Christian Socialist). Nobody but the weakest-willed amongst us would allow himself to be used in this way. It is not credible that Orwell would have participated in what he claimed to have been a mere show. Indeed, when Bernard Crick interviewed the curate's wife she was adamant that Orwell's belief had been genuine.[30] We know too from his own admission that Orwell took the *Church Times* regularly and that soon he began to 'like it more every week'. Why then did Orwell take this line with Eleanor Jacques? Not to beat about the bush, he was seeking to establish a relationship with her, and she was a religious agnostic and a freethinker. I suspect Orwell was being deviously economical with a rather complex truth. Finally, before he died, Orwell left instructions that he was to be buried according to the rites of the Church of England. Whilst we cannot be certain why Orwell gave this instruction, there are very few plausible possibilities that exclude the obvious: that when it really mattered his Church was important to him.

But let us be clear: Orwell was no card-carrying Anglican. He never acknowledged an attachment to Christianity, quite the opposite in fact, and it is clear why. First, he would not have found it politically convenient: it would have limited his room for manoeuvre because his arguments would have been regarded as *parti pris*. Moreover, a religious affiliation would have challenged his credibility amongst those he sought to influence. More importantly, association with any '-ism' was something Orwell abstemiously avoided. Just as he saw some socialists as the chief objection to socialism, he certainly saw some (probably most) Christians as the chief objection to Christianity. Institutions, based as they are upon '-isms' were anathema to him. He remained a firm opponent of institutional Christianity; indeed, he had a hatred bordering on neurosis of Roman Catholicism. He wrote of a seventeenth-century Italian crucifix which, when unfastened, revealed a stiletto. 'What a perfect symbol of the Christian religion', he wrote.[31] Moreover, he acknowledged unambiguously on a number of occasions the finality of the demise of formal Christian teaching.[32] We can conclude no more than this: Orwell's unwillingness to acknowledge any attachment to Christianity did not represent an unambiguous stance to say the least, and he never stopped thinking that it was essential for modern man to realise that he could not construct any 'worthwhile picture of the future unless [he] realises how much we have lost by the decay of Christianity'.[33] All the same the questions that worried him were: how to sustain moral sensibility and a commitment to freedom and justice, and how to retain a spiritual dimension to socialism after the demise of Christianity? Both had a clear religious connotation.

I said earlier that, unlike other chapters, this one would not be based upon a major work. However, we cannot leave this matter of religious sentiment without referring to the one work that bears exactly on some of these issues, *A Clergyman's Daughter*. In the novel, Dorothy Hare, the young woman of the title, finds herself acting as a general factotum for her self-absorbed father, the Reverend Charles Hare, who had a country living. Orwell managed to paint a sympathetic picture of her plight. She had contrived to come to terms with a stultifying, suffocating ritual of petty chores and physical hardship but only by practising masochistic forms of self-discipline. From April to November, for example, she took only cold baths. When she found her mind wandering during prayers she would prick herself sharply with a hat pin.[34] The best remembered example of Dorothy's self-discipline tells of when she found herself likely to have to take communion wine from the chalice after the only other communicant, Miss Mayfill, whose unsavoury oral hygiene was described in great detail by the writer. Dorothy succumbed to praying fervently not to have to take the chalice after Miss Mayfill. Suddenly, however, full of remorse, she drove the pin into her arm so fiercely she could hardly suppress a cry, and forced herself to kneel behind Miss Mayfill so that she, and not Dorothy, would receive the wine first.[35] She did her duty. Not so frequently remembered, however, is what happened next. A sudden shaft of sunlight, some 'jewel of unimaginable splendour' bathed the doorway in a green light. 'A flood of joy ran through Dorothy's heart' reawakening her love of God. Orwell describes Dorothy's own view of her faith as 'deeper than reason'.[36]

Dorothy's story loses credibility around the same time as she loses her memory, after the unsolicited sexual advances of a neighbour. There is little point in following the story that took her to London, where she slept rough, to the hop fields of Kent and then finally to the recovery of her senses and a return to her old life. Ironically she was escorted back to her home by Warburton, the very man whose unwelcome advances had been responsible for the onset of her amnesia. When she confessed regret at her loss of faith, Warburton was dismissive. If she was worried about living with hypocrisy, she need not, for almost all of the clergy were in that condition. But she should nevertheless think herself out of a position that offered her the worst of both worlds, Anglican atheism: Christianity without the prospect of paradise.[37] Dorothy responded by trying to argue that it would be less selfish to pretend to faith in order to help others to sustain their own faith. On later reflection she thought that what she should have said was that though her faith had gone, *she* had not changed. 'Beliefs change, thoughts change, but there is some inner part of the soul that does not change. Faith vanishes, but the need for faith remains the same as before.'[38] At the end of the novel we find Dorothy just where we discovered her at the beginning, gluing together Julius Caesar's breastplate for a church pageant. Now, however, she does not prick herself with pins, but instead her conscience stabs her into action. And action is the answer to her problem, for 'faith and no faith are very much the same provided that one is doing what is customary, useful and acceptable'.[39] The smell of glue, she thought, was the answer to her prayer. How ironic that a scholar of religion could write: 'From Feuerbach to Durkheim, the liberals have known that faith was nothing except its function as glue.'[40] For Dorothy, by contrast, it is glue that functions as faith. It is nugatory to consider whether Dorothy's loss of faith and her reaction to it represented a similar process in Orwell himself, but in many respects it did represent Orwell's perception of what was happening generally in the Western world. One could not serve two masters and had to choose, he said, between God and man. His own choice, man, was unambiguous.[41] What Orwell took from Christianity was a code of social conduct, not a religion.

Orwell's mind turned increasingly to man's moral condition and he regarded as supremely ironic the notion that modern man had been liberated from superstition.[42] Writers from Voltaire to Joyce, he said, had been 'saboteurs' destroying traditional values, sawing away the branch on which man was seated. Too late it was realised that underneath the branch was no bed of roses but a 'cesspool full of barbed wire'.[43] That cesspool stood for the general disposition towards mindless hedonism on the one hand and power worship, totalitarianism, on the other: so much for liberation. What was to be done? As Orwell saw it, the problem was to sustain the moral values of Christianity whilst acknowledging that belief in eternal punishment and reward had collapsed. But was it not already too late? No: after all, Orwell wanted to convince us, or at least himself, that he had seen these attitudes in operation amongst the working-class. Mr. Average, he wrote, had long forgotten the Christian texts, but he retained the belief that Christianity was about unselfishness and loving one's neighbour; above all, he held on to the essential truth, that might is not right.[44] This is the importance of Orwell's decency myth: it links to the ancient wisdom of what today we would call Judaeo-Christian morality, and for Orwell that link constituted socialism, a socialism that, because it represented the only long-term alternative to hedonistic self-indulgence, or worse, totalitarianism, might save the world.

Orwell, like Röpke, or Herzen before either of them,[45] was consumed with the effect on Western man of the perceived decline of Christian moral values, and time and again in his writing he turned to the real spectre haunting his Europe, the post-Christian society. Röpke spoke of 'an unequalled moral and intellectual decadence, a spiritual chaos' following the decline of Christianity which, he said, had nourished the essentially secular concepts of progress, rationalism, liberty and humanity.[46] Perhaps the most arresting metaphor in all of Orwell's writing, so powerful that he used it twice,[47] concerned a wasp eating jam from Orwell's breakfast plate. The breakfaster fastidiously cut the creature in two with his table knife but the wasp, unaware of his misfortune, continued to eat, the jam spewing out of its oesophagus. Only when it tried to fly away did the wasp understand its dreadful fate. 'It is the same with modern man', wrote Orwell, 'the thing that has been cut away is his soul . . .'[48] He tells us that abandoning the traditional form of religious belief was necessary, but it is hard to reconcile this reassurance with his own apparent fear of a world from which Christian morality had been excluded. In losing his belief in an afterlife, Orwell went on; modern man had lost his soul. Now a traditional believer can accommodate himself to the fact that 'man that is born of woman hath but a short time to live and is full of misery';[49] after all, it is the next life that counts. But, says Orwell, to accept that life is miserable when you believe that only this life counts, well, that is quite another matter. This became Orwell's most abiding concern:

how to encourage men to act morally, especially in a totalitarian age, when there remained no fear of everlasting retribution for wrongdoing and no everlasting reward for doing right. How can men be encouraged to act as brothers when they own no common father? How can men build a Kingdom of Heaven on Earth when they know they are mortal? Orwell became fixated by the real spectre haunting Europe: post-Christian morality. How could it resist totalitarianism? 'What we are moving towards', he went on, 'is something like the Spanish Inquisition, and probably far worse, thanks to the radio and the secret police'.[50] This fate is probably inescapable unless we manage to 'reinstate the belief in human brotherhood without the need for a "next world" to give it meaning'.[51] These more general fears, I believe, give a broader context to Orwell's despair regarding totalitarianism that we discussed in the last chapter. We shall be returning to totalitarianism shortly, but we need to be aware that it was not the only danger in the cesspool.

The other main danger was what Orwell referred to as 'sluttish antinomianism'. He used this phrase in a review of his old friend Cyril Connolly's book *The Rock Pool*.[52] The story concerned a young superior kind of Englishman, a 1930s version of a young Bernard Shaw, who found himself in a colony of artistic expatriates on the French Riviera. Soon he was indulging in the drinking and lechering that consumed his new friends. Orwell was appalled at Connolly. 'Even to want to write about so-called artists who spend on sodomy what they have gained by sponging betrays a kind of spiritual inadequacy.' His advice to his friend was that he should concern himself more with ordinary people. 'The fact to which we have got to cling, as if to a life belt, is that it *is* possible to be a normal decent person and yet to be fully alive.'[53] When he reviewed Henry Miller's *Tropic of Cancer*,[54] Orwell concluded that though Miller's ordinary man was not exactly a Yahoo, he quite resembled one. Orwell expressly linked the 'monstrous soppification of the sexual theme' that Miller depicted with the decline of Christian values. It is difficult not to elide Orwell's metaphors and come up with a lifebelt of post-Christian values in a cesspool as depicting Orwell's view of the only hope for modern man seeking to lead a 'decent' life.

It seems fair to ask whether Orwell would have regarded his own life, with his sexual adventures in Burma[55] and his later extra-marital philandering,[56] as decent. It is apparent in his review of Henry Miller's work[57] that Orwell was ambivalent about such matters, and at first sight it seems that he might be guilty simply of hypocrisy – not that this would have invalidated his argument. It is not clear whether Orwell considered that decency need not extend to the sphere of one's private life, or more specifically heterosexual relationships, because he never confronted the issue. He remarked of McGill's postcards (of which he claimed to have a personal collection) that they portrayed the lives of ordinary decent people who tried to act morally, though not too morally.[58] It would be difficult to fit Julia into such a category, especially since Winston relished her professed promiscuity. However, Orwell used the words hedonism and sluttish antinomianism to denote the 'spiritual inadequacy' that he despised and feared, words that seem more appropriate for describing the vices of the rich and powerful and not the poor and powerless. The poor may stray, said Orwell, but they recognise the social and political importance of the institution of marriage, and so once again it is the decency of ordinary people that provides a barrier against the spiritual inadequacy that lurked in the cesspool.

Perhaps we should not be entirely swept away by the force of Orwell's metaphors. It hardly needs pointing out that the practitioners of the Christian religion have been guilty of the most appalling atrocities, some carried out quite intentionally in the name of their God. Moreover, if we read the *Divine Comedy* or the *Canterbury Tales*, it is impossible to believe that the characters about whom Dante and Chaucer wrote were in any significant way constrained in their often brutal actions by a belief in an afterlife of eternal damnation. A correspondent wrote to Orwell privately in response to one of his attacks on the value system of the post-Christian world wondering how he knew that the majority of ordinary people 'whatever that means' no longer believed in an afterlife. There were many Christians who had acted immorally in the past, she went on, and many present-day atheists who behaved as decently as any believer. These are obvious criticisms, but the question she put to him raised a more profound difficulty: how to inculcate religious attitudes without a formally structured religion.[59] Another writer posed a question that went to the very heart of Orwell's claim for Christian morality based on a belief in the afterlife. 'Have you ever met', he asked, 'a Christian who was as afraid of Hell as he was of cancer?' The writer posing that probing question was none other than Orwell.[60] Elsewhere a writer took issue with the idea that a decent society must be structured along Christian lines – such an idea, he said, would limit 'decent' societies to the fringes of the Atlantic. That argument, together with its characteristic geographic licence, came, once again, from none other than Orwell.[61] None of this is to deny, even for a moment, that Christianity has had a generally benign and indeed uplifting effect on human behaviour, but so have other world religions. Indeed, if we are to believe McIntyre, the greatest moral influence upon virtuous behaviour, in the West anyway, has always been Aristotle.[62]

4

If Orwell was right in arguing that power politics, or 'bully-worship', had become a universal religion,[63] then Western society had more to fear than just the growing influence of Russia, for totalitarianism becomes more than just a state-sponsored political system; it becomes an attitude of mind born of the death of Christian values, an attitude that was becoming ever more pervasive. Nowhere was this theme more fully developed than in the article 'Raffles and Miss Blandish'.[64] In this essay Orwell sought to compare 'for sociological purposes' the moral atmosphere of two books, *Raffles, A Thief in the Night* (1900) and *No Orchids for Miss Blandish* (1939). In short, he sought to compare the moral values of the pre-1914 world and his own. Both books in their different ways glamorised crime but there the similarities ended. Raffles was a gentleman. He had played cricket for England. He was a burglar but his only remorse was social: he had let the school down and forfeited his right to enter decent society (he was in society but not of it, he told his friend Bunny). Nevertheless, everything that Raffles did was measured against certain social conventions; he would never contemplate any action that was 'not cricket'. The Raffles books, Orwell concluded, were representative of a time when people had standards. There was a clear line between good and evil. It might have been a silly line but the important fact was that it was not crossed. Having dealt with Raffles, Orwell then turned his attentions to Miss Blandish with the arresting phrase: 'Now for a header into the cesspool'.

The story centred round the abduction of a millionaire's daughter and entailed two rapes, a beating with a hosepipe, the extermination of two entire criminal gangs, and finally the suicide of Miss Blandish herself. Orwell concluded that, in the whole story, there was only one theme: the pursuit of power. In another of Hadley Chase's books, Orwell tells us, the hero, who was intended to earn our respect, stamped on somebody's face and then ground his heel round and round in the broken mouth. It is noteworthy, too, that the role of the police in both books is entirely different. In Raffles they represented society and its sense of moral propriety; in the latter, there was no difference between the police and the criminals beyond the fact that the police were better paid. No distinction was drawn, that is to say, between the values of good and evil, but only between strength and weakness. In short, the escapism of Raffles took the reader into the world of crime not of evil; that of Miss Blandish into a world of cruelty and sexual perversion.

Orwell claimed not to have been guilty of idealising the world of Raffles; it was, he said, a world of snobbishness and hypocrisy and Raffles had no morals, only the reflexes of a gentleman. But *No Orchids*, by contrast, constituted a 'day-dream appropriate to a total-itarian age' in which people had come to worship power. Before 1914 the heroes of the liberal intelligentsia were sympathetic figures, whereas in the 1930s a *New Statesman* reader 'worships Stalin'. Now here Orwell began to make a conceptual switch from identify-ing totalitarianism as a general attitude towards power and cruelty, ever more prevalent with the decline of traditional Christian values, to identifying these attitudes specifically with British socialist intel-lectuals. Amongst those who 'kiss the arse of Stalin', the cult of power 'tends to be mixed up with a love of cruelty and wickedness *for their own sakes*'.[65] He took as 'merely the first example that comes to mind' the case of Bernard Shaw. In reality Shaw was not merely a convenient example. We know Orwell's earlier attachment to Shaw's work, which he knew backwards. Moreover, Shaw's great talent was to dramatise his political and social views unapologetically and in a way that made him an easy target for the critics, of whom there were many.[66] Never-theless that master of hyperbole had been a founder member of the Fabian Society, had visited the Soviet Union and met Stalin and had, as his telegram address, 'Socialist, London'. Orwell was justified in claim-ing that nobody else had identified what he called the 'sadistic element' in Shaw's work, still less connected it with his admiration for dictators. It is not easy to come to terms with Orwell's fear of the influence of the Soviet Union unless we realise the extent to which intellectuals like Shaw were supportive of the Soviet Union. (We have only to reflect on the wide-scale infiltration of the British security system by pro-Soviet spies during and after the Second World War to recognise that Orwell's fears were not groundless.) So what were Shaw's politics?

Shaw had been one of those young intellectuals who had gone to Henry George's celebrated lecture to the London Zetetical Society on the nationalisation of land in 1883. Having subsequently attended meetings of Hyndman's Democratic Federation to discuss these issues further, he found himself introduced to the work of Karl Marx. This was an event which, it has been claimed, 'converted him to socialism, turned him into a revolutionary writer, made him a political agitator, changed his outlook, directed his energy, influenced his art, gave him a religion, and, as he claimed, made a man of him'.[67] Shaw joined a group known as the Fellowship of the Good Life which, in 1884, transmogrified into the Fabian Society. The Fabian Society was formally dedicated to 'educate, agitate and organise' so as to bring about, according to Shaw, a 'tremendous smash up of society'.[68] In fact, an insurrection on behalf of the working-class was never likely to have appealed to Shaw. His hatred of poverty, so clearly expounded in his early works,[69] seemed in many respects to extend to a hatred of the poor themselves, as this extract from one of Shaw's speeches shows:[70]

> As to the working-classes I believe neither in their virtues nor their intelligence, on the contrary my objection to the existing order is precisely that it inevitably produces this wretched, idolatrous, sentimental, servile, anti-socialist mass of spoiled humanity which we call the proletariat and which neither understands, believes in us or likes us. I am no friend of the working-class. I am its enemy to the extent of ardently desiring its extermination.

For Shaw, socialism was like a spoonful of malt to be forced down the throat of a reluctant working-class by a strong-armed, well-meaning Fabian care assistant. Shaw rightly claimed that the Fabians had never advanced any pretension to represent the working man,[71] and when challenged on the obvious lack of democracy implied by this disclaimer, he countered that the only meaningful definition of democracy was a political system that aimed for 'the greatest available welfare for the whole population'.[72] Power to the people? Not for Shaw! Orwell castigated Shaw's hero worship as a philosophy that extolled the virtues of Giant the Jack Killer.[73] He was right, as the following shows: 'Now in Herr Hitler', Shaw remarked in 1938, 'we have clearly no raving lunatic to deal with. He is a very able ruler and on most subjects a very sane one.'[74] As late as 1940 Shaw declared himself to have been a National Socialist before Hitler had been born and he expressed the hope that Britain would soon 'emulate and surpass his achievements'.[75] It is not surprising, then, that Shaw declared the Russian people to be the freest in the world[76] or that his elemental Puritanism caused him to argue that 'compulsory labour with death as the final penalty is the keystone to socialism'.[77]

Shaw's public correspondence with the Italian historian Salvemini showed him to be strongly supportive of Mussolini and dismissive of the mistreatment of liberals who opposed Mussolini.[78] There is also a revealing personal correspondence with a woman whose husband had been incarcerated by the Stalin regime who, on hearing that Shaw was to visit the Soviet Union, pleaded with him to seek her husband's release. Shaw assured her that she had been misinformed: there were no labour camps in the Soviet Union, but even if there were, her husband would be better off there, where he would be safe from her nagging.[79]

Whatever allowances we may make for Shaw's natural instinct to dramatise, we cannot mistake the bald fact that when Shaw described himself as a National Socialist or alternatively as a totalitarian democrat, he was telling the simple truth. Orwell's point, then, was well made, though he did not himself bother to develop it. Moreover, although Shaw might have been the most flamboyant exponent of what sympathisers today might call tough love, Orwell was right to classify him as exemplifying a totalitarian strain in intellectual socialism in Britain. We should not forget the Webbs' advocacy of measures to eliminate what they called moral lassitude in the Minority Report of the Poor Law in the debate over national insurance prior to the National Insurance Act of 1911 (a good example of tough love),[80] nor their massive tome written in support of Stalin, *Soviet Communism: A New Civilisation?*[81] Shavian and Fabian élitism were the very antithesis of Orwell's socialism. But does this make the jump from these British intellectual socialists to O'Brien any less preposterous?

There were two factors that distanced O'Brien from Shaw *et al.* The first was that, for all his talk, it was never likely that Shaw or any of his fellow Fabians would have had the stomach for the kind of action they championed in theory. The second was that, unlike O'Brien, Shaw and other British intellectuals of the Left were ideologically motivated. Some of them may indeed have been real or imagined sadists, just as some may have been insomniacs, or left-handed, but what characterised them and drove them on was ideology. O'Brien, on the other hand, was driven not by an ideology but a psychosis. His Hadley Chase-like picture of the future, unlike Shaw's garden city set out in detail in his élitist play *Major Barbara*,[82] represented pure sadism: 'a boot stamping on a human face – forever'.[83] O'Brien was no Fabian paternalist. When Winston Smith, acknowledging O'Brien's apparent intellectual ascendancy, proposed that the Inner Party ruled over society for its own good, from some kind of Shavian sense of social obligation, O'Brien responded by sending a bolt of electricity through Winston's body. He replied: 'We are not interested in the good of others; we are interested solely in power.'[84] The object of power was not some version of universal betterment imposed from above, or the attainment of any kind of utopia; 'the object of power is power'. And O'Brien went on to define power: 'Power is in inflicting pain and humiliation. Power is in tearing human minds to pieces and putting them together again in new shapes of your own choosing.'[85]

There are inconsistencies in O'Brien's position. For example, he told Winston that he was the last man in Europe, the guardian of the human spirit (that very spirit that Winston had believed the Party could never overcome). He made Winston look in the mirror. 'You are rotting away, you are falling to pieces. What are you? A bag of filth . . . Do you see that thing facing you? That is the last man . . .'[86] Yet he also claimed that 'the heretic, the enemy of society, will always be there, so that he can be defeated and humiliated over again'.[87] Was it conceivable that, unknown to Winston, O'Brien had been devoting seven years of his life to getting inside the minds of other last men? Surely not. After all, Winston tells us that O'Brien's mind contained his own. 'There was no idea that he had ever had, or could have that O'Brien had not long ago contained, examined and rejected.'[88] Theirs was clearly a special relationship. But the real weakness in the characterisation of O'Brien was that he simply did not ring true. Brutal regimes in every age and at every point of the compass have employed sadists to torture prisoners and to enforce their laws. Yet if we compare O'Brien to the two members of the Old Guard (the equivalent of the Inner Party) that we meet in Koestler's *Darkness at Noon*, neither, though they had been guilty of great brutality, was simply a sadist, and both had been motivated in their brutality by an ideological vision.[89] Even the Neanderthal Gletkin, a man with no scruples at all, used his power to attain ends that were essentially ideological. He had arranged to have peasants shot for trifles, because if he did not 'the whole country would come to a standstill'.[90] The very future of mankind depended upon the industrial success of the Soviet Union and no idle peasants were going to threaten that. None of these characters stretches our credulity the way that O'Brien does. Even the infamous Pol Pot was motivated by a vision and did not personally inflict torture on his abject victims.

In short, in portraying power as a kind of psychosis through the characterisation of O'Brien, Orwell leapt from the reality of an élitist pro-Russian British intelligentsia into a world of violence as graphic and as pointless as anything that Hadley Chase wrote. The picture that Orwell painted tells us nothing about his real enemies. Nor does it tell us much about power as a political concept. Isaac Deutscher declared that Orwell had plagiarised Zamyatin and dowsed the result in the 'mysticism of cruelty',[91] but if this had been all Orwell had done the book would never have lasted. Orwell had early castigated Burnham for equating power simply with force,[92] but he seemed to have forgotten the distinction himself. Steven Lukes identified one-, two- and three-dimensional power in his seminal work and warned against 'reductive and simplistic pictures of binary power relations'.[93] He contrasted power with 'the securing of compliance to domination', and we can easily see that O'Brien's exercise of power over Winston falls substantially into the latter category.

In most respects, Orwell's discussion of the nature of power is, in Lukes' terminology, one-dimensional. It fails to distinguish between power and domination, for example, as Gramschi did. Gramschi showed the limits of direct physical coercion *à la* O'Brien, when compared with power as generated through the combination of state propaganda and control of the various agents of civil society – the family, religion, education and so on – and above all, the media and advertising.[94] Marcuse, too, in his own iconic text of the late 1960s and 1970s, *One Dimensional Man*,[95] envisaged the modern totalitarian state exercising unlimited power through technology, consumerism and the media and (like Orwell) language. He saw this power as being able to indoctrinate and manipulate, to promote a false consciousness that was so inured as to be immune to invalidation and thus to be permanent.

Finally, on this subject it is worth pointing to Foucault's version of control mechanisms in the modern state, such as social welfare programmes, education, institutions treating mental illness, prisons, all of which seek to suppress 'deviancy' and to 'normalise' (Foucault's word) individuals.[96] Like Marcuse, Foucalt believed that these much more sophisticated aspects of power in the modern state were permanent features that tended towards totalitarian control. Orwell himself had criticised as unrealistic Aldous Huxley's picture of a future totalitarian society in *Brave New World*, likening it on one occasion to nothing more than a massive Riviera hotel.[97] Huxley had replied in a letter to Orwell upbraiding him for the primitiveness of his boot-on-the-face philosophy, his depiction of power as sadism.[98] Orwell was convinced that he and not Huxley better understood the real nature of power. For Orwell, power was primitive, brutally decisive and one-dimensional in its nature. In fact, his depiction of power in *Nineteen Eighty Four* has more in common with H. G. Wells' Dr Moreau's experimentation with live animals in the 'bath of pain'[99] than with the way power has been exercised by modern collectivist states. It is not surprising that Orwell's depiction of power is not discussed by Lukes at all. Orwell wrote of Jack London, an author whom he greatly admired, that he had a fascist streak in his character and was fascinated by cruelty: this was why he had been able to predict fascism.[100] Biographies of Orwell consistently show a similar sadistic streak, especially in his treatment of animals.[101] Perhaps it was this that gave Orwell greater insight into the mind of O'Brien than that of Shaw. Not only is O'Brien's account of the 'why?' of power simply unconvincing, but Winston's understanding of the 'how?' is seriously deficient.

5

I began this chapter with the admission that it would not be based on a major work. I want to conclude it by pointing out that, nevertheless, it is the clarity of Orwell's prose that obliges us to mull over the arguments concerning faith, morality and power that consumed him in his later years. The portrayal of Dorothy Hare is distinctly unconvincing, but her solution to the problem of her own loss of faith is not. The depiction of the generously angry Dickens and the discussion of his belief in ordinary people; the investigation of modern man's loss of faith, unforgettably captured in metaphor by the dissected wasp; the analysis of power in 'Miss Blandish' and *Nineteen Eighty Four*, all force themselves upon our attention not primarily through their inherent intellectual interest but through the uncompromising, often muscular and sometimes brutal quality of Orwell's prose.

We set out on a quest in this chapter to establish what Orwellian socialism was and what its underlying values were. We began by identifying reasons why many on the Left were unsympathetic towards Orwell, especially in respect of his alleged desertion from the colours of socialism. I sought to save him from his enemies by establishing a thematic consistency in his work that many do not recognise. Orwell was always a champion of the powerless and an enemy of the powerful, and he was able to theorise this disposition through his analysis of the consequences of imperialism and capitalism. In the process he contrived to construct what we called in Chapter 3 the decency myth, an idealisation of working-class values centred upon the notions of equality and common decency. He called the myth democratic socialism and remained unabashed in making this somewhat dubious link. This myth sustained Orwell through his harrowing wartime experiences in Spain. However, his time in Spain prompted Orwell to return with even greater confidence to his mistrust of the powerful. We could say that he created an 'indecency myth' to capture his increasing distaste for intellectuals generally and ideologists in particular. These were the twin poles that guided Orwell on his political odyssey through even the bleakest days of *Nineteen Eighty Four*. When he wrote in his diary 'if there is hope it lies with the proles', Winston reflected that this was both a 'mystical truth and a palpable absurdity',[102] and Orwell's pictures of proles in that book are as unflattering in some cases as they are flattering in others. O'Brien managed later to convince Winston that the proles would never revolt, not in a million years, and Orwell's fellow socialists might claim that this is where Winston finally betrayed his democratic socialism. But we should bear in mind that O'Brien also convinced Winston that two and two made five. Electric currents make compelling arguments. Before his capitulation to torture, Winston – and Orwell – held on to the decency myth, but only with difficulty. In fact, Orwell might have borrowed T. S. Eliot's lines to describe the small triumph of his ordinary people 'Who are undefeated/Because we have gone on trying'.[103] His proletariat had remained true to their values.

But we are left with a problem. It lies in the vague and inconsistent definition of those whose values Orwell championed. In *Wigan Pier* it was the northern industrial proletariat, particularly the miners, who were admired. Yet he made it clear that it was only the better-off working-class about whom he was writing.[104] The Brookers of this world received only his contempt. In *Coming Up for Air* it was the petit bourgeoisie whose values Bowling, and presumably Orwell, admired. Frequently, Orwell used the phrase 'the ordinary people', apparently to encompass these groups and perhaps others, but the only common characteristic of each group seems to have been their relative powerlessness. Even Orwell himself was aware of his loose usage, though he did nothing to tighten it.[105] If we were to conclude that Orwell's only hope was to give power to the powerless we might, with half an eye on Acton's dictum, want to make use of Bernard Shaw's criticism of such aspirations, that they represented a *reductio ad absurdum* of democratic socialism. In fact, we don't have to go to Shaw or even Acton. Orwell himself, when reviewing a book by the working-class author Jack Common, wrote: 'one is almost driven to the cynical conclusion that men are only decent when they are powerless'.[106]

Like all myths, then, Orwell's decency myth contained substantial contradictions, confusions and inadequacies, but perhaps it also contained a fundamental truth: that if there was any hope for a decent society based upon recast 'Christian' values, it lay with ordinary people. The word 'decency', it is true, has little political resonance, but it has a moral one. The judge in the film of Vidal's *Bonfire of the Vanities* berated his courtroom with, 'I'll tell you what justice is. Justice is the law. Law is man's feeble attempt to set down the principles of decency. And decency is not a deal, an angle, a contract or a hustle. Decency is . . . in your bones. Now you go home. Go home and be decent people.' About ten years after Orwell died, the revolutionary Ernesto 'Che' Guevara made a plea to his fellow middle-class medical students in Cuba that they could best learn what the values of the revolution were by getting to know ordinary people: they should live amongst them and imbibe their values.[107] Then they would understand. There is a long and honourable tradition of thinkers who found virtues in the lives of ordinary people, from Dickens, Herzen and Tolstoy back to Christ himself, and they included a number of self-proclaimed socialists. But what kind of socialist would this make Orwell?

We have already noted Crick's matter-of-fact classification, that Orwell was a Tribunite socialist.[108] This classification has an obvious virtue; we know what a Tribunite socialist is: someone on the left wing of the army of parliamentary socialism. Moreover, we know that Orwell worked for *Tribune*. Crick himself referred to Orwell as the Dr Johnson of the Tribunite Left,[109] a picture more vivid than useful, the equivalent of 'the Genghis Khan of Oxfam'. But Orwell was not greatly interested in parliamentary socialism. He became enthusiastic about the parliamentary Labour Party only when he believed that Stafford Cripps was about to take it over and turn it into a revolutionary force.[110] Newsinger, by contrast, rejected this classification and instead called Orwell a literary Trotskyite,[111] though it is never made explicit what this means. Newsinger's definition is: someone who debates the ideas of the revolutionary Left within a fictional framework. This is unhelpful; a fascist could do this. Let us try to make more sense of it for ourselves. Does the adjective qualify the noun and if so how? We might understand it to mean, for example, that Orwell was a Trotskyite but only in his writing, that is, not really a Trotskyite. Much more likely, Newsinger meant rather to convey that Orwell was both a Trotskyite and a writer. However, he says very little about Orwell as a writer and so we are simply not able to form any view as to what he thinks Orwell's being a writer and a Trotskyite signified that, say, being a professional wrestler and a Trotskyite might not. Neither does he define 'Trotskyite', and yet this has become one of those famous 'Humpty Dumpty' words, which means just what the user says it means. If Newsinger really means that Orwell was a left-wing writer and socialist who had sympathy with Trotsky's critique of Stalin's state socialism, then we might feel inclined to accept this as a rudimentary but recognisable portrait. After all, it cannot be inconsequential that Winston Smith's critique of Oceanian society is informed by Goldstein's *The Theory and Practice of Oligarchical Collectivism* (though we could hardly say that it shapes Winston's attitude). It is equally clear that Goldstein's book is modelled on Trotsky's *The Revolution Betrayed*, written in 1936. But there is no evidence that Orwell actually was a supporter of Trotsky. We know Orwell's aversion to '-isms', and anyway Orwell himself, in 1945, described Trotskyism as an essentially negative idea. Because they tended to be a persecuted minority, Trotskyites gave a false impression of being intellectually and morally superior to communists, he said, but in fact 'it is doubtful whether there is much difference'.[112]

An alternative view, and not a new one, is that Orwell is in fact not best thought of as a Tribunite, or a Trotskyite, but as an ethical socialist. My reading of Taylor and Bowker leads me to conclude that this is pretty much how they see Orwell, and from what I have written so far it might be thought that I too would be willing to classify Orwell in these terms. Certainly I would be willing to accept that ethical socialism was the camp that Orwell came closest to following, and in making this identification I could claim to be saving Orwell from his friends, such as Crick and Newsinger, as I promised earlier. But before going beyond this provisional recognition and proclaiming Orwell to be an ethical socialist, I intend first to avoid the hole into which I believe Newsinger fell, and to define my terms more fully than he did. Only then can we finally decide whether the description 'ethical socialist' is appropriate for Orwell. Only then and not before will we be in a position to contemplate the third and crucial objective of saving Orwell from himself.

8   Orwell's social and political thought

> The Kingdom of Heaven has somehow got to be brought on to the surface of the earth. We have got to be children of God, even though the God of the prayer book no longer exists.
>
> George Orwell, 'Notes on the Way', in Peter Davison's *The Complete Works of George Orwell*, Vol. 12 (London: Secker and Warburg, p. 126).

In this concluding chapter we shall begin exactly where Chapter 7 left off, by considering the claim that Orwell is best viewed as an ethical socialist, and there are clearly good *prima facie* grounds for advancing such a claim. In their book *English Ethical Socialism*,[1] Dennis and Halsey selected Orwell as one of six champions of that branch of socialism. However, an early indication that the classification may not be as tight as we might have hoped comes from the authors' choice of ethical socialism's other heroes, St. Thomas More, William Cobbett, L. T. Hobhouse, T. H. Marshall and R. H. Tawney. Only one of these would have a serious claim to be any kind of mainstream socialist. But Dennis and Halsey are nothing if not ingenious; they have discovered a political tradition that appears to unite these men and it goes beyond the ideology of any socialist political party. The keystone of that tradition, they claim, rests 'above all [on] the good sense of ordinary people'.[2]

It stresses the importance of a degree of individual autonomy and regards the exercise of choice at the personal level as crucial to ethical socialism. Choice brings into play the individual's conscience, that badge of what they call the Judaeo-Christian moral inheritance that Winston Smith fought to sustain. Only by allowing the full participation of the individual could communities be considered democratic and socialist. The banner of such a brand of socialism would surely be inscribed with words of the eponymous cleric from William Morris' *A Dream of John Ball*:[3] 'Fellowship is heaven', said the hedge priest, 'and the lack of fellowship is hell. Fellowship is life and the lack of fellowship is death, and the deeds that ye do upon the earth, it is for fellowship's sake that ye do them.'[4] The word that Dennis and Halsey use to characterise ethical socialism, however, is not Morris' 'fellowship', which is of Norse origin and a word that ordinary people would use, but the Latinate word 'fraternity', which intellectuals would be likely to use, and which many, Orwell included, would have thought gave it less force. Fraternity, they say, is 'the ethical socialist's *sine qua non*'.[5] On the one hand, ethical socialism believes in the efficacy of a social commitment which would allow for the allocation of tasks in a society as the outcome of rational uncoerced exchange (to each according to need; from each according to ability); and on the other hand, ethical socialism 'abhors idleness and is suspicious of intellectuals'.[6] But fraternity and liberty are sustainable only in conjunction with equality. Dennis and Halsey quote approvingly from *The Magnificat*: the mighty were to be put down from their seat and the humble and meek were to be exalted. They might equally profitably have turned to Morris' Father John Ball again. 'What shall ye lack when ye lack masters?' he queried, 'Ye shall not lack for the fields ye have tilled, not the houses ye have built, not the cloth ye have woven; all these shall be yours and whatsoever ye will of all that the earth beareth.'[7] Morris, like Orwell, longed for a society in which there would be no masters and no masters' men.

In short, ethical socialists believe in a non-ideological socialism that is rooted in the values of ordinary people, especially those of fraternity or fellowship. These values, our authors claim, have traditionally provided the bedrock on which much of the thinking of the British Labour Party was built. It is not difficult, in the light of the conclusions we drew in Chapter 7, to understand why Dennis and Halsey should have chosen Orwell as one of the champions of this ethical socialism. They note the emphasis that Orwell placed on terms like decency, equality and justice, which he, like they, understood as representing a personal ethic; they note too that decency is associated most directly with the values of ordinary people. Orwell recognised, they said, that:[8]

> The good society must have its foundation in a commitment to decency amongst its members. The code of conduct denoted by that essential word – love of truth, respect for persons, and hatred of injustice and inequality – must then run as the working principle of all human institutions.

But historically, as Orwell himself noted, those in power have always betrayed the people and their values.[9]

> It would seem that what you get over and over again is a movement of the proletariat which is promptly canalised and betrayed by astute people at the top, and then the growth of a new governing class. The one thing that never arrives is equality. The mass of people never get the chance to bring their innate decency into the control of affairs. . . .

This ethical socialism has long held currency in British political debate, but Dennis and Halsey's attempt constitutes one of only a few actually to define it. Now I have no quarrel with Dennis and Halsey's definition as far as it goes, but to my mind it is not rigorous or detailed enough and does not focus as it really should on the one historical period when ethical socialism was a political force to be reckoned with in Britain. They do well roundly to refute the loose assumption of many on the Left, that ethical socialism constituted what remained when scientific or state socialism was removed from the socialist tradition; that it was synonymous with either reformist or utopian socialism.[10] Equally often, the authors note, it is used as a synonym for Christian Socialism. Strictly speaking it is none of these. Many ethical socialists were, indeed, Christians, and many were reformers or utopians rather than revolutionaries or practical men and women of the world, but by no means all. We need to be more precise if we wish to know enough about ethical socialists to judge whether Orwell was one.

1

The obvious place to start the quest for precision is with the growth of the ethical socialist movement of late Victorian and Edwardian times, a growth energised by the visit to Britain of the American land reformer Henry George. George aroused wide interest amongst British intellectuals of all classes, who attended his lectures and read his famous pamphlet *Progress and Poverty*. Amongst the intellectuals who met in London to discuss George's ideas was H. M. Hyndman, one of not many in Britain who had read Marx's *Das Kapital*. He found it easy to persuade those with enough German or French to try Marx, and a number who did became converts to socialism, if not always to the Marxist version. Amongst them were Bernard Shaw and William Morris. For Shaw, Marx's message was principally that governing was a science and that socialists should study it. The working-class was the victim of capitalism, disadvantaged in every way and so to saddle the cause of progress with the necessity of securing working-class support was nothing more than infantile romanticism. Morris, on the other hand, as a founder of the Arts and Crafts movement, took a very different moral from Marx. Capitalism was doomed and though it might take a violent revolution to prise government from the capitalists' grasp, and necessitate a short period of strong central government to reshape the nation's affairs thereafter, there would follow what Engels called[11] a withering away of the state and a flourishing of smaller, self-governing communities. For both Shaw and Morris, economic and social equality was a prime goal, but only Morris sought equality of power too, through decentralising and not centralising government. Morris' view of socialism, like Orwell's, was rooted in the values of ordinary people and sought, with their help, to establish a society based on fellowship. Morris' influence was great, not only in the field of political thought but in its direct application to forms of artistic endeavour. The Arts and Crafts movement worldwide was rooted in the Morrissonian concept of community. Other thinkers, such as Edward Carpenter[12] and J. Bruce and Katherine Glazier,[13] also played important roles in the development of ethical socialism.

Amongst those who listened to and subsequently read Morris, and was greatly moved, was the journalist Robert Blatchford. He decided to establish, with the help of his brother and a few friends, a socialist weekly *The Clarion*. This paper was and remains the best example of successful socialist journalism in Britain, and, until the First World War, was highly influential. The socialism it proclaimed was Morrissonian ethical socialism. The first leading article that Blatchford published was markedly Orwellian. It had this to say: 'The policy of *The Clarion* is a policy of humanity, a policy not of party, sect or creed; but of justice, reason and mercy.'[14] After the editorial board moved to London in 1895, circulation grew steadily to over 80,000 by 1908.[15] It had no rival. Blatchford's socialism was not dogmatic or sectional, but rather spoke to a way of living based on the principles associated with fellowship. These principles soon bore fruit in a variety of working-class activities. The first was the Clarion Cycle Club, formed in Birmingham in 1894 to 'combine the pleasures of cycling with the propaganda of Socialism'.[16] For twenty years these Clarion cyclists, known as the Scouts, spread socialism around Britain, though chiefly the north and Midlands of England and central Scotland. Their task became more important after the publication of Blatchford's *Merrie England*,[17] a book purporting to comprise a series of letters to one John Smith of Oldham, a hard-headed working man, to convince him of the case for socialism. This book eventually sold over two million copies, including editions in Danish, Dutch, German, Hebrew, Italian, Norwegian, Spanish and Welsh. It was justly said in Labour Party circles that for every socialist converted by Marx, Blatchford converted a hundred. In addition to the Scouts, there were Clarion Vocal Unions, socialist brass bands, choirs, Clarion dramatic societies (whose stated aim was to develop dramatic art and to propagate socialist ideas), camera clubs, handicraft groups, swimming clubs, ramblers and a number of other sports groups. Finally, there were Cinderella Clubs, created by Blatchford himself, to entertain the children of the urban poor and to provide them with a cheap summer holiday in the country. The whole structure of this working-class movement represented the embodiment of fellowship; represented the effort to build socialism into the structure of working-class and lower-middle-class life; represented the embodiment, in short, of ethical socialism. It represented the very flowering of ethical socialism and constituted an expression of the principles of which Orwell was later to become a champion.

The Clarion Movement was not the only popular socialist movement. Another such was the Socialist Sunday School Movement founded in Glasgow in the 1890s. These Sunday Schools were not specifically Christian in character. Socialist and more generally revolutionary songs and not hymns were sung, including the *Red Flag* and the *Marseillaise*. If not Christian, the teaching was ethical in nature and it sought to put emphasis on the social significance of morality. In addition to the Sunday schools, there were the Labour and Socialist churches, a movement begun in Manchester in 1891 by John Trevor, a former Unitarian minister. Trevor and his followers regarded themselves as Christians and socialists who believed that the Labour movement should be the driving force in establishing the 'Kingdom of God upon Earth', and indeed many leading figures in the Labour movement were active in the Labour Church. In fact, the first meeting of the Independent Labour Party in 1893 was held in the Bradford Labour Church building. This brings us finally to the Christian Socialist Movement itself, founded by a group of Christian apologists including the theologian F. D. Maurice,[18] Charles Kingsley[19] and Thomas Hughes.[20] Maurice's *The Kingdom of Christ* provided a theological rationale for Christian Socialism. He argued that politics and religion were inseparable and that the Church should involve itself fully in confronting issues of social justice. Their influence has always been, and indeed still is, considerable in Labour Party circles.[21] All in all, then, ethical socialism struck deep roots in the lives and values of the ordinary people. Although none of the groups mentioned above considered themselves to be party creations, they gave general support to various socialist groups and especially the Independent Labour Party. Their primary aim, if we may generalise, was to establish a bedrock of socialist values amongst ordinary people, on which a socialist state might later be built. In short, their aim was just the same as Orwell's. But they failed.

In attempting to account for this failure, a number of theories have been put forward. The first, the standard explanation, is that the socialist movements were hijacked by the trade unions and manoeuvred into the struggle for parliamentary representation.[22] A second explanation suggests that in fact the decline of ethical socialism owed more to the advent and popularity of professional soccer, of the music hall and the associated consumption of alcohol, of the seaside holidays and of the cinema. All took the general public's mind off the prospect of the Kingdom of God on earth.[23] No doubt both these developments were influential, but the most decisive influence on the decline of ethical socialism was the obvious one, the First World War. The working -class was bitterly divided between the claims of international brotherhood and those of patriotism. On Christmas Eve 1914, British and German troops sang carols together and organised a soccer game. Perhaps that was the last gesture of a civilisation in which hope was more normal than despair and cynicism, an age in which many ordinary people believed not only in the desirability but the practicability of progress towards an equal and just society. It was very hard to believe anything of the sort after the horrors of the trenches that had brutalised so many of those whom they did not kill.

I have given a reasonably full account of the ethical socialist movement for two principal reasons. First was to show that, Dennis and Halsey notwithstanding, ethical socialism was not, of its nature, some abstract political theory that could hold together thinkers as diverse as R. H. Tawney and St. Thomas More, but a practical form of socialism which, though it failed in its objective to transform society from the bottom, nevertheless left its mark on British working-class life, especially in the north of England, and on the general development of British socialism. The second was to give us something against which to measure the extent to which Orwell could be considered an ethical socialist, and it is to this task that we now turn.

We have noted, as we have gone along, the many similarities between Orwell's thinking and the main ideas of the ethical socialists. They are fundamental. He saw socialism as primarily an instrument of justice. In writing about the socialism of working-class people, Orwell called it 'a body of belief, one might almost say a way of life'.[24] This had been exactly the view of Blatchford, and he did much more than Orwell to make it a reality. It is therefore almost unbelievable to report that nowhere in the corpus of his work did Orwell use the phrase 'ethical socialism'. Nowhere did he show any interest in or knowledge of the various parts of the movement of ethical socialism that I have identified. Orwell wrote extensively about the northern proletariat but he said nothing about any of the activities that made up the Clarion movement or Socialist Sunday Schools or the Labour Church movement, and yet these institutions and activities helped to shape the northern working-class and the form of socialism that it supported. It is true that the only political movement that Orwell ever joined was the ILP, proud of its ethical socialist connections. It is also true that he distanced himself from the movement because of its pacifism, but this was later on. He worked in a bookshop owned by the Westropes, prominent ILP members. As a member himself, Orwell had attended *Adelphi*-sponsored summer retreats in which discussions of the Christian Socialist legacy had frequently been prominent.[25] Moreover, he wrote for A. J. Orage's *New Age*, a champion of ethical socialism, especially in its early years, and for *The Adelphi*, which under Middleton Murry had become a mouthpiece for the ILP.[26] We can only conclude that avoiding any reference to ethical socialism was a conscious choice. He did, however, recount his 'sensations of horror' when attending his first ILP branch meeting in London. 'Are *these* mangy little beasts . . . the champions of the working-class? For every person there, male and female, bore the worst stigmata of sniffish middle-class superiority.'[27]

As for the great names of ethical socialism, they hardly received a mention. In one review, Morris' *News from Nowhere* was considered to be a useful book because it took the reader beyond the present and immediate future,[28] but elsewhere Orwell criticised the book for confusing socialism's goal. Morris' utopian society was static, like Wells', which Orwell described destructively as 'a hygienic garden suburb infested by nude schoolmarms'.[29] On Morris' *Nowhere* he was equally decisive: 'Everyone is kind and reasonable, all the upholstery comes from Liberty's and the impression left behind is of a watery melancholy.' Morris himself was dismissed as a 'dull, empty windbag'.[30] Orwell's spiteful anti-utopianism earned him a criticism from one reader: 'George – please keep off these vast and untrue generalisations and red herrings.'[31] Though not using the phrase, it is clear that Orwell partly had ethical socialists in mind in his devastating critique of middle-class socialists in *Wigan Pier*. In a letter to Jack Common, he attacked those 'eunuch types with a vegetarian smell who go about spreading sweetness and light' and see the working-class, ideally, as all teetotallers and washed behind the ears, people who read Edward Carpenter or 'some other pious sodomite'.[32] Moreover, although Orwell knew Tawney socially, there is no analysis of any of his writings anywhere in Orwell's work. What we can say with a reasonable degree of certainty, then, is that Orwell did not see himself as an ethical socialist, even though he chided fellow socialists who, with their eyes fixed on economic matters, had proceeded on the (presumably erroneous) assumption that 'man has no soul';[33] even though he himself argued that the real goal of socialism was not happiness but human brotherhood;[34] even though he wrote admiringly of German and Austrian socialists that they had tried to build a socialism that constituted 'a way of life, a moral attitude, and not simply a political and economic theory'.[35]

I suggested earlier that we should also consider what, if anything, Orwell contributed to the development of ethical socialism. It seems that we must address this question at two levels. At the theoretical level, we surely have to conclude that Orwell contributed nothing to that development. We can hardly help but recognise that his central concern, working-class socialism – what I have called the decency myth – was also the concern of ethical socialists, but it cannot be said that Orwell developed this theory in any important sense. Indeed, quite the contrary: in introducing the concept of the 'ordinary man' without adequately defining it, Orwell only exposed a lack of clarity in his thinking about ethical socialist issues.[36] Blatchford, like Orwell, became disillusioned with the ordinary man, however defined, and wondered whether attributing their politics to concepts like decency was not entirely misplaced. Orwell had correspondence, only part of which remains, with a Christian Socialist, a Jesuit, Fr. Martindale. Martindale had written expressing his support for the moral stance Orwell had taken in *Wigan Pier* but wondered whether the concepts of liberty and justice could not be further 'crystallised'; he offered his help as a philosopher.[37] But this was not Orwell's game, as Harold Laski forcefully observed, noting that Orwell's 'basic error is the belief that we all mean the same things by liberty and justice. Most emphatically we do not.'[38] Nothing appears to have come of the correspondence with Fr. Martindale. Christopher Small was more dismissive of Orwell's 'decency', which he described as nothing more than a device to block off further ethical discussion.[39] In his essay 'What is Socialism?', Orwell had the opportunity to connect his thinking to any tradition of socialism that he chose. He came closest to ethical socialism, recognising socialism's origins as a doctrine amongst the early Christians and even amongst the slaves of Rome,[40] and pursuing it through the millenarian movements of the English Civil War, through Rousseau and William Morris, up to the 'Christian Reformers' of his own times. Underneath this tradition lay the belief that 'human nature is fairly decent and is capable of infinite development'.[41] This is by no means an incisive analysis of socialism, and though it shows some sympathy with ethical or more precisely Christian socialism, in no sense could it be said to represent a detailed exposition, or even a general awareness of the spectrum of that tradition.

At the second, and to my mind the deeper, level, it is clear that Orwell contributed substantially to our understanding of ethical socialism because of the sheer power of the prose in which he depicted or discussed the central ideas of ethical socialism, even though he never identified them as such. Neither *News from Nowhere*, nor Blatchford's *The Sorcery Shop*, nor Carpenter's *The Promised Land* have had the impact that Orwell's imaginative writing has enjoyed. If this argument is accepted, then it leads us back to the fundamental point that I have argued throughout this analysis: that the most significant aspect of Orwell's political thought was the product of his power as a writer. Now it is time to grasp the full implication of this argument.

I want to suggest that Orwell is not adequately described by either of the terms 'Tribunite' or 'Trotskyite', however loosely employed, or even, as the above argument demonstrates, by the term 'ethical socialist'; in fact, he is best understood as not being primarily any kind of socialist or political thinker at all, but rather as a moralist. I suggest, moreover, that this idea of Orwell as a moralist rather than a political thinker fits better with the notion with which we began and which we should never lose sight of; that Orwell was first and last an imaginative writer. Moralist and writer – two sides of the same coin. In one way this claim, if granted, would constitute a break with the tradition of Orwell scholarship, which chiefly contests the nature and consistency of his politics. In another way, it would do nothing so radical, constituting only a readjustment to our focus. I take a moralist to be a writer who is chiefly interested in the values and behaviour of individuals and groups rather than in institutions, systems or events. As a moralist his interest in politics would therefore be only indirect, long-term and general in nature. This was just how Orwell saw Dickens, and I think it is appropriate to see Orwell in much the same kind of light. Although he was critical of Dickens in many respects, Orwell clearly recognised much in Dickens' approach to which he was himself instinctively drawn. His basic concern, like Dickens', was with human conduct. If we look for keywords in Orwell's writing, decency is the one that leaps out at the reader time and again. But his writing is replete with notions such as brotherhood, fair-play, justice, and honesty. Of the values he championed, only equality had an immediate political resonance, but even equality was almost invariably used as a moral rather than a political signifier. Orwell's interest, like Dickens', was not so much in political institutions or indeed outcomes as in human conduct. A. J. Ayer said of Orwell: 'Though he held no religious belief himself, there was something of a religious element in George's socialism.' He saw socialism, Ayer continued, as primarily an instrument of justice.[42] It is true that in most of his writing Orwell's focus was on the nature of political life and his hopes and fears for its future, but specific political agendas are very few indeed and usually confused. In *The English People*,[43] for example, where he probably comes closest to providing such an agenda, Orwell urged Britain to fulfil its political mission by breeding faster, working harder, living more simply and getting rid of class distinctions. 'We need, too, to be less centralised', he added, and then immediately argued for the equalisation of wealth and the teaching of a national accent ('maybe a modification of Cockney'), policies that could only be pursued by a strong (and in the case of the latter project, demented) central government. Elsewhere he wrote that it was 'obvious' that industry would have to be centralised to achieve socialist goals.[44] The reader will look in vain here and any-where for a coherent strategy for a socialist government or even a coherent exposition of socialist doctrine. When the Christian socialist Fr. Martindale had sought to draw him out, to crystallise his themes of decency, justice and equality, he simply was not interested.

If we contrast Dickens, or indeed Orwell himself, to Bernard Shaw, we get a clear picture of the difference between a moralist and a political writer. Shaw gave a considerable amount of time to public speaking, an activity that did not come naturally to him at first. He was also an active St Pancras vestryman; indeed, his political accomplish-ments included being instrumental in the installation of the first public urinals for women in Britain.[45] Shaw was a political man through and through. This passion for politics is to be found in nearly all his plays, each of which contains a substantial preface setting out the political issues with which the play deals and spelling out in some detail the relevant political theories. Shaw had a formidable grasp of Marxist and Jevonian economics, of Nietzsche's thought, of the vitalist school of philosophy from Schopenhauer to Bergson. Orwell had no comparable interest in theories. Moreover, the inconsistencies and shortcomings that we have discovered in Orwell's politics become somewhat less disabling if we view Orwell as primarily a writer and a moralist. If we see Orwell's work as principally an exhortation to base our behaviour, and hence our institutions and policies, on a value system that I have called the decency myth and he called democratic socialism (even if he did not himself show us how this might be done), then he would have achieved what he set out to achieve.

If we were to ask a political theorist a question about an aspect of human nature or of a political institution, we would have the right to expect some kind of philosophical or socioeconomic analysis in the answer. Were we to ask a writer a similar question, we would expect the response to be: 'Let me tell you a story.' And stories lend themselves to moral exhortation; indeed, some have said that is what they are.[46] When he was drawing his essay on Dickens to its conclusion, Orwell wrote:[47]

> That is the difference between being a moralist and a politician. He has no constructive suggestions, not even a grasp of the nature of the society he is attacking, only an emotional perception that something is wrong. All he can finally say is, 'Behave decently . . .'

I do not think that Orwell's approach was significantly different.

Now I do not wish for a moment to be thought of as implying that Orwell himself would have accepted this argument. I have no doubt that he saw himself as a political writer; thought of himself as much more sharply focused on political and economic issues than Dickens. It is for this reason that, in advancing the proposition that we see Orwell as a writer and a moralist, and not a political theorist or writer, that I can justify a claim to be fulfilling the third task I set myself in the previous chapter: to save Orwell from himself.

2

I said earlier that if we took Orwell to be a writer and a moralist rather than a political thinker, this would both constitute a break with the tradition of Orwell scholarship and from another perspective amount only to a shift of focus. To throw more light onto this apparent contradiction, we need to know what it is that distinguishes a writer from, say, a political thinker or historian; we need to get a hold on what literature is. Auden indicated in very general terms what it is that distinguishes a writer's analysis from that of a political theorist or a political scientist. He wrote: 'In grasping the character of a society, as in judging the character of an individual, no documents, statistics, "objective" measurements can ever compete with the single intuitive glance.'[48] This does little more, though, than point us in the right direction; we need to be more rigorous. Kenneth Quin debated this issue in *How Literature Works*.[49] 'We expect poets or novelists to be particular about the words they use. The more particular they are . . . the better the novel or poem is likely to be. But there is more to it than that. A bad novel is still a novel of sorts . . . all such texts have something in common: they work in a particular way . . . it is because they work that reading them becomes a literary experience.'[50] We can distinguish between literary texts and other forms of literature (such as works of political thought or history) as follows: they occupy different places in our lives. Quin offers the analogy of cars and trucks, for example; we expect different things from them, we put them to different uses. Recognising a text as literature means recognising that we are being offered an aesthetic experience. We tend to approach a novel with different expectations than those with which we might approach, say, a gardening manual, or indeed a work of history or political thought. We put them to different uses. Dr Johnson was disparagingly clear about the differences he recognised between literary and historical works.[51]

Creative or imaginative writing is first and foremost an aesthetic enterprise. It adopts a position to which one is invited, cajoled even, to react. Imaginative literature constitutes the reorganisation of the writer's experience into a body of words and ideas that can be said to provide an expression of both art and of life that is essentially true to experience. But we should also remember that, as William Golding observed, this kind of 'truth' is essentially artificial, because life itself is formless.[52] The writer discovers an ontology where none existed, and imbues experience with a value of his or her own choosing. Literary boundaries are neither as easily demarcated nor as clearly distinguishable as Quin seems to think (nor are trucks and cars, for that matter; cars that pretend to be trucks are currently very fashionable), but he is surely right to want to distinguish between the aims of creative or imaginative writing and those of other forms of writing. His principal argument stands: recognising a text as literature means recognising that reading it will offer readers an aesthetic experience. Reading imaginative literature is a process of interpretation and what the reader takes from a novel is unlikely to be just what the author intended. As a consequence of subsequent historical or cultural events, the reader cannot help taking a sense of a word or phrase that the author could not have intended; history alters the meaning and significance of words and phrases. And not just history: as Eagleton has argued, the reader has a 'socially structured way of seeing the world'.[53] Literary works, he goes on, 'are not mysteriously inspired, or explicable simply in terms of their author's psychology. They are forms of perception . . . and as such they have a relation to the dominant way of seeing the world which is the "social mentality" or ideology of the age.'[54]

So writers and readers alike are at least to some degree prisoners of their own time, of their own history, of their own social system and indeed of other forces such as religion or ethnicity. Some literary theorists in the 1950s held that there were no novels, only novelists, and that all readings were misreadings, though some were more interesting than others. But there is an obvious logical contradiction here: if there is no 'official' reading, there can be no misreading. If everything is open to individual interpretation and any reader's interpretation is as valid as the author's, then Hirsch is right: there really can be no inherent difference between a page of *Paradise Lost* and a Rorschach blot.[55] Perhaps we can agree that there can never be a completely 'right' way of reading a novel, but there can certainly be any number of wrong ways. We are not free agents but 'have to come to terms with the restraints the text itself imposes'.[56] It is clear that writers think and write within a particular historical and conceptual framework that is unlikely to be the same as the reader's, and so the reader's perspective will place a different emphasis on the author's intentions within the text. Reading *The Road to Wigan Pier*, for example, we, unlike Orwell, will have *Animal Farm* and *Nineteen Eighty Four*, not to mention the subsequent history of the period, to inform our understanding of Orwell and our interpretation of his intentions. But to claim seriously that one may interpret a work of imaginative literature simply as one chooses is a piece of nonsense. Quin is right to insist that 'in every sentence of a novel or a poem, if we know how to read it, we feel the speaking voice of the writer' (what Steiner called their 'real presence'). A text, then, for Quin, could be said to have a will of its own, to have what Umberto Eco referred to as an intention, and we must strive to comprehend that intention.

That intention refers to an act of communication, certainly, but of what? The intention does not seem to be concerned primarily with the communication of factual information but rather with the sharing of an experience. Orwell made just this point in his essay 'Why I Write',[57] when he spoke about the 'desire to share an experience which one feels is valuable and ought not to be missed'. For Orwell, and indeed for all imaginative writers, these experiences represented a fusion of the aesthetic and political. 'My starting point is always a feeling of partisanship, a sense of injustice', he wrote.[58] If he wishes to communicate that feeling successfully, he knows that it must be transmitted through a shared aesthetic experience: 'so long as I remain alive and well I shall continue to feel strongly about prose style'. He continues 'Animal Farm was the first book in which I tried, with full consciousness of what I was doing, to fuse political purpose and artistic purpose into one whole.'[59] Looking back through his works, he continued, he thought that it was where he lacked what he called a political purpose that he wrote lifeless books and 'was betrayed into purple passages, sentences without meaning, decorative adjectives and humbug generally'.[60] Orwell's aesthetic purpose was to produce what he called 'prose like a windowpane', but this was not principally to expose a body of fact or information but an experience – the experience of injustice. He went on to talk about communicating a 'pleasure in the impact of one sound on another, in the firmness of good prose or the rhythm of a good story' or a 'perception of beauty in the external world'. The aesthetic nature of this experience is crucial. 'Insight into the human condition in the absence of any special ability to create with words', said Quin, 'is clumsy, if possible at all.'[61]

Imaginative writers, then, are concerned to communicate an experience rather than to transmit a body of information, and for this to be successful the experience has to be a shared aesthetic one. It may be argued that other writers – the best historians and a few of the best philosophers, for example – are similarly committed. But their primary task is to present and explain facts or ideas. Historians, however eloquently and empathetically they may write, would simply cease to be read if their account of events proved unreliable or their judgements seriously flawed; philosophers, especially political philosophers, would soon be forgotten if their theories were demonstrably inconsistent. But the imaginative writer is concerned with what might be thought of as different kinds of 'truths'; we might say that their concern was to be true-to-experience. We discussed Orwell's Burmese essays, 'A Hanging' and 'Shooting an Elephant', for example. Were they authentic, in the sense of true accounts of actual events? We concluded that this was not the most important consideration, and that Orwell had more important fish to fry. He wanted to communicate an experience of the destructive nature of imperialism; this was far more important than historical authenticity. This suggests that the stories could be both phoney and yet authentic, untrue and yet true.

Truth in this context seems to be a property of statements concerning human experience. What gives a work literary force is that this experiential truth is expressed aesthetically. Self-evidently what we might call truth-to-experience (the truth of 'A Hanging', for example) is not the same thing as factual truth. A literary account may contain factual statements that are demonstrably false, and other factual statements that are true, but nevertheless tangential or even irrelevant to the writer's main purpose. E. M. Forster claimed that it is the *internal consistency* of a work that makes it true to experience. When we enter the world of literature, he said, we begin to inhabit 'a universe that only answers to its own laws, supports itself, internally coheres, and has a new standard of truth'. A work of literature, then, is 'true if it hangs together'.[62] On the other hand, if such a work, though apparently coherent and internally consistent, bore no relation at all to the readers' experience, how could they possibly make a judgement on its 'truth'? What measure or model could they use except their own experience?

How can we codify truth-to-experience? We can say that a novel, for example, though it might not convey truth in the sense of presenting verifiable factual evidence, might nevertheless give us important information about human experience. The significance of this potentiality becomes clear as soon as we acknowledge that some general statements about human experience cannot easily be stated objectively, and the whole point of turning to imaginative literature is 'to convey by illustration a general truth that cannot be stated explicitly'.[63] Auerbach's claim, that in conveying general social truths literature had 'taken over the methods and duties of science',[64] is nevertheless an exaggeration, and Althusser is more modest and more accurate in asserting that whereas science gives us knowledge, art gives us experience. But all the same, this experiential truth provides an important dimension to our full understanding of history and politics. When John Barrell explored the ideas of experience and literary truth, he too spoke of 'truth to experience' and implied that a fictional experience was only valid (true) if it resembled an actual experience. This would not make 'A Hanging' untrue (even if we assume that Orwell had *not* participated in the event) because he was reflecting the actual (true) experience of imperialism, in which such events regularly occurred. Walter Benjamin argued that the whole purpose of narrative was to communicate and share such experiences.[65] Indeed, a literary work could be said to succeed largely to the extent that it represented or corresponded with experiences which we have had ourselves, or with which we are vicariously familiar, and so helps us better to understand those experiences. There is more to be said, though. A literary account of an experience might pass the test of authenticity and be expressed in an aesthetically pleasing form, but we still expect something more. We expect insight! In Tolstoy's description of a public execution by guillotine, for example, he spoke of understanding what was happening 'not with my mind but my whole being'. It was this experience that he sought to convey, and he wanted also to provide the reader with an insight into what was 'really' happening. Barrell suggests that to judge a text's truth-to-experience is, after all, 'the same thing as to judge its value', but surely such a judgement would encompass more than that truth-to-experience: it would encompass insight. In the full sense, experiential truth consists of a successful attempt to encapsulate an understanding of some important aspect of human experience and to make a statement about it. Such literary truths might possess a veracity and significance, which both the elaboration of theory or the accumulation of factually supportive statements might not possess. History seeks accuracy and is based upon verifiable evidence. Political thought or theory seeks above all consistency and relevance in explication. Both are, to some extent, localised in space and time: not so imaginative literature. This is not to imply that all imaginative writers are careless of factual truths. Dickens, Kingsley or Gaskell, for example, attempted to convey truths to their audiences about the evils of social conditions in England that, as far as they were concerned, were both experiential and factual (indeed, Gaskell said apropos *Mary Barton*: 'I'm sure I *believe* I wrote the truth'), but their themes had wider and long-term moral and political significance. Other imaginative writers might manipulate factual truths for moral and aesthetic purposes, as we saw Orwell do in *Wigan Pier*, and yet still be, in a deeper sense, true to experience. Imaginative writers, as Sartre argued, write for all people of all times. They strive after truths of their own but they want, above all, to make them available to us all. Eagleton might argue that even Gaskell's 'truth' was ideological in the Marxist sense, but this is surely not a problem. Readers would reinterpret Gaskell in terms of their own ideological experience and accept, modify or reject it accordingly.

A literary text, according to Quin, is the product of a decision: to tell us certain things and not to tell us others.[66] This decision, he continued, must be a *moral* one because it reflects the conscious reorganisation of experience so as to make a clearer and more insightful statement about some aspect of reality. Unlike political thinkers or philosophers, imaginative writers do not always put their cards on the table; but they do have a game plan all the same. Some profess no moral authority, though even to say this much is clearly to adopt implicitly a moral position. Mordecai Richler did not beat about the bush: 'every serious writer is primarily a moralist and only incidentally an entertainer'.[67] Whilst it is unarguable that some writers are more 'serious', more concerned to influence us through their insights than others, the primary expertise of all is with words. We see an imaginative work as part of some philosophical and literary tradition, and knowledge of that tradition tends to shape the way we think about it. Orwell's tradition was fundamentally a moralistic one; reading Orwell might lead us to 'see life with a new clarity [because] our insight has been sharpened, our understanding of the human condition subjected to a significant renewal'.[68] This is what is meant by the identification of Orwell as primarily a writer and a moralist.

Before continuing, it is worth tracing once again the implications of stressing Orwell's status as a writer and a moralist. When he was engaged in creating a work of literature, Orwell was at his most incisive and influential. But as we have seen, he also wrote innumerable essays and reviews and in these, though his passionate concern for the meaning and structure of language would have added differing degrees of aesthetic value, the more general kinds of consideration concerning imaginative literature that we have been discussing would not necessarily apply. That is why, in the corpus of this study, I have tried to distinguish between those pieces of writing that are primarily works of imaginative literature and pieces that are primarily journalism. I have tended to treat the more obviously factual writings on their own terms, which is to say as straightforward contributions to moral or political debate, and not as works of imaginative literature. The boundary is unclear, as I have acknowledged, but it exists and is important.

3

Our final challenge is to attempt to frame a conclusion to this study of Orwell. If I have been critical of some of the central ideas of Orwell's social and political thought, it was primarily because I did not really think it best to understand it as political thought at all. If we take Orwell as a political thinker, then, immediately, basic shortcomings, inconsistencies and apparently irresolvable tensions appear, but if we shift our focus, a different picture emerges. In categorising Orwell as a moralist and a writer, I do not wish for a moment to suggest that he was not, therefore, a socialist sympathiser or, more simply, a socialist. But what I want to stress is that he approached socialism, not as a spokesman for this or that ideological stratum or substratum, but as a moralist and a writer, and that is how he should be considered. A similar case is advanced, I believe, by the following. In response to an article that Orwell had written for *The New Republic* in 1941, one American respondent replied, 'I think it important that your readers understand that George Orwell is expressing only his own opinions. From what facts they are deduced, or on what philosophy based, I am unable to discover.'[69]

Though he wrote with passion and conviction for what he took to be justice, it needs to be said that as an individual Orwell was opinionated, frequently very wrong in his judgements about people and events, prejudiced, often ill-informed, misogynistic, homophobic and sadistic. He was abruptly dismissive of opponents', and indeed allies', views and his reputation for integrity as a writer, not always well founded, was frequently opportunistically traded on. In a letter to a clergyman who had taken exception to Orwell's criticism of Gandhi, for example, Orwell had declared that pacifism was always to be found in maritime countries and thus there was a quite substantial pacifist movement in Japan but, by extension, no room for the pacific policy of *satyagraha*, or civil disobedience, in non-maritime India. Far from being considered to pose a real threat to the future of British rule through his active pacifism, he went on, Gandhi was, in fact, seen by the authorities as 'one of the government's right-hand men'. Orwell concluded this gallimaufry of piffle with the stern admonition: 'I know what I am talking about – I used to be an officer in the Imperial Police.'[70] In the same year, Orwell assured his American readers of *Partisan Review* that 'very soon we shall all be in uniform or doing some kind of compulsory labour and probably eating communally'.[71] A year earlier he had suggested that *Brave New World*, though a brilliant caricature of the present, casts no light at all on the future.[72] These are all failures of political judgement and imagination. But his claim that he 'never met a genuine working man who accepted Marxism'[73] was no error of judgement; it was an untruth. We know from Woodcock that in London Orwell used to frequent a working-class pub but made a quick exit whenever a young Marxist came in.[74] His claim, in the introduction to the Ukrainian edition of *Animal Farm*, that he had spent 'many months' in the north of England studying the 'condition of the miners'[75] was certainly an untruth. He was there for approximately six weeks, taking a break of about a week in the middle of his stay to visit his sister and brother-in-law in a Leeds suburb. All the same, he managed to convince intellectuals (though never working men) that he had truly 'gone native in his own country' and had become an expert on working-class politics.[76]

Finally, here is an example of Orwell's contrariness towards potential allies, in this case a potential ally in a cause especially dear to his heart.

In 1939 Orwell wrote a review of Wyndham Lewis' *The Mysterious Mr Bull*, in which the author painted a picture of the English as peace-loving, kindly and unassuming. Orwell, who was himself to write about English gentleness in *The Lion and the Unicorn* (and more especially in Part 1, 'England Your England') only a year later, pointed out in this review that Wyndham Lewis' kind-hearted and gentle English have 'exploited their fellow creatures with a callous selfishness unparalleled in history',[77] an opinion that he mysteriously contrived not to deploy in his own work.

Nowadays it is frequently asked, on issues such as the invasion of Iraq, the use of closed-circuit television in public places, the intrusiveness of censuses and other bodies of information on individuals, or the carrying of identity cards in Britain: 'what would Orwell have thought about this?' All the evidence suggests that in order to answer this question it would first be necessary to find out what other prominent left-wing intellectuals thought about it. We could then be confident that, irrespective of what it was they thought, Orwell would think something quite different. Those who do not know Orwell's work very well are likely to be more confident in their expectations about 'what Orwell would have thought' than those who do. Pearce concluded of Orwell that he was always prepared to tell small lies to help substantiate what he believed were big truths, and in doing so was 'guilty of the sort of double standards which he was so quick to spot – and condemn – in others. In short he sometimes wrote with more artistry than honesty.'[78]

Near the beginning of this study, reference was made to Richard Rees' perceptive comparison between Orwell and the French writer and moralist Simone Weil: both, it will be remembered, understood the balance of society and were prepared at any time to add their weight to the lighter scale.[79] Orwell, like Weil, assumed the character of Justice, that 'fugitive from the victor's camp', and attempted to take a stand with and for those he considered to be defeated or powerless. Perhaps this represents a more realistic and certainly less judgemental way of dealing with Orwellian inconsistency, but it proposes very clearly that we regard Orwell as a moralist, like Weil, and not as a political thinker from whom greater consistency and predictability could be expected. Raymond Plant has observed that one of the fundamentally important problems confronting post-modern politics, and it is essentially a moral one, has been to know in what values to ground a conception of the good life.[80] Orwell professed to have such a conception and such a ground, and he claimed them for what he called democratic socialism, his decency myth, strictly a moral and not a political construct.

Moreover, George Orwell was also one of the greatest exponents of written English in the twentieth century; indeed according to George Woodcock, the best writer of prose since Swift.[81] He was no great novelist, being generally an unsympathetic man who seemed not to have nor want to have insights into the sympathies of others, and he had little feeling for structure (as was said of Dickens – 'rotten architecture but wonderful gargoyles'[82]); but as a writer of exceptional power and an exponent of lucid prose, he was unsurpassed.[83] It is Western man's lasting good fortune, however, that Orwell chose to use what he did have, his unique narrative talents, in the field of public morality, championing virtues that will always be crucial to the quest for the good life, and attacking evils that will always be inimical to the individual liberties that provide the *sine qua non* of that good life. It should come as no surprise, given Orwell's concern as a writer with language and its usage, that one of his major preoccupations was with the abuse of language by politicians. As George Steiner pointed out, Orwell, more than any other writer, recognised that 'to abuse, inflate or falsify the meaning of words is to devalue the political process. Political sanity and the ability of a community to view and communicate issues are clearly dependent on the integrity of syntax . . . The right for meaningful speech is a fight for moral and political life.'[84] Critics picked up on Orwell's concerns, applying them to the abuse of language in totalitarian regimes,[85] but as we have seen Orwell's concerns remain just as relevant in Blair's Britain and Bush's America. The adjective 'Orwellian' is still in constant use and, if not always employed properly or unambiguously, it is at least nearly always brought to bear against expressions or acts of injustice, and on behalf of ordinary people and plain language, however loosely these may sometimes be defined. For Orwell, what Hitchens described as 'a common language with mutually accepted and mutually understood rules' was a precondition of democracy.[86] In fact, as far as Orwell was concerned, lucidity and concision in language meant that ordinary people could not easily be excluded from political debates or easily lied to by leaders. He himself strove always, and with complete success, to write in a manner that anyone who wished could understand. This represented a profound achievement.

Yet there is more than this to Orwell's legacy. The searing and poignant pictures he painted helped to awaken us to the broader dangers of totalitarianism from the Left and the Right; his depiction of poverty and injustice were of such force as to throw readers' complacency in their faces. It is principally for these reasons that Orwell merits greater acclaim than Stephen Spender's portrayal of him as a twentieth-century English Candide allows. Spender spoke of Orwell's truth and decency driving 'like a drill through the façade of his generation'.[87] Nothing Panglossian about Orwell in this characterisation. Perhaps he is better portrayed as more Voltaire than Candide![88] Vaclav Havel once wrote that if a better world were to be created, then 'it must derive from profound existential and moral changes in society ... a better system will not automatically ensure a better life. In fact the opposite is true; only by creating a better life can a better system be developed.'[89] This mirrors exactly the decency myth that Orwell propounded for most of his adult life, a myth that represented a belief in ordinary people and a disbelief in élites. This might appear at first glance to be little more than an exercise in sentimentalism, but a substantial recent study of the common sense of ordinary people, James Surowiecki's *The Wisdom of Crowds*,[90] shows it to be a belief with some substance. Surowiecki, it has to be said, does not consider whether the wisdom of which he writes might have a moral base, but it would not be unreasonable to fit such an assumption into what he says. For Orwell, of course, the wisdom of ordinary people is rooted in their values, and the moral vision that inspired his belief finds its fullest expression in his last and bleakest book:[91]

> What mattered were individual relationships, and a completely helpless gesture, an embrace, a tear, a word spoken to a dying man, could have a value in itself. The proles, it suddenly occurred to him, had remained in this condition. They were not loyal to a party or a country or an idea, they were loyal to one another. For the first time in his life he did not despise the proles or think of them merely as an inert force which would one day spring to life and regenerate the world. The proles had stayed human. They had not become hardened inside. They had held on to the primitive emotions which he himself had to learn by conscious effort ... 'The proles are human beings', he said aloud.

If this vision has helped in the past, and continues to help today, to nudge forward the kind of cultural awakening that Havel had in mind, thus giving some kind of voice to the voiceless,[92] and if at the same time Orwell's chief and lasting hope was sustained, that 'the common people ... never parted company with their moral code',[93] then Orwell the moralist would have achieved as much as any writer could reasonably hope for, giving a firm notice to quit to all the Napoleons and Squealers in parliamentary chambers and other institutions of power everywhere.

Notes

Abbreviations

In the following sets of notes two sources will be referred to very frequently in shortened form:

The four-volume *Collected Essays, Journalism and Letters of George Orwell*, edited by Sonia Orwell and Ian Angus, published in 1968 by Secker and Warburg in London. Throughout they will be referred to as *CEJL* 3, pp. xx–yy.

The twenty-volume *The Complete Works of George Orwell*, edited by Peter Davison, published between 1996 and 1998 by Secker and Warburg in London. Throughout, these volumes will be referred to as *CW* 18, pp. xx–yy.

1 In search of Orwell

1 See Stephen Ingle, 'Socialism and Literature: The Contribution of Imaginative Writers to the Development of the British Labour Party', *Political Studies* XX11 (2), June 1974, pp. 158–68.
2 George Orwell, 'Wells, Hitler and the World State', *CEJL* 2, pp. 139–45.
3 Some of the facts here are taken from Jeffrey Meyers, *Orwell: Wintry Conscience of a Generation*, New York: Norton, 2000.
4 Eliot was a reader for Faber and Faber and had written to Orwell praising the book but pointing out the political inappropriateness of its timing.
5 Fred Inglis, *The Cruel Peace*, New York: Basic Books, 1992, pp. 103–4.
6 John Rodden, *The Politics of Literary Reputation: The Making and Claiming of 'St. George' Orwell*, Oxford: Oxford University Press, 1989, chapter 1.
7 For example, Margaret Attwood, 'Why *Animal Farm* Changed My Life', *The Age*, 12 July 2003; Terry Eagleton, 'Reach-Me-Down Romantic', *London Review of Books*, 19 June 2003.
8 For example, the Washington Branch of the society adopted '1984' as the final four digits of its telephone number.
9 Rupert Murdoch, *The Century of Networking*, *http://1khht.com/huber/orwell/mursch.html*
10 Bernard Crick, *George Orwell: A Life*, Harmondsworth: Penguin, 1992, p. 18.

11 Crick, *Orwell: A Life*, p. 30.

12 Michael Shelden, *Orwell: The Authorised Biography*, London: Heinemann, 1991.

13 Crick, *Orwell: A Life*, p. 38.

14 Lionel Trilling,*The Opposing Self*, London: Secker and Warburg, 1955.

15 Michael Shelden, *Weekend Telegraph*, 16 September 1989.

16 Rodden, *Literary Reputation*, p. 40.

17 Richard Rees, *George Orwell: Fugitive from the Camp of Victory*, London: Secker and Warburg, 1961.

18 Rees described the tribulations of the long and tedious journey to Barnhill, and the unprepossessing state of the farmhouse. He believed that nevertheless Orwell was keen to put down roots on Jura. (Rees, *Fugitive*, p. 179.)

19 George Orwell, 'Charles Dickens', *The Penguin Book of Essays of George Orwell*, Harmondsworth: Penguin, n.d., pp. 35–77.

20 George Orwell, review of *Mein Kampf, New English Weekly*, 21 March 1940, CW 12, pp. 116–18.

21 George Orwell, CW 14, p. 67.

22 George Orwell, review of *The Rock Pool, CEJL* 1, pp. 225–7.

23 For example, George Orwell, CW 14, p. 132.

24 W. H. Auden, 'Spain', in Robin Skelton (ed.), *Poetry of the Thirties*, Harmondsworth: Penguin, 1971, pp. 133–6.

25 'Blair's Babe: Did Love for this Woman turn Orwell into a Government Stooge?' *The Guardian*, 21 June 2003.

26 Orwell wrote to Anthony Powell on 11 May 1949 that he had been 'beastly ill on and off' and had even put off a visit from his future wife. *CEJL* 4, p. 499.

27 Christopher Hollis, *Study of George Orwell: The Man and his Works*, London: Hollis and Carter, 1956, p. 86.

28 George Woodcock, *The Crystal Spirit*, London: Jonathan Cape, 1967.

29 Woodcock, *Crystal Spirit*, p. 11.

30 Woodcock, *Crystal Spirit*, p. 28.

31 Woodcock, *Crystal Spirit*, p. 51.

32 Woodcock, *Crystal Spirit*, p. 275.

33 'Politics versus Literature', *Penguin Essays*, p. 379.

34 Woodcock, *Crystal Spirit*, p. 153.

35 Woodcock, *Crystal Spirit*, p. 221.

36 Robert A. Lee, *Orwell's Fiction*, London: University of Notre Dame Press, 1969.

37 Lee, *Orwell's Fiction*, p. 25.

38 Lee, *Orwell's Fiction*, p. 89.

39 Raymond Williams, *Orwell*, London: Fontana Modern Masters, 1971.

40 Williams, *Orwell*, p. 18.

41 Williams, *Orwell*, p. 38.

42 Williams, *Orwell*, p. 77.

43 P. Stansky and W. Abrahams, *The Unknown Orwell*, London: Constable, 1972.

44 Stansky and Abrahams, *Unknown Orwell*, p. 39.

45 Stansky and Abrahams, *Unknown Orwell*, p. 57.

46 Geoffrey Meyers, *George Orwell: The Critical Heritage*, London: Routledge and Kegan Paul, 1975.

47 Christopher Norris (ed.) *Inside the Myth, Orwell: Views from the Left*, London: Lawrence and Wishart, 1984.
48 Daphne Patai, *The Orwell Mystique: A Study of Male Ideology*, Amherst: University of Massachusetts Press, 1984.
49 Patai, *The Orwell Mystique*, p. 16.
50 For example, Patsy Schweikhart's review of *The Orwell Mystique* in *Women's Review of Books* 2, November 1984, which she described as just 'one more book about one more obnoxious male writer'. Jenni Calder was more tolerant, accepting that Orwell 'simply didn't see feminism as a larger issue' and reminding readers that Orwell was an active parent after his wife's death. (Both quoted in Rodden, *Literary Reputation*, p. 218.) See also Jenni Calder, *Chronicles of Conscience*, London: Secker and Warburg, 1968.
51 Christopher Hitchens, *Orwell's Victory*, London: Penguin, 2002, chapter 6.
52 Quoted in Bowker, *George Orwell*, p. 128.
53 Quoted in Taylor, *Orwell: The Life*, p. 143.
54 Stefan Collini, 'The Grocer's Children: The Lives and Afterlives of George Orwell', *Times Literary Supplement*, 20 June 2003.
55 John Newsinger, *Orwell's Politics*, London: Palgrave, 1999.
56 Newsinger, *Orwell's Politics*, p. 19.
57 Crick, *Orwell: A Life*, p. 399.
58 Newsinger, *Orwell's Politics*, p. 39.
59 Michael Collins,*The Likes of Us*, London: Granta Books, 2004, p. 115.
60 Newsinger, *Orwell's Politics*, p. 41.
61 George Orwell, *The Road to Wigan Pier*, Harmondsworth: Penguin, 1963, p. 160.
62 Newsinger, *Orwell's Politics*, pp. 63–66.
63 Orwell, *The Lion and the Unicorn*, *Penguin Essays*, p. 174.
64 Orwell, 'Looking Back on the Spanish War', *Penguin Essays*, pp. 216–33.
65 Crick, *George Orwell*, pp. 396–401.
66 Newsinger, *Orwell's Politics*, p. 109.
67 Newsinger, *Orwell's Politics*, p. 116.
68 Letter to Dwight Macdonald, 5 December 1946, quoted Newsinger, *Orwell's Politics*, p. 118.
69 Orwell, 'Arthur Koestler', *Focus* 2, 1946, *CEJL* 3, pp. 234–44.
70 Arthur Koestler, *The Gladiators*, London: Vintage, 1965, p. 293.
71 Koestler, *The Gladiators*, p. 310.
72 Newsinger, *Orwell's Politics*, p. 124.
73 Newsinger, *Orwell's Politics*, p. 89.
74 John O'Callaghan, 'George Orwell's Political Education', a paper presented at the European Consortium of Political Research (ECPR) Conference, Marburg, September 2003. Session: 'Aspects of Orwell'.
75 Jeffrey Meyers, *Orwell: Wintry Conscience of a Generation*, New York: Norton, 2000.
76 Gordon Bowker, *George Orwell*, London: Abacus, 2003.
77 Bowker, *George Orwell*, p. 48.
78 Stephen Spender was later to say that Orwell despised women and thought of them as inferior and stupid (interview, quoted in Bowker, *George Orwell*, p. 128).
79 Orwell, 'Wells, Hitler and the World State', *CEJL* 2, pp. 139–45.

80 Bowker, *George Orwell*, p. 46.
81 Bowker, *George Orwell*, p. 53.
82 Bowker, *George Orwell*, p. 93.
83 Bowker, *George Orwell*, p. 94.
84 Bowker, *George Orwell*, pp. 131–2.
85 Bowker, *George Orwell*, p. 235.
86 Bowker, *George Orwell*, p. 324.
87 Bowker, *George Orwell*, p. 331.
88 Letter to Frederick Warburg, 4 May 1946, *CW* 18, p. 305.
89 As a nine-year-old, Orwell had introduced himself to new friends, the Buddicom children, by standing on his head in a field. He later explained that by standing on one's head one got noticed more. He went on to tell that he intended to become a FAMOUS AUTHOR, in capitals. (See Jacintha Buddicom, *Eric and Us*, London: Leslie Frewin, 1974, p. 38.)
90 D. J. Taylor, *Orwell: The Life*, London: Chatto and Windus, 2003.
91 George Orwell, *A Clergyman's Daughter*, Harmondsworth: Penguin, 1964.
92 Taylor, *Orwell: The Life*, p. 176.
93 Taylor, *Orwell: The Life*, p. 215.
94 Taylor, *Orwell: The Life*, p. 213.
95 Taylor, *Orwell: The Life*, p. 206.
96 Orwell, *Wigan Pier*, p. 115.
97 Orwell, *Wigan Pier*, p. 173.
98 Taylor, *Orwell: The Life*, p. 340.
99 Peter Davison, *The Complete Works of George Orwell*, London: Secker and Warburg, 1998.
100 Jennie Lee, letter to Miss Goalby, 23 June 1945, *CW* 2, p. 5.
101 Rodden, *Literary Reputation*, p. 403.
102 Rodden, *Literary Reputation*, p. 404.
103 Ronald Thiemann, 'The Public Intellectual as Connected Critic', in Thomas Cushman and John Rodden (eds), *George Orwell into the Twenty-First Century*, Boulder, Co: Paradigm Publishers, 2004, p. 105.
104 See Bowker, *George Orwell*, p. 333.
105 Terry Eagleton, 'Reach-me-Down Romantic', *London Review of Books*, 19 June 2003, 6–9.
106 Anna Vaninskaya, 'After a Century of Orwell: Politics, Postmodernism and Reputation', a paper presented to the Language, Communication and Culture Conference, Lisbon, November 2003.
107 Orwell, 'The English People', *CEJL* 3, pp. 1–38.
108 'As I Please', *Tribune*, 19 May 1944, *CEJL* 3, pp. 150–3.
109 Ibid.
110 'As I Please', *Tribune*, 3 December 1943, *CEJL* 3, pp. 181–3.
111 Orwell's original article appeared in 'As I Please', *Tribune*, 14 April 1944. *Tribune* published the reply on 28 April.
112 'As I Please', *Tribune*, 3 December 1943.
113 'Words and Henry Miller', *Tribune*, 22 February 1946, *CW* 18, pp. 117–22.
114 'Boys Weeklies', *Penguin Essays*, pp. 78–100.
115 *Horizon*, March 1940, *CW* 12, pp. 79–85.
116 Orwell, *CW* 12, p. 128.

2 The shadow of imperialism

1 See Stephen Wadhams, *Remembering Orwell*, Harmondsworth: Penguin Books, 1984, p. 21.
2 Gordon Bowker, *George Orwell*, London: Abacus, 2003, p. 94.
3 John Newsinger, *Orwell's Politics*, London: Palgrave Macmillan, 1999, p. 2.
4 Jacintha Buddicom, 'The Young Eric', in Miriam Gross (ed.), *The World of George Orwell*, London: Weidenfeld and Nicolson, 1971, pp. 143–4.
5 For example, Maung Htin Aung, 'Orwell of the Burma Police', *Asian Affairs* 60, 1973, 182–6; Shamsul Islam, *Chronicles of the Raj*, London: Macmillan, 1979, pp. 63–5; D. C. R. A. Goonetelleke, *Images of the Raj*, London: Macmillan, 1998, pp. 112–31.
6 Christopher Hollis, *A Study of George Orwell: The Man and His Works*, London: Hollis and Carter, 1956, pp. 27–8.
7 Bowker, *George Orwell*, p. 153.
8 George Orwell, *Burmese Days*, Harmondsworth: Penguin, 1969, p. 93.
9 See, for example, the debate generated by David Beatham 'The Legitimisation of Power', in *Political Studies* 41 (3), 1993, 488–92 and 42 (1), 1994, 101–5.
10 *Burmese Days* was first published by Gollancz in 1935.
11 Orwell, *Burmese Days*, p. 24.
12 Orwell, *Burmese Days*, p. 23.
13 Orwell, *Burmese Days*, p. 24.
14 Orwell, *Burmese Days*, p. 28.
15 Orwell, *Burmese Days*, p. 41.
16 Orwell, *Burmese Days*, p. 39.
17 Shaw had once pleaded with his compatriots: 'War if you must – but no more war songs!'
18 When Orwell later gave permission for the dramatisation of *Burmese Days* in the USA he suggested as a title *The Black Man's Burden*.
19 Orwell, *Burmese Days*, p. 29.
20 Orwell, *Burmese Days*, p. 37.
21 Orwell, *Burmese Days*, p. 66.
22 Orwell, *Burmese Days*, p. 223.
23 Orwell, *Burmese Days*, p. 144.
24 Orwell, *Burmese Days*, p. 174.
25 W. H. Auden, 'A Communist to Others', in Robin Skelton (ed.), *Poetry of The Thirties*, Harmondsworth: Penguin Books, 1971.
26 Orwell, *Burmese Days*, p. 228.
27 Orwell, 'A Hanging', *CEJL* 1, pp. 44–8.
28 Orwell, 'A Hanging', p. 45.
29 Orwell, *The Road to Wigan Pier*, Harmondsworth: Penguin, 1963, p. 128.
30 Orwell, *Wigan Pier*, p. 128.
31 Orwell, *Wigan Pier*, p. 129.
32 Jorge Fernandes, 'Beyond the City: An Aesthetics of Gendered Detection', given at the Language, Communication, Culture Conference, Beja, Portugal, November 2004.
33 Orwell, 'Shooting an Elephant', *CEJL* 1, pp. 235–42.
34 Orwell, 'Shooting an Elephant', p. 236.

35 Orwell, 'Shooting an Elephant', p. 239.
36 D. J. Taylor, *Orwell: The Life*, London: Chatto and Windus, 2003, p. 79.
37 Bowker, *George Orwell*, pp. 90–1.
38 Taylor, *Orwell*, pp. 79–80.
39 Orwell, 'Shooting an Elephant', p. 239.
40 Orwell, 'Not Counting Niggers', *Adelphi*, July, 1939, *CEJL* 1, pp. 394–8.
41 Taken from 'The Echoing Green', in Blake's *Songs of Innocence*.
42 Orwell, 'Such, Such Were the Joys', *CEJL* 4, pp. 330–69.
43 Orwell, 'The Joys', p. 433.
44 Orwell, 'The Joys', p. 440.
45 Orwell, *Wigan Pier*, p. 119.
46 Orwell, 'Rudyard Kipling', *Penguin Essays*, Harmondsworth: Penguin, n.d., pp. 203–15.
47 Orwell, 'Kipling', p. 204.
48 Orwell, 'Kipling', p. 206.
49 Orwell, 'Kipling', p. 215.
50 See W. J. West (ed.), *Orwell: The War Broadcaster*, London: Duckworth/ BBC, 1985; Douglas Kerr, 'Orwell's BBC Broadcasts; Colonial Discourse and the rhetoric of propaganda', *Textual Practice* 16 (3), December 2002; C. Fleay and M. L. Sanders, 'Looking at the Abyss: George Orwell at the BBC', *Journal of Contemporary History* 24, 1989.
51 Orwell, review of Robert Duval's 'Whitehall to Mandalay', *Tribune*, 2 April 1943, *CW* 15, p. 48.
52 Reply to Orwell's review, *Tribune*, 16 April 1943, *CW* 15, p. 48.
53 Orwell, letter to the editor, *Tribune*, 23 April 1943, *CW* 15, p. 49.
54 Alok Rai, *Orwell and the Politics of Despair*, Cambridge: Cambridge University Press, 1988, p. 109.
55 Orwell, *The Lion and the Unicorn*, *The Penguin Essays of George Orwell*, Harmondsworth: Penguin, n.d., p. 171.
56 Review of Lionel Fielden, 'Beggar My Neighbour,' Horizon, September 1943, *CW* 15, p. 211. Fielden, who became a celebrated BBC producer, had been the Controller of Broadcasting for All India Radio, and thus a man with some knowledge of sub-continental and imperial politics.
57 Fielden's reply to Orwell, *CW* 15, p. 221.
58 Fielden's reply to Orwell, *CW* 15, p. 222.
59 In fairness to Orwell, he later wrote a generally supportive essay on Gandhi. He thought him unrealistic and unworldly in the pejorative sense, and did not much like him, but he recognised that if Britain and India were to settle down to a mutually supportive relationship it would be because Gandhi had conducted his struggle for independence without rancour ('Reflections on Gandhi', *Partisan Review*, January 1949, *CEJL* 4, pp. 463–70).
60 Orwell, *Time and Tide*, 31 May 1941.
61 Christopher Hitchens, *Orwell's Victory*, Harmondsworth: Penguin, 2001, p. 25.
62 Near the end of his life, for example, Orwell quoted a representative of a minority people in Burma telling him that he hoped the British would rule for 200 years so that his people would not be ruled by the Burmese ('As I Please', *Tribune*, 7 February 1947).
63 Terry Eagleton, *The Rise of English*, quoted in Kenneth Quin, *How Literature Works*, London: Palgrave Macmillan, 1992, p. 22.

64 In an interview published in *The Times Higher Educational Supplement*, 26 July 1996.
65 Quin, *How Literature Works*, p. 34.
66 The future Labour Cabinet Minister R. H. S. Crossman always claimed that as a student in the 1930s he had been greatly influenced by Auden's poetry.

3 The poor, the workers and the 'decency myth'

1 George Orwell, review of Philip Henderson, *The Novel Today*, *New English Weekly*, 13 December 1935, *CW* 19, p. 533.
2 Orwell, 'Inside the Whale', *Penguin Essays*, Harmondsworth: Penguin, n.d., p. 115.
3 Orwell, *The Road to Wigan Pier*, Harmondsworth: Penguin, 1963, pp. 29–30.
4 Bernard Crick, *George Orwell: A Life*, Harmondsworth: Penguin, 1992, p. 179.
5 Letter from T. S. Eliot to George Orwell, 19 February 1932. Orwell's difficulty in securing publication, including his response to Eliot, is set out in his letter to his agent-to-be, Leonard Moore, dated 29 April 1932, *CEJL* 1, pp. 77–8.
6 Orwell, *Down and Out in Paris and London*, Harmondsworth: Penguin, 1969, p. 17.
7 Orwell, *Down and Out*, p. 14.
8 Ibid.
9 Orwell, *Down and Out*, p. 69.
10 Robert Tressell, *The Ragged Trousered Philanthropists*, London: Grafton Books, 1965.
11 Orwell, review of *The Ragged Trousered Philanthropists*, *Manchester Evening News*, 25 April 1946, *CW* 18, pp. 255–7.
12 Letter to *Times* from H. Possenti, 31 January 1933, quoted in Gordon Bowker, *George Orwell*, London: Abacus, p. 148.
13 Orwell, *Down and Out*, p. 72.
14 Orwell, *Down and Out*, p. 106.
15 See, for example, Lynette Hunter, *George Orwell: The Search for a Voice*, London: Open University Press, 1984.
16 Letter to Rayner Heppenstall on the birth of his daughter, 16 April 1940, *CW* 12, p. 146.
17 Orwell, *Down and Out*, pp. 146–7.
18 Orwell, *Down and Out*, p. 115.
19 Orwell, *A Clergyman's Daughter*, Harmondsworth: Penguin, 1964.
20 Orwell, *Keep the Aspidistra Flying*, first published in London by Gollancz, 1936.
21 George Gissing, *New Grub Street*, London: Bodley Head, 1967.
22 Adapted from St Paul's *First Letter to the Corinthians*, Ch.13, v. xiii.
23 Orwell, *Keep the Aspidistra Flying*, p. 102.
24 Orwell, *Keep the Aspidistra Flying*, p. 37.
25 Orwell, *Keep the Aspidistra Flying*, p. 53.
26 Raymond Williams, *Orwell*, London: Fontana Modern Masters, 1971, pp. 46–9.

27 Walter Greenwood and his *Love on the Dole* makes an honourable exception.
28 George Woodcock, *The Crystal Spirit*, London: Jonathan Cape, 1967, p. 104.
29 Orwell, *Keep the Aspidistra Flying*, p. 81.
30 Ruth Pitter, BBC talk, 1956, quoted in Bowker, *George Orwell*, p. 124.
31 See Peter Lewis, *George Orwell*, London: Heinemann, 1981, p. 149.
32 Bowker, *George Orwell*, p. 180.
33 Orwell, *The Road to Wigan Pier*, Harmondsworth: Penguin, 1963, p. 15.
34 H. G. Wells, *The Time Machine, Selected Short Stories*, Harmondsworth: Penguin, 1970, pp. 45–8.
35 Orwell, *Wigan Pier*, p. 64.
36 Orwell, *Wigan Pier*, p. 68.
37 Orwell, *Wigan Pier*, p. 76.
38 Orwell, *Keep the Aspidistra Flying*, p. 49.
39 Jack London, *The People of the Abyss*, London: The Journeyman Press, 1977.
40 Orwell, *Wigan Pier*, p. 98.
41 Orwell, review of *A Coat of Many Colours*, by Herbert Read, *CEJL* 4, pp. 48–52.
42 Philip Toynbee, in *Encounter*, August 1959, quoted in Jeffrey Meyers, *George Orwell: The Critical Heritage*, London: Routledge and Kegan Paul, 1975.
43 Orwell, *Wigan Pier*, p. 102.
44 Orwell, *Wigan Pier*, p. 103.
45 Orwell, *Wigan Pier*, p. 104.
46 Orwell, *Wigan Pier*, p. 102.
47 Stephen Ingle, *George Orwell: A Political Life*, Manchester: Manchester University Press, 1993, p. 50.
48 Orwell, *Wigan Pier*, p. 19.
49 See 'The English People', *CEJL* 3, pp. 1–37.
50 Orwell, 'The Art of Donald McGill', *CEJL* 2, pp. 155–64.
51 Orwell, *Time and Tide*, 21 December 1940, *CW* 12, p. 313.
52 Orwell, 'Donald McGill', p. 161.
53 Orwell's analysis identifies the essence of McGill's philosophy with deftness and perspicacity: indeed he proved to be way ahead of his time. In 1954, at Lincoln, McGill was prosecuted under the Obscene Publications Act of 1857. On legal advice McGill pleaded guilty to four of twenty-one charges of obscenity and escaped with a fine. Had his learned counsel read Orwell's essay he would certainly have been able to mount a far more resolute defence of his client.
54 Orwell, 'Donald McGill', p. 164.
55 Orwell, 'The English People', *CEJL* 3, p. 9.
56 Orwell, review of *Caliban Shrieks* by Jack Hilton, *CEJL* 1, pp. 148–50.
57 Orwell, letter to Henry Miller, 26 August 1936, *CEJL* 1, pp. 227–9.
58 Wyndham Lewis, 'Climax and Change', in Samuel Hynes (ed.), *Twentieth Century Interpretations of Nineteen Eighty Four*, Englewood Cliffs: Prentice Hall, 1971, p. 107.
59 Walter Greenwood, *Tribune*, 12 March 1937.
60 John Newsinger, *Orwell's Politics*, London: Palgrave, 1999, pp. 38–9.
61 D. H. Lawrence, *Sons and Lovers*, Harmondsworth: Penguin, 1981.

62 Orwell, *Wigan Pier*, p. 112.
63 Orwell, *Wigan Pier*, p. 114.
64 Orwell, *Wigan Pier*, p. 119.
65 This story was reported by John Morris of the BBC (see Woodcock, *The Crystal Spirit*, p. 26).
66 Orwell, *Wigan Pier*, p. 119.
67 Peter Lewis, *George Orwell*, London: Heinemann Quixote Press, 1981, p. 50.
68 This was what Stalin hoped for too, and indeed he put considerable effort into persuading the bourgeoisie to become proletarians. (See Paul Heywood, *Political Ideologies*, Basingstoke: Palgrave/Macmillan, 1998, p. 134.)
69 Orwell, *Wigan Pier*, p. 155.
70 Marxists would surely reply that Marx himself only rarely spoke of the dialectic; it is more frequently to be found in Engels' writing. Moreover, the negation of the negation, to which Orwell later unflatteringly refers, is Hegelian rather than Marxian. We should read Orwell to be attacking Marxists here rather than Marx. Marxists would also stress that Marx was well aware of the strength of working-class values; he sought to transcend them not ignore or destroy them. Rather like Orwell.
71 Orwell, *Wigan Pier*, p. 155.
72 Ibid.
73 Orwell, *Wigan Pier*, p. 157.
74 Orwell, *Wigan Pier*, p. 184.
75 Orwell, *Wigan Pier*, p. 193.
76 Newsinger, *Orwell's Politics*, p. 39.
77 Orwell, *Wigan Pier*, pp. 202–3.
78 Orwell, *Wigan Pier*, p. 195.
79 Dietrich Bonhoeffer, *Ethics*, London: Fontana, 1968, pp. 85–6.
80 Orwell, review of *Freedom of the Streets* by Jack Common, *CEJL* 1, pp. 355–6.
81 John McNair, 'The George Orwell I Knew', *Controversy* 1(1), Autumn, 1962.
82 Vaclav Havel, 'The Power of the Powerless', in J. Vladislav, *Vaclav Havel, or Living from Truth*, London: Faber and Faber, 1987, pp. 36–122.
83 Orwell, 'Not Enough Money: A Sketch of George Gissing', *Tribune*, 2 April 1943.
84 Ibid.
85 Orwell, review of Graham Greene's *The Heart of the Matter*, *CEJL* 4, p. 442.
86 Aldous Huxley, *Point Counter Point*, Harmondsworth: Penguin, 1971, p. 59.
87 Michael Collins, *The Likes of Us*, London: Granta Books, 2004, p. 255.
88 In the new intake of Labour MPs following the 1997 landslide there were as many millionaires as there were manual workers. (See Stephen Ingle, *The British Party System*, London: Pinter, 2000, p. 157.)
89 Stephen Ingle, *Narratives of British Socialism*, London: Palgrave/Macmillan, 2002, p. 169.
90 Orwell, Diary Entry for 15 February 1936, *CEJL* 1, pp. 177–8.
91 Ibid.

92 Ibid.
93 Orwell, *Wigan Pier*, p. 17.
94 Newsinger, *Orwell's Politics*, p. 37.
95 Orwell, *Wigan Pier*, pp. 94–5.
96 Quoted in Bowker, *George Orwell*, p. 185.
97 In fact, Gollancz felt obliged to include a foreword dissociating himself from some of Orwell's views. (See Robert Pearce, 'Revisiting Orwell's *Wigan Pier*', *History: The Journal of the History Association*, July 1997, pp. 410–24.)
98 Orwell, *Wigan Pier*, p. 152.
99 Orwell, *Wigan Pier*, p. 195.
100 Orwell, *Wigan Pier*, p. 156.
101 Orwell, *Wigan Pier*, pp. 194–5.
102 Orwell, *Wigan Pier*, p. 190.

4 To the barricades and back

1 It should be noted that in fact Orwell fought on the side of the democratically elected Spanish government, not on the side of the rebels or insurgents. In Catalonia a government more revolutionary than the Madrid government took power and Orwell took his stand with the Partido Obrero de Unification Marxista (POUM), said to be the most politically conscious of the militias. Orwell was absolutely clear that what he was fighting for was 'the revolution'.
2 Letter to Cyril Connolly, 8 June 1937, *CEJL* 1, pp. 268–9.
3 Baboeuf's own attempts to establish a proletarian republic were crushed by Napoleon in 1796. Subsequently condemned to death, he took his own life.
4 Neil Harding, 'Socialism and Violence', in Bhiku Parekh, *The Concept of Socialism*, London: Croom Helm, 1975, p. 204.
5 Sorel set these ideas out most fully in *Reflections on Violence* (1908). For a full discussion of his theories, see Jack J. Roth, *The Cult of Violence: Sorel and the Sorelians*, London: University of California Press, 1980.
6 Harding, 'Socialism and Violence', p. 209.
7 See Frantz Fanon, *The Wretched of the Earth*, London: MacGibbon and Kee, 1965, passim.
8 Quoted in Eldridge Cleaver, *Post-Prison Writings and Speeches*, London: Panther Books, 1971, p. 55.
9 See Stephen Ingle, *The British Party System*, London: Continuum, 2001, pp. 103–8.
10 George Orwell, *Homage to Catalonia*, Harmondsworth: Penguin, 1966, p. 119.
11 Quoted in Alan Chappelow, Shaw: 'The Chucker Out', London: Allen and Unwin, 1969, p. 181.
12 Orwell, *Homage*, p. 9.
13 Orwell, *Homage*, p. 7.
14 Ibid.
15 Orwell, *Homage*, p. 59.
16 Orwell, *Homage*, p. 10.
17 Orwell, *Homage*, p. 15.

18 Orwell, *Homage*, p. 46.
19 Arthur Koestler, *Darkness at Noon*, Harmondsworth: Penguin, 1969, pp. 81–133.
20 Its leader Andrés Nin had been a close ally of Trotsky.
21 Orwell, *Homage*, p. 29.
22 Orwell, *Homage*, p. 42.
23 Orwell, *Homage*, p. 99.
24 Orwell, 'You and the Atom Bomb', *CEJL* 4, pp. 6–10.
25 See Stephen Ingle, 'Politics and Literature: Means and Ends in Arthur Koestler', *Political Studies*, 47(2), June 1999, pp. 329–44.
26 Orwell, 'Notes on the Spanish Militias', *CEJL* 1, pp. 316–28.
27 Orwell, *Homage*, p. 59.
28 Orwell, *Homage*, p. 60.
29 See Stephen Ingle, *George Orwell: A Political Life*, Manchester: Manchester University Press, 1993, pp. 70–2.
30 Orwell, *Homage*, p. 67.
31 Orwell, *Homage*, p. 47.
32 Orwell, letter to Jack Common, October 1937, *CEJL* 1, pp. 288–9.
33 Orwell, Letter to Victor Gollancz, 9 May 1937, *CEJL* 1, p. 267.
34 Orwell, Letter to Frank Jellinek, 20 December 1938, *CEJL* 1, pp. 363–6.
35 Ibid.
36 Letter from Eileen to her brother Dr Laurence O'Shaugnessy, 1 May 1937, *CW* 11, p. 20.
37 Gordon Bowker, *George Orwell*, London: Abacus, 2003, p. 217.
38 The Communist Party, PUSC, declared that POUM were 'our worst enemies. We shall treat them as such.' (Quoted in Newsinger, *Orwell's Politics*, Basingstoke: Palgrave, 1999, p. 52.)
39 Eileen had joined her husband in March 1937, having arranged the details of the publication of *Wigan Pier*. She worked as a secretary in the ILP office in Barcelona.
40 Michael Shelden, *Orwell: The Authorised Biography*, London: Heinemann, 1991, p. 295.
41 Peter Davison, 'Analysis of the Report of the Tribunal for Espionage', 13 July 1937, *CW* 11, p. 32.
42 William Morris, *News from Nowhere*, in A. L. Morton (ed.), *Three Works by William Morris*, London: Lawrence and Wishart, 1973, pp. 286–317.
43 Remarque's *All Quiet on the Western Front* and Robert Graves' *Goodbye to All That* are obvious examples of books that de-bunk the 'glories' of war.
44 See Ingle, *George Orwell*, p. 72.
45 Orwell, Letter to Cyril Connolly, 8 June 1937, *CEJL* 1, pp. 268–9.
46 Daphne Patai, *The Orwell Mystique*, Amherst: University of Massachusetts Press, 1984, p. 15.
47 'Spilling the Spanish Beans', *New English Weekly*, 29 July and 2 September 1937, *CEJL* 1, pp. 269–76.
48 Orwell uses this phrase in 'Spilling the Spanish Beans', *CEJL* 1, pp. 269–76. He used it again in a review of Russia Under Soviet Rule', *CEJL* 1, pp. 378–81.
49 The *New Statesman* refused to publish an article and a review by Orwell because his anti-communist stance did not fit the periodical's editorial policy. (Orwell letter to Rayner Heppenstall, 31 July 1937, *CEJL* 1, pp. 278–80.)

50 Orwell, letter to Geoffrey Gorer, 15 September 1937, *CEJL* 1, pp. 283–5.
51 Ibid.
52 Orwell, 'Why I Joined the ILP', *CW* 11, p. 168.
53 John Callaghan, 'George Orwell's Political Education', a paper read to the ECPR Conference at Marburg, September 2003. Session: 'Aspects of Orwell'.
54 *New English Weekly*, 26 May 1938, *CEJL* 1, pp. 330–32.
55 George Orwell, 'Political Reflections on the Crisis', *The Adelphi*, December 1938, *CW* 11, p. 244.
56 Review of Franz Borkenau's *The Communist International*, *CW* 11, p. 203.
57 Orwell, letter to Yvonne Davet, 18 August 1938, *CW* 11, pp. 188–9.
58 Orwell, *Coming Up for Air*, first published by Gollancz in 1939.
59 *The Penguin Essays of George Orwell*, Harmondsworth: Penguin, 1994, pp. 138–88.
60 Orwell, 'Wells, Hitler and the World State, *CEJL* 2, pp. 139–45.
61 W. B. Yeats, *The Second Coming*, written in 1921.
62 Orwell, 'London Letter to Partisan Review', November–December 1942, *CEJL* 2, p. 230.
63 Franz Borkenau, author of *The Spanish Cockpit*, much admired by Orwell, also wrote a history in 1938 of the Communist International.
64 Orwell, letter to John Skeats, *CEJL* 1, pp. 357–9.
65 Orwell, 'My Country Right or Left', *Penguin Essays*, pp. 133–8.
66 Orwell, *New English Weekly*, 21 July 1938, *CEJL* 1, pp. 330–2.
67 Orwell, 'London Letter', *Partisan Review*, Winter 1945, *CEJL* 3, pp. 293–9.
68 Ibid.
69 Orwell, 'Catastrophic Gradualism', *Common Wealth Review*, November 1945, *CEJL* 4, pp. 15–19. For a fuller examination of Orwell's attitude to revolution, see Stephen Ingle, *George Orwell*, pp. 57–82.
70 Orwell, letter to Geoffrey Gorer, 15 September 1937, *CEJL* 1, pp. 283–5.
71 Orwell, *The Lion and the Unicorn, Penguin Essays*, p. 155.
72 Orwell, lecture to the Fabian Society, 22 November 1941, *CW* 13, pp. 70–1.
73 Orwell, 'The Novel Today', *CEJL* 1, p. 259.
74 Orwell, 'London Letter', *Partisan Review*, July–August 1942, *CEJL* 2, pp. 207–16.
75 After Dunkirk there had been a measurable shift to the Left amongst ordinary British people, according to Angus Calder in *The People's War*, London: Pimlico, 1992. Nevertheless, Paul Addison, in *The Road to 1945*, London: Quartet, 1977, dismissed Orwell's observations and predictions as far-fetched. Addison's argument is given substance by Orwell's urging of fellow socialists to join the Home Guard so as to turn it into a 'democratic guerrilla force' ('The Home Guard and You', *Tribune*, 20 December 1940, *CW* 12, p. 309). Although these days we would be inclined to wonder how this message might have gone down in Warminster-on-Sea, Crick assures us that the Home Guard did acquire a political if not a revolutionary dimension. (Crick, *George Orwell: A Life*, Harmondsworth: Penguin, 1992, pp. 398–402.)
76 Orwell, *Animal Farm*, Harmondsworth: Penguin, 1958. First published in 1945.

77 Eliot was a reader for Faber and Faber and had written to Orwell praising the book but pointing out the political inappropriateness of its timing.
78 Orwell, letter to Dwight MacDonald, 3 January 1946, CW 18, p. 11.
79 Letter from Eliot to Orwell 13 July 1944, CW 16, pp. 282–3.
80 Orwell, *Animal Farm*, p. 19.
81 Orwell, *Animal Farm*, p. 29.
82 Orwell, *Animal Farm*, p. 21.
83 Orwell, *Animal Farm*, p. 32.
84 Orwell, *Animal Farm*, p. 23.
85 A central tenet of animalism was that society should produce according to need and not to make profit. But in order to trade society must produce a surplus above needs, or it will have nothing to exchange.
86 In reality Stalin did indeed defend his opposition to Trotsky's plans, and managed to win over the other reluctant party leaders. At the X1Vth Congress Bukharin declared that they would have to build socialism at a snail's pace, but that it would be built.
87 Orwell, *Animal Farm*, p. 114.
88 H. M. Hyndman, *Record of an Adventurous Life*, London: Macmillan, 1911, p. 432.
89 St Paul's *Second Letter to the Thessalonians*, Ch.3 vs. 7–11.
90 Orwell, *Animal Farm*, p. 79.
91 Orwell, *Animal Farm*, p. 111.
92 Orwell, *Animal Farm*, p. 104.
93 See Crick, *George Orwell: A Life*, pp. 291–2.
94 Orwell was somewhat dismayed that some readers had drawn this conclusion. (See his Preface to the Ukrainian edition of *Animal Farm*, CW 19, pp. 86–9.)
95 Quoted by Leonard Wolf, in C. M. Joad, *Shaw and Society*, London: Odhams, 1953, p. 44.
96 André Malraux, *Man's Estate*, Harmondsworth: Penguin, 1975, p. 167.
97 Aldous Huxley, *Eyeless in Gaza*, Harmondsworth: Penguin, 1972, p. 207.
98 Orwell, 'Why I Write', *Penguin Essays*, p. 6.
99 Orwell, *Homage to Catalonia*, p. 153.
100 Bowker, *George Orwell*, p. 202.
101 Victor Alba, *El Marxisme a Catalunya 1919–39*, Barcelona: Pòrtic, 1974, p. 50. Miquel Berga's *Mil nou-cents vuitanta quatre: Radiografia d'un maison*, Barcelona: Edicions 62, 1984, gives other instances of the poor impression that Orwell made on POUM comrades.
102 Orwell, 'Why I Write', *Penguin Essays*, p. 6.
103 Preface to the Ukrainian Edition of *Animal Farm*, CW 19, pp. 86–9.
104 See Richard Rorty, 'The Last Intellectual in Europe', in *Contingency, Irony and Solidarity*, Cambridge: Cambridge University Press, 1989, pp. 169–88.

5 Family and nation

1 For example, John Rossi, in 'Orwell and Patriotism', *Contemporary Review*, August 1992.

2 George Orwell, *The Lion and the Unicorn, The Penguin Essays*, Harmondsworth: Penguin, n.d., pp. 138–87.

3 For example, James Kellas, *The Politics of Nationalism and Ethnicity*, Basingstoke: Macmillan, 1991. Kellas was primarily interested in Scotland, though his concepts are more broadly applicable.

4 Jeremy Paxman, *The English: A Portrait of a People*, Harmondsworth: Penguin Books, 1998.

5 See Anthony Easthope, *Englishness and National Character*, London: Routledge, 1999. For representations of Englishness in writing, see Judy Giles and Tim Middleton (eds), *Writing Englishness*, London: Routledge, 1995.

6 A. S. Byatt, 'What it means to be English', *The Times*, 6 April 1998.

7 David Milstead, *Brewer's Anthology of England and the English*, London: Cassell, n.d.

8 See George Shepperson, 'Livingstone the Scot', *Scottish Historical Review* 39 (2), 1960, pp. 113–21.

9 Cyril Connolly once said of Orwell that he could not blow his nose without moralising on conditions in the handkerchief industry.

10 Orwell, 'Such, Such Were the Joys', *Penguin Essays*, pp. 441–2.

11 Orwell, letter to Anthony Powell, 8 June 1936, *CEJL* 1, p. 223.

12 Bernard Crick, *George Orwell*, London: Penguin Books, 1992, p. 263.

13 Orwell, *Burmese Days*, Harmondsworth: Penguin, 1969, p. 38.

14 Orwell, *Burmese Days*, p. 181.

15 Orwell, Partisan Review, 3 January 1943, *CEJL* 2, p. 280.

16 Orwell, on Rayner Heptenstall's review of *Poetry Scotland, Tribune*, 7 April 1944.

17 Orwell, 'As I Please', *Tribune*, 7 February 1947, *CEJL* 4, pp. 283–7.

18 Orwell, 'Extracts from a Manuscript Notebook', *CEJL* 4, p. 515.

19 Orwell, 'Our Opportunity', *Left News* 55, January 1941, *CW* 12, pp. 343–50.

20 John Major, speech to Conservative Group for Europe, 22 April 1993.

21 Stanley Baldwin, *On England and Other Addresses*, Freeport, NY: Ayer Publishers, 1971, first published 1926.

22 Martin Wiener, *English Culture and the Decline of the Industrial Spirit*, Cambridge: Cambridge University Press, 1981.

23 D. H. Lawrence, 'Nottingham and the Mining Country', http://displace.dial.pipex.com/town/parable/obj76/PG/pieces/lawrence/Nottingham.html.

24 William Morris, 'The Lesser Arts', in A. L. Morton (ed.), *Political Writings of William Morris*, London: Lawrence and Wishart, 1973.

25 Friedrich Engels, *The Condition of the Working Class in England*, St Albans: Panther Press, 1969.

26 Charles Dickens, *Hard Times*, London: Odhams Press, n.d., Book 2, Ch.1, pp. 89–90.

27 Rupert Brooke, 'The Soldier'.

28 Orwell, 'The English People', *CEJL* 3, pp. 1–38.

29 Orwell, *The Lion and the Unicorn*, p. 140.

30 For a rather more measured discussion of English music, see J. Day, *Englishness in Music: From Elizabethan Times to Elgar, Tippett and Britten*, London: Thames, 1999.

31 Peter Ackroyd, unlike Orwell, is very much of the view that not merely is the range of English music of high quality but that it entails a distinctively English quality that might have been of interest to Orwell. (See his *Albion: The Origins of the English Imagination*, London: Chatto and Windus, 2002.)

32 For a more balanced view of English painting, see William Vaughan, *British Painting: The Golden Age from Hogarth to Turner*, London: Thames and Hudson, 1999, and for specifically English themes, see Kenneth Clarke, *On the Painting of English Landscape*, London: British Academy, 1935.

33 Letter dated April 13 1946, *CW* 18, p. 242.

34 Orwell, *Wigan Pier*, p. 128.

35 Orwell, *The Lion and the Unicorn*, p. 141.

36 Orwell, *The Lion and the Unicorn*, p. 153.

37 Orwell, *The Lion and the Unicorn*, p. 157.

38 His celebrated poem *Slough* begins with the stanza:

> Come friendly bombs and fall on Slough
> It isn't fit for humans now,
> There isn't grass to graze a cow
> Swarm over, Death!

39 Orwell, *The Lion and the Unicorn*, p. 159.

40 Orwell, *The Lion and the Unicorn*, p. 166.

41 Orwell, *The Lion and the Unicorn*, p. 188.

42 Orwell, *The Lion and the Unicorn*, p. 174.

43 Orwell, 'The English People', *CEJL* 3, pp. 1–38.

44 Orwell, 'The English People', p. 37.

45 Ibid.

46 Joyce Grenfell, letter to her mother, May 1944, *CW* 16, p. 197.

47 Charles Dickens, *Our Mutual Friend*, London: Odhams Press, n.d., Ch.11.

48 Sir Ernest Barker, *The Character of England*, Oxford: Clarendon Press, 1947. See also his *National Character and the Factors in its Formation*, London: Methuen, 1927.

49 Jeffrey Meyers, *National Review*, 29 November 1985.

50 Paxman, *The English*, p. 133.

51 Orwell, *Wigan Pier*, p. 104.

52 Orwell, *Wigan Pier*, p. 73.

53 For example, in his review of Fenner Brockway's *Workers' Front*, Orwell argues that to concentrate as Brockway does on the industrial proletariat as the class that does not benefit from capitalism is to miss out 'many others in the same boat'. These others are the ordinary people, the powerless (*CW* 14, p. 105).

54 Orwell, *Coming Up for Air*, Harmondsworth: Penguin, 1990, pp. 9–11.

55 Orwell, *Coming Up for Air*, p. 140.

56 Orwell, *Coming Up for Air*, p. 11.

57 Orwell, *Coming Up for Air*, p. 24.

58 Orwell, *Coming Up for Air*, p. 49.

59 Orwell, *Coming Up for Air*, p. 66.

60 Orwell, *Coming Up for Air*, p. 82.

61 Orwell, *Coming Up for Air*, p. 66.

62 In their Shabbat morning prayers, Jewish men thank God who has made

them men and not women, whereas women give thanks to God who has made all things according to his will (*http://www.acs.ucalgary.ca/-elsegal/ Shokel/991021_DubiousBlessing.html*)

63 Orwell, *Coming Up for Air*, p. 112.
64 Orwell, *Coming Up for Air*, p. 192.
65 Orwell, *Coming Up for Air*, p. 214.
66 Orwell was concerned that his novel would be seen as 'watered down Wells' and he admitted his admiration of Wells to Julian Symons (letter 10 May 1948, *CEJL* 4, pp. 421–3).
67 For example, when Bowling's car turns from the familiar road, signifying that he was finally on his way, he had a powerful feeling of being followed. All the forces of modern life were conspiring to restrain him. He could almost hear them shouting: 'There's a chap who thinks he's going to escape! There's a chap who says he won't be streamlined! He's going back to Lower Binfield! After him! Stop him!'
68 William Morris, *News from Nowhere, Three Works by William Morris*, A. L. Morton (ed.), London: Lawrence and Wishart, 1973, p. 257.
69 George Gissing, *Demos: A Story of English Socialism*, Brighton: Harvester Press, 1972.
70 Fishing was an activity favoured by the Conservative philosopher Michael Oakshott, who extolled its virtues in the celebrated essay 'On Being Conservative' (see his *Rationalism in Politics and Other Essays*, London: Methuen, 1962).
71 Orwell, *Coming Up for Air*, p. 143.
72 Orwell, *Coming Up for Air*, p. 26.
73 Orwell, *Animal Farm*, Harmondsworth: Penguin, 1958, p. 7.
74 Orwell, *Animal Farm*, p. 75.
75 Orwell, *Animal Farm*, p. 76.
76 Orwell, *Nineteen Eighty Four*, Harmondsworth: Penguin, 1960, p. 11.
77 Orwell, *Nineteen Eighty Four*, p. 23.
78 Orwell, *Nineteen Eighty Four*, p. 187.
79 Orwell, *Nineteen Eighty Four*, p. 27.
80 Orwell, *Nineteen Eighty Four*, pp. 53–4.
81 Orwell, *Nineteen Eighty Four*, p. 183.
82 Orwell, *Nineteen Eighty Four*, pp. 174–5.
83 Orwell, *Nineteen Eighty Four*, p. 176.
84 Daphne Patai's *The Orwell Mystique* has already been discussed. See also Beatrix Campbell, 'Orwell – Pater Familias or Big Brother?' in Christopher Norris, *Inside the Myth: Orwell – Views from the Left*, London: Lawrence and Wishart, 1984.
85 Hitchens, *Orwell's Victory*, London: Penguin, 2002, pp. 109–10.
86 Orwell, 'On Housing', *Tribune*, 25 January 1946, *CW* 18, pp. 75–8.
87 Orwell, 'As I Please', *Tribune*, 9 February 1945, *CEJL* 4, pp. 329–32.
88 Bernard Crick, *Orwell: A Life*, pp. 266–7.
89 Orwell, *The Lion and the Unicorn*, p. 150.
90 Not everyone shares my concern. In 'Orwell and Patriotism', Rossi refers to the analogy as 'one of Orwell's most brilliant insights'. He does not develop this point.
91 Joseph, Heller, *Catch 22*, London: Vintage edn., 1994, p. 525.
92 Roger Scruton, *England: An Elegy*, London: Chatto and Windus, 2000.

93 Roundtable: 'Britain Rediscovered', *Prospect*, April 2005, 20–25.
94 See Margaret Canovan, *G. K. Chesterton: Radical Populist*, New York: Harcourt Brace, 1977.
95 Robert Benewick, *The Fascist Movement in Britain*, London: Allen Lane, 1972, passim.
96 Orwell, *The Lion and the Unicorn*, p. 139.
97 Ibid.

6 Two plus two equals four

1 Frederick Warburg's report, 13 December 1948, CW 19, pp. 479–81.
2 David Farrer's report, 15 December 1948, CW 19, p. 482.
3 Gollancz quoted widely a letter from Orwell, who at the time was very sick, objecting to the view that his novel was anti-Labour, CW 20, p. 136.
4 George Orwell, 'Second Thoughts on James Burnham', *Polemic*, 3 May 1946, CW 18, pp. 268–84.
5 Orwell, *The Road to Wigan Pier*, Harmondsworth: Penguin, 1963, pp. 191–204.
6 James Burnham, *The Managerial Revolution*, London: Putnam, 1942.
7 Orwell, *Wigan Pier*, pp. 152–7.
8 Orwell, review of *The Road to Serfdom*, *Observer*, 4 September 1944.
9 Orwell, unpublished review of H. Laski's *Faith, Reason and Civilisation*, CW 16, pp. 122–3.
10 Orwell, 'War-Time Diary', 3 July 1941, CW 12, p. 552.
11 Orwell, 'London Letter', *Partisan Review*, November–December 1941, CEJL 2, pp. 145–54.
12 John Newsinger, *Orwell's Politics*, Basingstoke: Palgrave/Macmillan 1999, p. 145.
13 Orwell, 'Culture and Democracy', CW 13, p. 78.
14 First published in 1897 as a serial, this book became a bestseller when Heinemann reproduced it one year later in volume form.
15 Anthony West, 'George Orwell', in his *Principles and Persuasions*, London: Eyre and Spottiswoode, 1958, pp. 150–9.
16 Alan Sandison, *The Last Man in Europe*, London: Macmillan, 1974, and *George Orwell: After Nineteen Eighty Four*, London: Macmillan, 1986.
17 George Orwell, 'Looking Back on the Spanish War', *The Penguin Essays*, pp. 216–23.
18 Quoted in Bernard Crick, *Orwell: A Life*, Harmondsworth: Penguin, 1992, p. 567.
19 Rodden, *The Politics of Literary Reputation: The Making and Claiming of 'St George' Orwell*, Oxford: Oxford University Press, 1989, p. 26.
20 J. Burnham, *The Managerial Revolution*. Orwell also read Burnham's *The Machiavellians* (1943).
21 George Orwell, review of 'We', *Tribune*, 4 January 1946, CEJL 4, pp. 72–5.
22 Yefgeny Zamyatin, *We*, London: Penguin, 1993, p. 13.
23 See Clarence Brown's introduction to the Penguin edition of *We*.
24 Zamyatin, *We*, pp. 19–20.
25 Orwell, *Nineteen Eighty Four*, Harmondsworth: Penguin, 1960, p. 239.
26 Irving Howe, 'The Fiction of Anti-Utopia', in *Orwell's Nineteen Eighty Four*, New York: Harcourt Brace, 1963, p. 149.

27 Orwell, *Nineteen Eighty Four*, pp. 109–10.

28 Ibid.

29 Orwell, 'The Case for the Open Fire', *Evening Standard*, 8 December 1945, CW 1, pp. 419–21.

30 Ibid.

31 Orwell wrote an essay extolling the virtues of junk shops, to be distinguished from antique shops by the fine film of dust over the window, the fact that the proprietor shows no signs of wanting to sell his goods, and by the gamut of goods for sale – including, in one case, ominously, a glass paperweight (*Evening Standard*, 5 January 1946).

32 Orwell, *Nineteen Eighty Four*, p. 126.

33 Orwell, *Nineteen Eighty Four*, p. 123.

34 In 'Looking back on the Spanish War', Orwell including the poem on the Italian militiaman, which concluded:

> But the thing I saw in your face
> No power can disinherit.
> No bomb that ever burst
> Shatters the crystal spirit.

35 Orwell, *Nineteen Eighty Four*, p. 177.

36 Orwell, *Nineteen Eighty Four*, p. 26.

37 Milan Kundera, *The Book of Laughter and Forgetting*, London: Penguin, 1983, p. 157.

38 Orwell, *Nineteen Eighty Four*, p. 215.

39 Orwell, *Nineteen Eighty Four*, p. 103.

40 Irving Howe, 'History of nightmare in politics', *Politics and the Novel*, New York: Columbia University Press, 1992.

41 Orwell, *Nineteen Eighty Four*, p. 51.

42 Ibid.

43 Orwell, *The Lion and the Unicorn, Penguin Essays*, Harmondsworth: Penguin, n.d., p. 141.

44 George Orwell, *Down and Out in Paris and London*, Harmondsworth: Penguin, 1969, p. 147.

45 Sandison argues that if Winston Smith was the 'last man' in Europe, Martin Luther was the first.

46 The Second Vatican Council's Decree on Ecumenism (p. 215) states: 'For it is through Christ's Catholic Church alone, which is the universal help toward salvation, that the fullness of the means of salvation can be obtained.'

47 Orwell, *Nineteen Eighty Four*, p. 68.

48 Isaiah Berlin, *Four Essays on Liberty*, London: Oxford University Press, 1969, p. 174.

49 Russell makes no reference whatever to Orwell or any of his work in his three-volume autobiography, published in London by Allen and Unwin, 1969, though there are numerous references to other authors. A. J. Ayer, however, records having read most of Orwell's major works and, although Orwell had referred to him as a good friend, felt he knew little about Orwell, and felt that was how Orwell had wanted things (*A Part of My Life*, London: Oxford University Press, 1977, p. 286).

50 Orwell, letter to Richard Rees, 3 March 1949, *CW* 20, p. 52.
51 Orwell, letter to Julian Symonds, 29 October 1948, *CW* 20, p. 461.
52 Gottfried Wilhelm Leibniz, *The Monadology* 33, London: Oxford University Press, 1898.
53 David Hume, *A Treatise of Human Nature*, Book One, Appendix B, London: Fontana, 1962.
54 Bernard Crick, *George Orwell*, p. 27.
55 According to A. J. Ayer, Poincaré argued that mathematics 'cannot amount to anything more than an immense tautology' (see his *Language, Truth and Logic*, Harmondsworth: Penguin, 1971, Ch.4).
56 Hannah Arendt, *The Origins of Totalitarianism*, London: Allen and Unwin, 1957, p. 477.
57 Ayer, *Language, Truth and Logic*, Ch. 2.
58 Orwell, *Nineteen Eighty Four*, p. 67.
59 It is no coincidence that G. E. Moore, whose ideas Orwell follows elsewhere, wrote an essay entitled 'Common Sense' from a similar standpoint (G. E. Moore, 'Common Sense', *Philosophical Papers*, New York: Macmillan, 1959).
60 Orwell, *Nineteen Eighty Four*, p. 68.
61 Zamyatin, *We*, p. 65.
62 N. Chernychevsky, *What is to be Done?* (trans. Michael Katz), Ithica: Cornell University Press, 1989.
63 Orwell, 'Good Bad Books', *Tribune*, 2 November 1943, *CEJL* 4, pp. 19–23.
64 Orwell argues convincingly that many British intellectuals, themselves champions of reason, failed to see the unreason of totalitarianism, chiefly because the 'order of the State' was based upon reason; but it was employed in the service of unreason. See Orwell's 'Wells, Hitler and the World State', *Horizon*, August 1941, *CEJL* 2, pp. 139–54.
65 Fyodor Dostoevsky, *Notes from the Underground*, Harmondsworth: Penguin, 1972.
66 Dostoevsky, *Notes*, pp. 30, 31.
67 Dostoevsky, *Notes*, p. 41.
68 Dostoevsky, *Notes*, pp. 33–4.
69 William Steinhoff, for example, discusses these issues in *George Orwell and the Origins of Nineteen Eighty Four*, Ann Arbor: University of Michigan Press, 1975, pp. 173–5.
70 Orwell, *Nineteen Eighty Four*, p. 160.
71 Orwell, *Nineteen Eighty Four*, p. 127.
72 Orwell, *Nineteen Eighty Four*, pp. 125–8.
73 George Orwell, 'As I Please', *Tribune*, 4 February 1944, *CEJL* 3, pp. 87–9.
74 Orwell, *Nineteen Eighty Four*, pp. 199–209.
75 G. E. Moore, 'Proof of an External World', *Philosophical Papers*, p. 272.
76 Orwell, *Nineteen Eighty Four*, pp. 63–7.
77 Orwell, *Nineteen Eighty Four*, pp. 39–42.
78 Kundera's *Laughter* begins with a story of senior Czech political figures appearing before a Prague crowd. The leader has no hat on and a faithful lieutenant, careful of the leader's health, loans him his own fur hat to ward off the snow. Many copies of the resulting photograph were made. Four

years later the lieutenant was hanged for treason. 'The propaganda section immediately airbrushed him out of history, and, obviously, out of all the photographs as well', says Kundera. All that remained of him was his hat, on the leader's head (p. 3).

79 Orwell, *Nineteen Eighty Four*, p. 214.
80 J. S. Mill, *On Liberty*, London: Dent and Son, 1957, pp. 89–90.
81 Orwell, *Nineteen Eighty Four*, p. 68.
82 Orwell, *Nineteen Eighty Four*, p. 217.
83 *St Matthew's Gospel*, Ch. 6, v.3. The import of this advice, however, concerns the giving of alms, which the Christian is to undertake without 'the sound of a trumpet' like the hypocrites. It is only in this sense that the right hand should be ignorant of what the left is doing.
84 Orwell, *Nineteen Eighty Four*, p. 31.
85 For example, Mike Martin, 'Demystifying Doublethink: Self-Deception, Truth and Freedom', *Social Theory and Practice*, 10 (3), 1984, pp. 319–31.
86 David Rudrum, 'On Certainty and Doublethink: Orwell, and Wittgenstein', a paper delivered to the Language, Communication and Culture Conference, Lisbon: Session on George Orwell, November 2003.
87 Orwell, 'In Front of Your Nose', *Tribune*, 11 March 1946, CW 18, pp. 161–4.
88 Orwell, *Nineteen Eighty Four*, p. 171.
89 Orwell, review of Bertrand Russell's *Power: A New Social Analysis*, *The Adelphi*, January 1939, CW 14, p. 311.
90 Margaret Canovan, *Hannah Arendt*, Cambridge: Cambridge University Press, 1992, p. 123.
91 Orwell, *Nineteen Eighty Four*, p. 45.
92 Orwell, *Nineteen Eighty Four*, p. 47.
93 Arthur Koestler, 'The Initiates', in R. H. S. Crossman (ed.), *The God That Failed*, London: Hamish Hamilton, 1950, pp. 53–4.
94 These examples are taken from Douglas Kellner, 'From 1984 to One-Dimensional Man: Critical Reflections on Orwell and Marcuse', a paper presented to the American Political Science Association Convention, August 1984.
95 See Norman Fairclough, *New Labour, New Language*, London: Routledge, 2000, esp. Chs 3 and 4. The overall effect on political communications of the mass media and their manipulative models of narrative is discussed in Thomas Meyers' and Lew Hinchman's *Media Democracy*, Cambridge: Polity Press, 2002.
96 George Orwell, 'Catastrophic Gradualism', *Common Wealth Review*, November 1945, CEJL 4, pp. 15–19.
97 David P. Chandler, *Brother Number One: A Political Biography of Pol Pot*, Chang Mai, Thailand: Silkworm Books, 1999.
98 In *The Philosophy of History*, Hegel depicted history as rational. Through the process of the dialectic a stage would be reached when an organic society would reconcile the interests of the individual and the state, thereby transcending liberal individualism.
99 J. J. Rousseau, *Confessions*, Penguin, 1953, p. 333.
100 George Orwell, 'As I Please', *Tribune*, 28 April 1944, CEJL 3, pp. 131–4.
101 Mill, *On Liberty*, p. 82.

102 Orwell, *Nineteen Eighty Four*, pp. 140–1.
103 Hannah Arendt, *The Human Condition*, Chicago: University of Chicago Press, 1958, p. 7.
104 Edmund Burke, 'An Appeal from the new to the old Whigs', *Further Reflections on the Revolution in France*, Indianapolis: Liberty Classics Edition, 1992, p. 196.
105 It is pursued by Gordon Marsden in 'Orwell and Burke: Strange Bedfellows? *History Today*, 53 (7), July 2003, pp. 24–5.
106 See the work of John Keane, for example, *Democracy and Civil Society*, London: Verso, 1988 and *Civil Society and the State*, London: Verso, 1988. Keane focuses on the problems of social and political control in the modern democratic state.
107 Orwell, *The Lion and the Unicorn, Penguin Essays*, p. 141.
108 George Woodcock, *The Crystal Spirit*, London: Jonathan Cape, 1967, p. 166.
109 Quoted in Woodcock, *The Crystal Spirit*, p. 49.
110 Isaac Deutscher, 'The Mysticism of Cruelty', in Irving Howe, *Orwell's Nineteen Eighty Four*, New York: Harcourt Brace, 1963, p. 38.
111 *News Chronicle*, 13 December 1954.
112 Rodden, *Literary Reputation*, p. 279.
113 *New York Times*, 17 December 1954. See Rodden, ibid.
114 Orwell, *Wigan Pier*, p. 189.
115 Christopher Small, *The Road to Miniluv*, London: Gollancz, 1975, p. 207.
116 Patrick Reilly, *George Orwell: The Age's Adversary*, London: Macmillan, 1986, p. 294.

7 Orwell, socialism and the soul of man

1 George Orwell, *A Clergyman's Daughter*, Harmondsworth: Penguin, 1964.
2 In *Why Orwell Matters*, New York: Basic Books, p. 182, Christopher Hitchens argued that *A Clergymen's Daughter* was a 'finer novel than Orwell believed it to be', and Compton Mackenzie praised it, along with *Down and Out* and *Burmese Days* as being incomparable in their 'directness, vigour courage and vitality'. Others, for example, Jenni Calder, *Chronicles of Conscience*, London: Secker and Warburg, 1968, p. 89, described it as 'the least successful of Orwell's novels'.
3 Saul Below, *Mr Sammler's Planet*, New York: Viking, 1970, p. 46.
4 Richard Rees, *George Orwell, Fugitive From The Camp Of Victory*, London: Secker and Warburg, 1961. This, too, was the phrase by which Orwell described himself.
5 Christopher Hollis, *A Study of George Orwell: The Man and his Works*, London: Hollis and Carter, 1956.
6 Samuel Hynes, *Twentieth Century Interpretations of Nineteen Eighty - Four*, Englewood Cliffs: Prentice Hall, 1971, p. 3.
7 Isaac Deutscher, 'Nineteen Eighty Four: The Mysticism of Cruelty', in Irving Howe, *Orwell's Nineteen Eighty Four*, New York: Harcourt Brace, 1963.
8 George Woodcock, *The Crystal Spirit*, London: Jonathan Cape, 1967, p. 28.

9 George Orwell, *The Road to Wigan Pier*, Harmondsworth: Penguin, 1963, pp. 152–3.

10 This is a problem that has not gone away. See Noam Chomsky, 'The Responsibility of Intellectuals', in *American Power and the New Mandarins*, New York: The New Press, 2002.

11 Shaw believed that the people would accept the wisdom of their Platonic rulers as readily as they would accept the expertise of their dentist. He explained the relationship between governors and governed as similar to that between a traveller and a railway porter. 'When a railway porter directs me to Platform No. 10 I do not strike him to the earth with a cry of "Down with Tyranny" and rush violently to No.1 platform.' (George Bernard Shaw, *Intelligent Women's Guide to Socialism and Capitalism*, London: Constable, 1929, p. 376.)

12 G. B. Shaw, *Essays in Fabian Socialism*, London: Constable, 1932, p. 158. Here Shaw explained why the Fabians had 'never advanced the smallest pretension to represent the working-classes'. See also Shaw's Preface to *Widowers' Houses*, in *Prefaces by Bernard Shaw*, London: Odhams, 1938, pp. 699–715.

13 Orwell, *Wigan Pier*, p. 190.

14 Orwell, *Wigan Pier*, p. 155. See also 'Road to Wigan Pier Diary', *CEJL* 1, p. 173.

15 George Orwell, 'London Letter', *Partisan Review*, January 1944, CEJL 3, p. 78.

16 He wrote a short profile of Bevan, that 'architect of disloyalty' in which he said admiringly that Bevan 'thinks and feels like a workingman'. (*CW* 17, p. 311). He could have written so much more.

17 Orwell noted that as soon as a working man got a position in a trade union or the Labour party he 'becomes middle-class whether he will or no'. 'The Road to Wigan Pier Diary', *CEJL* 1, p. 173.

18 This is fully discussed in George Orwell, 'The Moral Outlook of the English People', in 'The English People', *CEJL* 3, pp. 1–38.

19 Orwell, 'Charles Dickens', *The Penguin Essays of George Orwell*, Harmondsworth: Penguin, n.d., pp. 35–77.

20 Orwell, 'Dickens', p. 38.

21 Ibid.

22 Orwell, 'Dickens', p. 47.

23 Ibid.

24 Orwell, 'Dickens', p. 76.

25 Ibid., footnote.

26 Orwell, 'Dickens', p. 73.

27 Orwell, 'Dickens', p. 78.

28 Letter to Denys King-Farlow, 9 June 1936, *CEJL* 1, pp. 224–5.

29 *CW* 10, p. 249.

30 *CW* 10, p. 227.

31 George Orwell, 'Extracts from a Manuscript Notebook', *CEJL* 4, p. 511.

32 For example, 'As I Please', *Tribune*, 3 March, 1944, *CEJL* 3, pp. 101–4.

33 Ibid.

34 George Orwell, *A Clergyman's Daughter*, Harmondsworth, Penguin, 1964, p. 11.

35 Orwell, *A Clergyman's Daughter*, p. 13.

36 Orwell, *A Clergyman's Daughter*, p. 14.
37 Orwell, *A Clergyman's Daughter*, p. 245.
38 Orwell, *A Clergyman's Daughter*, p. 252.
39 Orwell, *A Clergyman's Daughter*, p. 262.
40 J. S. Whale, *The Protestant Tradition*, Cambridge, Cambridge University Press 1960, p. 26.
41 George Orwell, 'Reflections on Gandhi', *Partisan Review*, January 1949, *CEJL* 4, pp. 463–70.
42 George Orwell, 'Notes on the Way', published in *Time and Tide*, 6 April 1940, *CEJL* 2, pp. 15–18.
43 Ibid.
44 George Orwell, 'The English People', *CEJL* 3, p. 7.
45 Alexander Herzen, *The Russian People and Socialism*, Oxford: Oxford University Press, 1979.
46 Wilhelm Röpke, *The Social Crisis of our Time*, London: William Hodge, 1950, p. 6.
47 He used it when reviewing Henry Miller's *Tropic of Cancer*, *CEJL* 1, pp. 154–6; he later used a fuller version in 'Notes on the Way', *Time and Tide*, 6 April 1940, *CEJL* 2, pp. 15–18.
48 Orwell, 'Notes on the Way', p. 17.
49 Orwell uses this quotation from the Prayer Book in his review of *Tropic of Cancer*, *CEJL* 1, pp. 154–6.
50 Orwell, 'Notes on the Way', p. 17.
51 Ibid.
52 Orwell, review of *The Rock Pool* and *Almayer's Folly*, *CEJL* 1, pp. 225–7.
53 Italics in the original.
54 Orwell, review of *Tropic of Cancer*, pp. 154–6.
55 See, for example, Gordon Bowker, *George Orwell*, London: Abacus, 2003 p. 82.
56 To take only one period of his life, when working at the BBC, see Bowker, *George Orwell*, pp. 284–5.
57 Orwell, review of *Tropic of Cancer*, pp. 154–6.
58 George Orwell, 'The Art of Donald McGill', *Horizon*, September 1941, *CEJL* 2, pp. 155–65.
59 Correspondence following Orwell's 'As I Please', *Tribune*, 28 April 1944, *CW* 16, p. 170.
60 George Orwell, 'As I Please', *Tribune*, 14 April 1944, *CW* 16, p. 158.
61 George Orwell, review of Alfred Noyes' *The Edge of the Abyss*, Observer 27 February 1944, *CW* 16, pp. 105–7.
62 Alasdair McIntyre, *After Virtue: a study in moral theory*, London: Duckworth, 1994.
63 Review of Bertrand Russell's *Power: A New Social Analysis*, *CEJL* 1, pp. 375–6.
64 George Orwell, 'Raffles and Miss Blandish', *Horizon*, October 1944, *CEJL* 3, pp. 212–24.
65 Italics in the original.
66 Oscar Wilde famously remarked of Shaw that had no enemies but that all his friends despised him.
67 Hesketh Pearson, *Bernard Shaw: His Life and Personality*, London: Methuen, 1961, p. 86.

68 Shaw, *Essays in Fabian Socialism*, p. 131.
69 For example *Widowers' Houses, Mrs Warren's Profession, Major Barbara*, in *The Complete Plays of Bernard Shaw*, London: Odhams, 1937.
70 Speech given on 26 March 1914, quoted in Chappelow, Alan, *Shaw 'The Chucker Out'*, London: Allen and Unwin, 1969, p. 288.
71 Shaw, *Essays in Fabian Socialism*, p. 158.
72 From *Time and Tide*, 2 February 1945, quoted in Chappelow, *Shaw*, p. 321.
73 Orwell, 'Miss Blandish', *CEJL* 3, pp. 222–3.
74 Quoted Chappelow, *Shaw*, p. 197.
75 A draft for a radio talk, quoted in Chappelow, *Shaw*, p. 199.
76 Bernard Shaw, *Tribune*, 25 April 1943.
77 Bernard Shaw, *Labour Monthly*, October 1921.
78 Their correspondence was conducted publicly in the *Manchester Guardian*, in October of 1927.
79 See Chappelow, *Shaw*, p. 199.
80 See Joan Simeon Clarke, 'The Break-Up of the Poor Law', in Margaret Cole (ed.), *The Webbs And Their Work*, London: Frederick Muller, 1949, pp. 101–18.
81 S. and B. Webb, *Soviet Communism: A New Civilisation?*, London: Longmans Green, 1935.
82 Bernard Shaw, *Major Barbara, Bernard Shaw: The Complete Plays*, pp. 460–503.
83 George Orwell, *Nineteen Eighty Four*, Harmondsworth: Penguin, 1960, p. 215.
84 Orwell, *Nineteen Eighty Four*, p. 211.
85 Orwell, *Nineteen Eighty Four*, p. 214.
86 Orwell, *Nineteen Eighty Four*, p. 219.
87 Orwell, *Nineteen Eighty Four*, p. 215.
88 Orwell, *Nineteen Eighty Four*, p. 205.
89 The reference here is to Ivanov, the first interrogator, and Rubashov, the novel's central character. (See Arthur Koestler, *Darkness at Noon*, Harmondsworth: Penguin Modern Classics, 1969, pp. 67–133.)
90 Koestler, *Darkness at Noon*, p. 181.
91 Isaac Deutscher, 'The Mysticism of Cruelty', in Irving Howe, *Orwell's Nineteen Eighty Four*, New York: Harcourt Brace, 1963.
92 George Orwell, 'Burnham's View of the Contemporary World Struggle', *New Leader*, 29 March 1947, *CEJL* 4, pp. 312–3.
93 Steven Lukes, *Power*, London: Palgrave/Macmillan, 2005, p. 109.
94 Antonio Gramsci, 'The Modern Prince', in Quintin Hoare and Geoffrey Nowell Smith (eds), *Selections from the Prison Notebooks of Antonio Gramschi*, London: Lawrence and Wishart, 1971, pp. 169–70.
95 Herbert Marcuse, *One Dimensional Man: studies in the ideology of advanced industrial societies*, London: Routledge and Kegan Paul, 1964, passim.
96 Michel Foucault, *Power-Knowledge: selected interviews and other writings*, Brighton: Harvester, 1980, passim.
97 George Orwell, 'Prophecies of Fascism', *Tribune*, 12 July 1940, *CEJL* 2, pp. 30–31.
98 See C. J. Kupig (ed.), *Nineteen Eighty Four to 1984*, New York: Carroll and Graf, 1984, pp. 165–6.

99 H.G. Wells, *The Island of Dr Moreau*, Harmondsworth: Penguin, 1971.
100 Orwell's refers to London's fascist tendencies twice, in his reviews of London's *Iron Heel, CW* 12, pp. 210–13 and *Love of Life, CW* 17, p. 356.
101 His 'Domestic Diaries' from Jura show that Orwell took pleasure in killing animals, an activity in which he exhibited considerable skill such that others remarked on it. Barnhill was by no means swamped by a sea of blood, but the reader sometimes gets the impression that Orwell was living out the imagined childhood of George Bowling (*CW* 19, passim).
102 Orwell, *Nineteen Eighty Four*, p. 69.
103 T.S. Eliot, *The Dry Salvages*, 1941. The third of Eliot's *Four Quartets*.
104 For example, Orwell was dismissive of the Brookers with whom he lodged in the early part of the book.
105 George Orwell, 'Inside the Whale', *Penguin Essays*, pp. 101–33.
106 George Orwell, review of Jack Common, *The Freedom of the Streets*, June 1938, *CEJL* 1, pp. 335–6.
107 Ernesto 'Che' Guevara, *The Motor Cycle Diaries*, New York: Ocean Press, 2004, Appendix.
108 Bernard Crick, *George Orwell: A Life*, Harmondsworth: Penguin, 1992, pp. 15–18 and passim.
109 Crick, *Orwell: A Life*, p. 444.
110 George Orwell, 'The British Crisis: London Letter', *Partisan Review* July–August 1942, *CEJL* 2, pp. 207–16.
111 See the concluding chapter to Newsinger's *Orwell's Politics*, London: Palgrave, 1999, pp. 155–8.
112 George Orwell, 'Notes on Nationalism', *Polemic* (1), October 1945, *CEJL* 3, pp. 361–80.

8 Orwell's social and political thought

1 Norman Dennis and A. H. Halsey, *English Ethical Socialism*, Oxford: Oxford University Press, 1988.
2 Dennis and Halsey, *Ethical Socialism*, pp. 4–5.
3 William Morris, *A Dream of John Ball*, in *Three Works* by *William Morris* (ed. A.L. Morton) London: Lawrence and Wishart, 1973, p. 51.
4 Ibid.
5 Dennis and Halsey, *Ethical Socialism*, p. 5.
6 Dennis and Halsey, *Ethical Socialism*, p. 4.
7 Morris, *John Ball*, p. 59.
8 Dennis and Halsey, *Ethical Socialism*, p. 121.
9 George Orwell, review of Jack Common, *The Freedom of the Streets*, June 1938, *CEJL* 1, pp. 335–6.
10 See for example Geoffrey Foote, *The Labour Party's Political Thought: A History*, London: Macmillan, 1997, pp. 36–9.
11 See Friedrich Engels, *Anti Dühring*, originally published in Vorwärts, 1877.
12 Edward Carpenter, *Civilisation: its cause and cure and other essays*, London: Swan Sonnenschein, 1903.
13 J. Bruce Glaser, *The Meaning of Socialism*, Manchester: The National Labour Press, 1919.
14 *The Clarion*, 12 December 1891.

15 Denis Pye, *Fellowship is Life*, Bolton: Clarion Publishing, 1995.
16 Ibid.
17 Robert Blatchford, *Merrie England*, London: Journeyman Press, 1977.
18 F. D. Maurice, *Theological Essays*, London: Macmillan, 1871.
19 Charles Kingsley, *Alton Locke: Tailor and Poet*, London: Dent, 1970.
20 Thomas Hughes, *Tom Brown's School Days*, London: S. W. Partridge & Co., 1917.
21 Alan Wilkinson, *Christian Socialism: Scott Holland to Tony Blair*, London: SCM Press, 1998.
22 Foote, *Labour's Thought*, Chs. 2, 3.
23 Jonathan Rose, *The Intellectual Life of the British Working Class*, London Yale University Press, 2002, p. 461.
24 George Orwell, review of Jack Common's *The Freedom of the Streets*, *CW* 11, p. 162.
25 Crick, *George Orwell: A Life*, Harmondsworth: Penguin, 1992, p. 273.
26 In the first 'new' edition in 1932 Murry had written a piece on Marx and William Morris.
27 George Orwell, *The Road to Wigan Pier*, Harmondsworth: Penguin, 1963, p. 153.
28 George Orwell, review of Wilde's *The Soul of Man under Socialism*, *Observer*, 9 May 1948, *CEJL* 4, pp. 426–8.
29 George Orwell, 'As I Please', *Tribune*, 24 December 1943, *CEJL* 3, pp. 63–5.
30 Orwell, *Wigan Pier*, p. 161.
31 In response to Orwell's 'As I Please' of 24 December 1943, *CW* 16, p. 37.
32 George Orwell, letter to Jack Common, *CEJL* 1, pp. 215–17.
33 In *Wigan Pier*, Orwell suggests that it is only this kind of moralistic socialism that can stand against Fascism. See pp. 187–90.
34 Written under a *nom de plume*, John Freeman, *CW* 16, p. 42.
35 George Orwell, review of Evelyn Andersen's *Hammer or Anvil: The Story of the German Working Class Movement* and Julius Brauntal's *Search for the Millennium*, *CW* 17, p. 273.
36 In 'Inside the Whale' Orwell himself admits: 'I have used the phrase "ordinary man" rather loosely, and I have taken it for granted that the "ordinary man" exists . . .' In fact Orwell took much more than this for granted. (*CEJL* 1, p. 501)
37 Unpublished letter, April 1939, Orwell archive. Orwell and Fr. Martindale had an exchange of opinion over the former's review of Karl Adam's *The Spirit of Catholicism*, *CW* 10, pp. 251–2. Ronald Thiemann pursued the Martindale connection in 'The Public Intellectual as Connected Critic: George Orwell and Religion', a paper prepared for the ECPR conference at Marburg in September 2003. Session: 'Aspects of Orwell'.
38 Laski went on to say that Orwell ignored the reality of class antagonism, said little about the role of the state, or the historic movement of the economic process. 'At bottom', he concluded, 'it is an emotional plea for socialism addressed to comfortable people'. (*Left News*, March 1937, quoted in Jeffrey Meyers (ed.), *The Critical Heritage*, London: Routledge and Kegan Paul, 1975, p. 105.)
39 Christopher Small, *The Road to Miniluv*, London: Gollancz, 1975, pp. 172–3.

40 He had written a review of Koestler's novel *The Gladiators* which depicts an unsuccessful attempt by escaped gladiators and slaves to form a free society. ('Arthur Koestler', *Focus* 2, 1946, *CEJL* 2, pp. 234–44.)
41 Orwell, 'What is Socialism', *CW* 18, pp. 63–6.
42 A. J. Ayer, *Part of My Life*, London: Oxford University Press, 1977, p. 287.
43 George Orwell, 'The English People', *CEJL* 3, pp. 1–38.
44 George Orwell, 'London Letter', *Partisan Review*, April 1944, *CEJL* 3, pp. 123–8.
45 Characteristically Shaw had chided his reluctant fellow-vestrymen by suggesting that they considered women to be inferior in every capacity except the size of their bladders.
46 Mordecai Richler, quoted in Georg Lukacs, 'The Ideology of Modernism', in John Barrell (ed.), *Poetry, Language and Politics*, Manchester: Manchester University Press, 1988, p. 210.
47 Orwell, 'Charles Dickens', *Penguin Essays of George Orwell*, Harmondsworth: Penguin, n.d., p. 75.
48 W. H. Auden, 'The American Scene', *The Dyers Hand*, London: Faber and Faber, 1948, p. 313.
49 Kenneth Quin, *How Literature Works*, London: Macmillan, 1992.
50 Quin, *How Literature Works*, p. 9.
51 Doctor Johnson is quoted as remarking: 'Great abilities . . . are not required for an Historian; for in historical composition, all the greatest powers of the human mind are quiescent, He has facts only to his hand; so there is no exercise of invention. Imagination is not required in any high degree . . . Some penetration, accuracy and colouring will fit a man for the task, if he can give the application which is necessary' (*Boswell's Johnson*, London: Cygnet Classics, 1968, p. 46).
52 William Golding, *Rights of Passage*, London: Faber and Faber, 1980.
53 Terry Eagleton, 'The Rise of English', in Walder (ed.), *Literature in the Modern World*, Oxford: Oxford University Press, 1990, p. 25.
54 Terry Eagleton, 'Marxist Criticism', in Barrell, *Poetry, Language and Politics*, p. 208.
55 E. D. Hirsch, Jnr, 'The Babel of Interpretation', in Walder, *Literature*, p. 64.
56 Quin, *How Literature Works*, p. 18.
57 George Orwell, 'Why I Write', *Penguin Essays*, pp. 1–6.
58 Orwell, 'Why I Write', p. 3.
59 Orwell, 'Why I Write', p. 6.
60 Orwell, 'Why I Write', p. 7.
61 Quin, *How Literature Works*, p. 93.
62 E. M. Forster, 'Anonymity: An Enquiry' in *Two Cheers for Democracy*, London: Edward Arnold, 1951, p. 89.
63 D. H. Mellor, 'On Literary Truth', *Ratio* 10, 1968, pp. 150–68.
64 Eric Auerbach, *Mimesis*, Princeton: Princeton University Press, 1968, p. 496.
65 Walter Benjamin, 'Theses on the Philosophy of History', in Hannah Arendt (ed.), *Illuminations*, New York: Schoken Books, 1969, p. 159.
66 Quin, *How Literature Works*, p. 212.
67 Extract from a Radio interview (1990) quoted in Lukacs, 'Modernism', p. 210.
68 Lukacs, 'Modernism', p. 103.

69 A response to 'English Writing in Total War', *The New Republic*, 14 July 1941, *CW* 12, pp. 527–31.

70 George Orwell, letter to the Rev. I. Jones, 18 April 1941, *CEJL* 2, pp. 109–12.

71 George Orwell, 'London Letter', *Partisan Review*, July–August 1941, *CEJL* 2, pp. 112–23.

72 George Orwell, review of *Brave New World*, *Tribune*, 12 July 1940, *CW* 12, pp. 210–13.

73 George Orwell, letter to Humphry House, 11 April 1940, *CW* 12, pp. 139–41.

74 George Woodcock, *The Crystal Spirit*, London: Jonathan Cape, 1967, p. 24.

75 See the Introduction to the Ukrainian edition of *Animal Farm*, published in 1947, *CW* 19, p. 87.

76 The phrase was coined by V. S. Pritchett.

77 George Orwell, review of Wyndham Lewis' *The Mysterious Mr Bull*, *CW* 11, pp. 353–4.

78 Robert Pearce, 'Orwell Now', *History Today*, 47(10), October 1997, pp. 4–6.

79 Richard Rees, *George Orwell: Fugitive from the Camp of Victory*, London: Secker and Warburg, 1961.

80 Raymond Plant, *Equality, Markets and the State*, Fabian Tract 494, 1984; see also *Citizenship, Rights and Socialism*, Fabian Tract 531, 1988.

81 Woodcock, *The Crystal Spirit*, p. 275.

82 Ibid.

83 Rebecca West said of *Animal Farm*: 'Every sentence was on the very highest level.' It was a 'complete work of art'. (Letter to Orwell *CW* 18, p. 121.) After reading Orwell's essay 'Some Thoughts on the Common Toad' John Betjeman called Orwell 'one of the best living writers of prose'. (Letter, *CW* 18, pp. 238–40.) John Dos Passos wrote to Orwell, a few months before his death, that: '*Nineteen Eighty Four* is a wonderful job. I read it with such cold shivers as I haven't had since as a child I read Swift about the Yahoos. Had nightmares all the next week . . .' (letter dated 8 October 1949.)

84 George Steiner, in *George Orwell: The Critical Heritage*, Jeffery Meyers (ed.), London: Routledge, 1975, pp. 139–51.

85 For example, John Wesley Young, *Totalitarian Language: Orwell's New-speak and its Nazi and Communist Antecedents*, London: University of Virginia Press, 1991.

86 Christopher Hitchens, *Orwell's Victory*, London: Penguin, 2002, p. 139.

87 Stephen Spender, *World Review*, June 1950, pp. 51–4.

88 Indeed Conor Cruise O'Brien likened Orwell's effect on the British intelligentsia to that of Voltaire on the French. (See *Writers and Politics*, New York: Pantheon Books, 1965, pp. 32–3.)

89 Vaclav Havel, 'The Power of the Powerless', in J. Vladislav, *Vaclav Havel, or Living from Truth*, London: Faber and Faber, 1987, pp. 36–122.

90 James Surowiecki, *The Wisdom of Crowds*, London: Little Brown, 2004.

91 George Orwell, *Nineteen Eighty Four*, Harmondsworth: Penguin, p. 135.

92 The phrase is Italo Calvi's. See his *The Uses of Literature*, New York: Harcourt, Brace, Jovanovic, 1986, p. 101.

93 George Orwell, letter to Humphry House, dated 11 April 1940, *CEJL* 1, pp. 529–32.

Bibliography

Ackroyd, Peter (2002) *Albion: The Origins of the English Imagination*, London: Chatto and Windus.

Alba, Victor (1974) *El Marxisme a Catalunya 1919–39*, Barcelona: Pòrtic.

Arendt, Hannah (1957) *The Origins of Totalitarianism*, London: Allen and Unwin.

Arendt, Hannah (1958) *The Human Condition*, Chicago: University of Chicago Press.

Arendt, Hannah (ed.) (1969) *Illuminations*, New York: Schoken Books.

Auerbach, Eric (1968) *Mimesis*, Princeton: Princeton University Press.

Ayer, A. J. (1971) *Language, Truth and Logic*, Harmondsworth: Penguin.

Baldwin, Stanley (1971, first published 1926) *On England and Other Addresses*, Freeport, NY: Ayer Publishers.

Barker, Ernest (1927) *National Character and the Factors in its Formation*, London: Methuen.

Barker, Ernest (1947) *The Character of England*, Oxford: Clarendon.

Barrell, John (ed.) (1988) *Poetry, Language and Politics*, Manchester: Manchester University Press.

Below, Saul (1970) *Mr Sammler's Planet*, New York: Viking.

Benewick, Robert (1972) *The Fascist Movement in Britain*, London: Allen Lane.

Berga, Miquel (1984) *Mil nou-cents vuitanta quatre: Radiografia d'un maison*, Barcelona: Edicions 62.

Berlin, Isaiah (1969) *Four Essays on Liberty*, London: Oxford University Press.

Blatchford, Robert (1977) *Merrie England*, London: Journeyman Press.

Bonhoeffer, Dietrich (1968) *Ethics*, London: Fontana.

Booth, Charles (1892–7) *Life and Labour of the People in London*, 10 vols, London: Macmillan.

Borkenau, Franz (1937) *The Spanish Cockpit*, London: Faber.

Bowker, Gordon (2003) *George Orwell*, London: Abacus Books.

Buckler, Steve (1993) *Dirty Hands: The Problem of Political Morality*, Aldershot: Avebury Press.

Buddicom, Jacintha (1974) *Eric and Us*, London: Leslie Frewin.

Burke, Edmund (1992) *Further Reflections on the Revolution in France*, Indianapolis: Liberty Classics Edition.

Burnham, James (1942) *The Managerial Revolution*, London: Putnam.

Calder, Jenni (1968) *Chronicles of Conscience*, London: Secker and Warburg.

Calvi, Italo (1986) *The Uses of Literature*, New York: Harcourt, Brace, Jovanovic.

Canovan, Margaret (1992) *Hannah Arendt*, Cambridge: Cambridge University Press.

Canovan, Margaret (1997) *G. K. Chesterton: Radical Populist*, New York: Harcourt Brace.

Carpenter, Edward (1903) *Civilisation: Its Cause and Cure and Other Essays*, London: Swan Sonnenschein.

Chandler, David P. (1999) *Brother Number One: A Political Biography of Pol Pot*, Chang Mai, Thailand: Silkworm Books.

Chappelow, Alan (1969) *Shaw 'The Chucker Out'*, London: Allen and Unwin.

Chernychevsky, N. (1989) *What is to be Done?* (trans. Michael Katz), Ithica: Cornell University Press.

Chomsky, Noam (2002) 'The Responsibility of Intellectuals', in *American Power and the New Mandarins*, New York: The New Press.

Clark, Kenneth (1935) *On the Painting of English Landscapes*, London: British Academy.

Cleaver, Eldridge (1971) *Post-Prison Writings and Speeches*, London: Panther Books.

Cole, Margaret (ed.) (1949) *The Webbs And Their Work*, London: Frederick Muller.

Collins, Michael (2004) *The Likes of Us*, London: Granta Books.

Connolly, Cyril (1961) *Enemies of Promise*, Harmondsworth: Penguin.

Coppard, Audrey and Crick, Bernard (eds) (1984) *Orwell Remembered*, London: Ariel Books.

Crick, Bernard (1992) *George Orwell: A Life*, Harmondsworth: Penguin.

Crossman, R. H. S. (1950) *The God That Failed*, London: Hamish Hamilton.

Davison, Peter (1996) *George Orwell: A Literary Life*, Basingstoke: Macmillan.

Davison, Peter (1998) *The Complete Works of George Orwell*, London: Secker and Warburg.

Day, J. (1999) *Englishness in Music: From Elizabethan Times to Elgar, Tippett and Britten*, London: Thames.

Dennis, Norman and Halsey, A. H. (1988) *English Ethical Socialism*, Oxford: Oxford University Press.

Deutscher, Isaac (1955) *Nineteen Heretics and Renegades and Other Essays*, London: Hamish Hamilton.

Deutscher, Isaac (1963) 'The Mysticism of Cruelty', in Irving Howe, *Orwell's Nineteen Eighty Four*, New York: Harcourt Brace.

Dickens, Charles (n.d.) *Hard Times*, London: Odhams Press.

Dostoevsky, Fyodor (1972) *Notes from the Underground*, Harmondsworth: Penguin.

Easthorpe, Anthony (1999) *Englishness and National Culture*, London: Routledge.

Engels, Friedrich (1987) *The Condition of the Working Class in England*, Harmondsworth: Penguin.

Fairclough, Norman (1995) *Critical Discourse Analysis: The Critical Study of Language*, London: Longman.

Fairclough, Norman (2000) *New Labour, New Language*, London: Routledge.

Fanon, Frantz (1965) *The Wretched of the Earth*, London: MacGibbon and Kee.

Foote, Geoffrey (1997) *The Labour Party's Political Thought: A History*, London: Macmillan.

Forster, E. M. (1951) 'Anonymity: An Enquiry', in *Two Cheers for Democracy*, London: Edward Arnold.

Foucault, Michel (1980) *Power-Knowledge: Selected Interviews and Other Writings*, Brighton: Harvester.

Fowler, Roger (1995) *The Language of George Orwell*, Basingstoke: Macmillan.

Giles, Judy and Middleton, Tim (eds) (1995) *Writing Englishness*, London: Routledge.

Gissing, George (1972) *Demos: A Story of English Socialism*, Brighton: Harvester Press.

Glaser, J. Bruce (1919) *The Meaning of Socialism*, Manchester: The National Labour Press.

Golding, William (1980) *Rights of Passage*, London: Faber and Faber.

Goodwin, Barbara and Taylor, Keith (1982) *The Politics of Utopia*, London: Hutchinson.

Goonetelleke, D. C. R. A. (1998) *Images of the Raj*, London: Macmillan.

Gramschi, Antonio (1971) 'The Modern Prince', in Quintin Hoare and Geoffrey Nowell Smith (eds), *Selections from the Prison Notebooks of Antonio Gramschi*, London: Lawrence and Wishart.

Greenwood, Walter (1975) *Love on the Dole*, Harmondsworth: Penguin.

Guevara, Ernesto 'Che' (2004) *The Motor Cycle Diaries*, New York: Ocean Press.

Heller, Joseph (1994) *Catch 22*, London: Vintage.

Herzen, Alexander (1979) *The Russian People and Socialism*, with an introduction by Isaiah Berlin, Oxford: Oxford University Press.

Hitchens, Christopher (2002a) *Orwell's Victory*, Penguin: London.

Hitchens, Christopher (2002b) *Why Orwell Matters*, New York: Basic Books.

Hollis, Christopher (1956) *A Study of George Orwell: The Man and his Works*, London: Hollis and Carter.

Howe, Irving (1963) *Orwell's Nineteen Eighty Four*, New York: Harcourt Brace.

Howe, Irving (1992) *Politics and the Novel*, New York: Columbia University Press.

Hughes, Thomas (1917) *Tom Brown's School Days*, London: S. W. Partridge & Co.

Hume, David (1962) *A Treatise of Human Nature*, London: Fontana.

Huxley, Aldous (1971) *Point Counter Point*, Harmondsworth: Penguin.

Huxley, Aldous (1972) *Eyeless in Gaza*, Harmondsworth: Penguin.

Hyndman, H. M. (1911) *Record of an Adventurous Life*, London: Macmillan.

Hynes, Samuel (1971) *Twentieth Century Interpretations of Nineteen Eighty Four*, Englewood Cliffs: Prentice Hall.

Ingle, Stephen (1979) *Socialist Thought in Imaginative Literature*, London: Macmillan.

Ingle, Stephen (1993) *George Orwell: A Political Life*, Manchester: Manchester University Press.

Ingle, Stephen (2000) *The British Party System (3)*, London: Continuum.

Ingle, Stephen (2002) *Narratives of British Socialism*, London: Palgrave/Macmillan.

Inglis, Fred (1992) *The Cruel Peace*, New York: Basic Books.

Islam, Shamsul (1979) *Chronicles of the Raj*, London: Macmillan.

Keane, John (1988a) *Civil Society and the State*, London: Verso.

Keane, John (1988b) *Democracy and Civil Society*, London: Verso.

Kellas, James (1991) *The Politics of Nationalism and Ethnicity*, Basingstoke: Macmillan.

Kingsley, Charles (1969) *Alton Locke: Tailor and Poet*, London: Dent.

Koestler, Arthur (1965) *The Gladiators*, London: Vintage.

Koestler, Arthur (1969) *Darkness at Noon*, Harmondsworth: Penguin.

Kundera, Milan (1983) *The Book of Laughter and Forgetting*, London: Penguin.

Laski, Harold (1944) *Faith, Reason and Civilisation*, London: Gollanz.

Lawrence, D. H. (1981) *Sons and Lovers*, Harmondsworth: Penguin.

Lee, Robert A (1969) *Orwell's Fiction*, London: University of Notre Dame Press.

Leibniz, Gottfried Wilhelm (1898) *The Monadology (33)*, London: Oxford University Press.

Lewis, Peter (1981) *George Orwell*, London: Heinemann.

London, Jack (1977) *The People of the Abyss*, London: The Journeyman Press.

Lukes, Steven (2005) *Power*, London: Palgrave/Macmillan.

McIntyre, Alasdair (1994) *After Virtue: A Study in Moral Theory*, London: Duckworth.

Malraux, André (1975) *Man's Estate*, Harmondsworth: Penguin.

Marcuse, Herbert (1964) *One Dimensional Man: Studies in the Ideology of Advanced Industrial Societies*, London: Routledge and Kegan Paul.

Maurice, F. D. (1871) *Theological Essays*, London: Macmillan.

Mellor, D. H. (1968) 'On Literary Truth', *Ratio*, December, 10(2).

Meyers, Jeffrey (ed.) (1975a) *George Orwell: The Critical Heritage*, London: Routledge and Kegan Paul.

Meyers, Jeffrey (1975b) *A Reader's Guide to George Orwell*, London: Thames and Hudson.

Meyers, Jeffrey (2000) *Orwell: Wintry Conscience of a Generation*, New York: Norton.

Meyers, Thomas and Hinchman, Lew (2002) *Media Democracy*, Cambridge: Polity Press.

Mill, J. S. (1957) *On Liberty*, London: Dent and Son.

Milstead, David (n.d.) *Brewer's Anthology of England and the English*, London: Cassell.

Moore, G. E. (1959) *Philosophical Papers*, London: Macmillan.

Morris, William (1973a) *A Dream of John Ball*, London: Lawrence and Wishart.

Morris, William (1973b) *News from Nowhere*, in A. L. Morton (ed.), *Three Works by William Morris*, London: Lawrence and Wishart.

Newsinger, John (1999) *Orwell's Politics*, London: Palgrave.

Norris, Christopher (1984) *Inside the Myth. Orwell: Views from the Left*, London: Lawrence and Wishart.

Oakshott, Michael (1962) *Rationalism in Politics and Other Essays*, London: Methuen.

O'Brien, Conor Cruise (1965) *Writers and Politics*, New York: Pantheon Books.

Orwell, George (1958) *Animal Farm*, Harmondsworth: Penguin.

Orwell, George (1960) *Nineteen Eighty Four*, Harmondsworth: Penguin.

Orwell, George (1963) *The Road to Wigan Pier*, Harmondsworth: Penguin.

Orwell, George (1964a) *A Clergyman's Daughter*, Harmondsworth: Penguin.

Orwell, George (1965) *Keep the Aspidistra Flying*, Harmondsworth: Penguin.

Orwell, George (1966) *Homage to Catalonia*, Harmondsworth: Penguin.

Orwell, George (1967) *Burmese Days*, Harmondsworth: Penguin.

Orwell, George (1990) *Coming Up for Air*, Harmondsworth: Penguin.

Orwell, George (1996) *Down and Out in Paris and London*, Harmondsworth: Penguin.

Orwell, George, *The Lion and the Unicorn* (n.d.) *Penguin Essays of George Orwell*, Harmondsworth: Penguin.

Parekh, Bhiku (1975) *The Concept of Socialism*, London: Croom Helm.

Patai, Daphne (1984) *The Orwell Mystique: A Study of Male Ideology*, Amherst: University of Massachusetts Press.

Paxman, Jeremy (2003) *The English: A Portrait of a People*, Harmondsworth: Penguin.

Pearson, Hesketh (1961) *Bernard Shaw: His Life and Personality*, London: Methuen.

Pye, Denis (1995) *Fellowship is Life*, Bolton: Clarion Publishing.

Quin, Kenneth (1992) *How Literature Works*, London: Macmillan.

Rai, Alok (1988) *Orwell and the Politics of Despair*, Cambridge: Cambridge University Press.

Rees, Richard (1951) *George Orwell: Fugitive From The Camp Of Victory*, London: Secker and Warburg.

Reilly, Patrick (1986) *George Orwell: The Age's Adversary*, London: Macmillan.

Rodden, John (1989) *The Politics of Literary Reputation: The Making and Claiming of 'St. George' Orwell*, Oxford: Oxford University Press.

Röpke, Wilhelm (1950) *The Social Crisis of Our Time*, London: William Hodge.

Rorty, Richard (1982) *The Consequences of Pragmatism: Essays 1972–80*, Brighton: Harvester.

Rorty, Richard (1989) 'The Last Intellectual in Europe', in *Contingency, Irony and Solidarity*, Cambridge: Cambridge University Press.

Rose, Jonathan (2002) *The Intellectual Life of the British Working Class*, London: Yale University Press.

Rousseau, J. J. (1953) *Confessions*, Harmondsworth: Penguin.

Russell, Bertrand (2004) *Power: A New Social Analysis*, London: Routledge.

Sandison, Alan (1974) *The Last Man in Europe*, London: Macmillan.

Sandison, Alan (1986) *George Orwell: After Nineteen eighty-four*, London: Macmillan.

Sartre, J. P. (1967) *What is Literature?*, London: Methuen.

Shaw, George Bernard (1929) *Intelligent Women's Guide to Socialism and Capitalism*, London: Constable.

Shaw, George Bernard (1932) *Essays in Fabian Socialism*, London: Constable.

Shaw, George Bernard (1937) 'Widowers' Houses, Mrs Warren's Profession, Major Barbara', in *The Complete Plays of Bernard Shaw*, London: Odhams.

Shaw, George Bernard (1938) *Prefaces by Bernard Shaw*, London: Odhams.

Shelden, Michael (1991) *Orwell: The Authorised Biography*, London: Heinemann.

Small, Christopher (1975) *The Road to Miniluv*, London: Gollancz.

Stansky, P. and Abrahams, W. (1972) *The Unknown Orwell*, London: Constable.

Steinhoff, William (1975) *George Orwell and the Origins of 1984*, Ann Arbor: University of Michigan Press.

Surowiecki, James (2004) *The Wisdom of Crowds*, London: Little Brown.

Taylor, D. J. (2003) *Orwell: The Life*, London: Chatto and Windus.

Tressell, Robert (1972) *The Ragged Trousered Philanthropists*, St Albans: Panther.

Trilling, Lionel (1955) *The Opposing Self*, London: Secker and Warburg.

Vaughan, William (1999) *British Painting: The Golden Age from Hogarth to Turner*, London: Thames and Hudson.

Vladislav, J. (1987) *Vaclav Havel, or Living from Truth*, London: Faber and Faber.

Wadhams, Stephen (1984) *Remembering Orwell*, Harmondsworth: Penguin Books.

Walder, Dennis (ed.) (1990) *Literature in the Modern World*, Oxford: Oxford University Press.

Webb, S. and B. (1935) *Soviet Communism: A New Civilisation?*, London: Longmans Green.

Wells, H. G. (1971) *The Island of Dr Moreau*, Harmondsworth: Penguin.

Wells, H. G. (1958) 'The Time Machine', in *Selected Short Stories*, Harmondsworth: Penguin.

West, W. J. (ed.) (1985) *Orwell: The War Broadcaster*, London: Duckworth/ BBC.

Wiener, Martin (1981) *English Culture and the Decline of the Industrial Spirit*, Cambridge: Cambridge University Press.

Wilde, Oscar (1991) 'The Soul of Man Under Socialism', *The Complete Illustrated Stories, Plays and Poems*, London: Chancellor Press.

Wilkinson, Alan (1998) *Christian Socialism: Scott Holland to Tony Blair*, London: SCM Press.

Williams, Raymond (1971) *Orwell*, London: Fontana Modern Masters.

Woodcock, George (1967) *The Crystal Spirit*, London: Jonathan Cape.

Young, John Wesley (1991) *Totalitarian Language: Orwell's Newspeak and its Nazi and Communist Antecedents*, London: University of Virginia Press.

Zamyatin, Yevgeny (1993) *We*, Harmondsworth: Penguin.

Zwerdling, Alex (1974) *Orwell and the Left*, Newhaven: Yale University Press.

Index